TABLE OF CONTENTS

Top 20 Test Taking Tips

1. Carefully follow all the test registration procedures
2. Know the test directions, duration, topics, question types, how many questions
3. Setup a flexible study schedule at least 3-4 weeks before test day
4. Study during the time of day you are most alert, relaxed, and stress free
5. Maximize your learning style; visual learner use visual study aids, auditory learner use auditory study aids
6. Focus on your weakest knowledge base
7. Find a study partner to review with and help clarify questions
8. Practice, practice, practice
9. Get a good night's sleep; don't try to cram the night before the test
10. Eat a well balanced meal
11. Know the exact physical location of the testing site; drive the route to the site prior to test day
12. Bring a set of ear plugs; the testing center could be noisy
13. Wear comfortable, loose fitting, layered clothing to the testing center; prepare for it to be either cold or hot during the test
14. Bring at least 2 current forms of ID to the testing center
15. Arrive to the test early; be prepared to wait and be patient
16. Eliminate the obviously wrong answer choices, then guess the first remaining choice
17. Pace yourself; don't rush, but keep working and move on if you get stuck
18. Maintain a positive attitude even if the test is going poorly
19. Keep your first answer unless you are positive it is wrong
20. Check your work, don't make a careless mistake

World History

Prehistory

Prehistory is the period of human history before writing was developed. The three major periods of prehistory are:
- Lower Paleolithic—Humans used crude tools.
- Upper Paleolithic—Humans began to develop a wider variety of tools. These tools were better made and more specialized. They also began to wear clothes, organize in groups with definite social structures, and to practice art. Most lived in caves during this time period.
- Neolithic—Social structures became even more complex, including growth of a sense of family and the ideas of religion and government. Humans learned to domesticate animals and produce crops, build houses, start fires with friction tools, and to knit, spin and weave.

Anthropology

Anthropology is the study of human culture. Anthropologists study groups of humans, how they relate to each other, and the similarities and differences between these different groups and cultures. Anthropological research takes two approaches: cross-cultural research and comparative research. Most anthropologists work by living among different cultures and participating in those cultures in order to learn about them.

There are three major divisions within anthropology:
- Biological and cultural anthropology
- Archaeology
- Linguistics

Archeology

Archeology studies past human cultures by evaluating what they leave behind. This can include bones, buildings, art, tools, pottery, graves, and even trash. Archeologists maintain detailed notes and records of their findings and use special tools to evaluate what they find. Photographs, notes, maps, artifacts, and surveys of the area can all contribute to evaluation of an archeological site. By studying all these elements of numerous archeological sites, scientists have been able to theorize that humans or near-humans have existed for about 600,000 years. Before that, more primitive humans are believed to have appeared about one million years ago. These humans eventually developed into Cro-Magnon man, and then Homo sapiens, or modern man.

Human development from the Lower Paleolithic to the Iron Age

Human development has been divided into several phases:
- Lower Paleolithic or Old Stone Age, about one million years ago—early humans used tools like needles, hatchets, awls, and cutting tools.
- Upper Paleolithic or New Stone Age, 6,000-8,000 BCE—also known as the Neolithic, textiles and pottery are developed. Humans of this era discovered the wheel, began to practice agriculture, made polished tools, and had some domesticated animals.

- Bronze Age, 3,000 BCE—metals are discovered and the first civilizations emerge as humans become more technologically advanced.
- Iron Age, 1,200-1,000 BCE—metal tools replace stone tools as humans develop knowledge of smelting.

Civilizations

Civilizations are defined as having the following characteristics:
- Use of metal to make weapons and tools
- Written language
- A defined territorial state
- A calendar

The earliest civilizations developed in river valleys where reliable, fertile land was easily found, including:
- Nile River valley in Egypt
- Mesopotamia
- Indus River
- Hwang Ho in China

The very earliest civilizations developed in the Tigris-Euphrates valley in Mesopotamia, which is now part of Iraq, and in Egypt's Nile valley. These civilizations arose between 4,000 and 3,000 BCE. The area where these civilizations grew is known as the Fertile Crescent. There, geography and the availability of water made large-scale human habitation possible.

<u>Importance of rivers and water</u>
The earliest civilizations are also referred to as fluvial civilizations because they were founded near rivers. Rivers and the water they provide were vital to these early groupings, offering:
- Water for drinking and cultivating crops
- A gathering place for wild animals that could be hunted
- Easily available water for domesticated animals
- Rich soil deposits as a result of regular flooding

Irrigation techniques helped direct water where it was most needed, to sustain herds of domestic animals and to nourish crops of increasing size and quality.

Fertile Crescent

James Breasted, an archeologist from the University of Chicago, coined the term Fertile Crescent to describe the area in the Near East where the earliest civilizations arose. The region includes modern day Iraq, Syria, Lebanon, Israel/Palestine and Jordan. It is bordered on the south by the Arabian Desert, the west by the Mediterranean Sea, and to the north and east by the Taurus and Zagros Mountains respectively. This area not only provided the raw materials for the development of increasingly advanced civilizations, but also saw waves of migration and invasion, leading to the earliest wars and genocides as groups conquered and absorbed each other's cultures and inhabitants.

Egyptian, Sumerian, Babylonian and Assyrian cultures

The Egyptians were one of the most advanced ancient cultures, having developed construction methods to build the great pyramids, as well as a form of writing known as hieroglyphics. Their religion was highly

- 6 -

developed and complex, and included advanced techniques for the preservation of bodies after death. They also made paper by processing papyrus, a plant commonly found along the Nile, invented the decimal system, devised a solar calendar, and advanced overall knowledge of arithmetic and geometry.

> ➤ **Review Video: Egyptians**
> *Visit **mometrix.com/academy** and enter **Code: 398041***

The Sumerians were the first to invent the wheel, and also brought irrigation systems into use. Their cuneiform writing was simpler than Egyptian hieroglyphs, and they developed the timekeeping system we still use today.

> ➤ **Review Video: The Sumerians**
> *Visit **mometrix.com/academy** and enter **Code: 939880***

The Babylonians are best known for the Code of Hammurabi, an advanced law code.

The Assyrians developed horse-drawn chariots and an organized military.

Hebrew, Persian, Minoan, and Mycenaean cultures

The Hebrew or ancient Israelite culture developed the monotheistic religion that eventually developed into modern Judaism and Christianity.

The Persians were conquerors, but those they conquered were allowed to keep their own laws, customs, and religious traditions rather than being forced to accept those of their conquerors. They also developed an alphabet and practicing Zoroastrianism, Mithraism and Gnosticism, religions that have influenced modern religious practice.

The Minoans used a syllabic writing system and built large, colorful palaces. These ornate buildings included sewage systems, running water, bathtubs, and even flush toilets. Their script, known as Linear Script A, has yet to be deciphered.

The Mycenaeans practiced a religion that grew into the Greek pantheon, worshipping Zeus and other Olympian gods. They developed Linear Script B, a writing system used to write an ancient form of classical Greek.

Phoenicians and early culture in India and ancient China

Skilled seafarers and navigators, the Phoenicians used the stars to navigate their ships at night. They developed a purple dye that was in great demand in the ancient world, and worked with glass and metals. They also devised their own phonetic alphabet, using symbols to represent individual sounds rather than whole words or syllables.

In the Indus Valley, an urban civilization arose in what is now India. These ancient humans developed the concept of zero in mathematics, practiced an early form of the Hindu religion, and developed a caste system which is still prevalent in India today. Archeologists are still uncovering information about this highly developed ancient civilization.

In ancient China, human civilization developed along the Yangtze River, starting as long as 500,000 years ago. These people produced silk, grew millet, and made pottery, including Longshan black pottery.

- 7 -

Civilizations of Mesopotamia

The major civilizations of Mesopotamia, in what is now called the Middle East, were:
- Sumerians
- Amorites
- Hittites
- Assyrians
- Chaldeans
- Persians

These cultures controlled different areas of Mesopotamia during various time periods, but were similar in that they were autocratic. This meant a single ruler served as the head of the government and often, the main religious ruler, as well. These, often tyrannical, militaristic leaders, controlled all aspects of life, including law, trade, and religious activity. Portions of the legacies of these civilizations remain in cultures today. These include mythologies, religious systems, mathematical innovations and even elements of various languages.

Sumer

Sumer, located in the southern part of Mesopotamia, consisted of a dozen city-states. Each city-state had its own gods, and the leader of each city-state also served as the high priest. Cultural legacies of Sumer include:
- The invention of writing
- Invention of the wheel
- The first library—established in Assyria by Ashurbanipal
- The Hanging Gardens of Babylon—one of the Seven Wonders of the Ancient World
- First written laws—Ur-Nammu's Codes and the Codes of Hammurabi
- The *Epic of Gilgamesh*—the first epic story in history

Kushite culture

Kush, or Cush, was located south of ancient Egypt, and the earliest existing records of this civilization were found in Egyptian texts. At one time, Kush was the largest empire on the Nile River, surpassing even Egypt.

In Neolithic times, Kushites lived in villages, with buildings made of mud bricks. They were settled rather than nomadic, and practiced hunting and fishing, cultivated grain, and also herded cattle. Kerma, the capitol, was a major center of trade.

Kush determined leadership through matrilineal descent of their kings, as did Egypt. Their heads of state, the Kandake or Kentake, were female. Their polytheistic religion included the primary Egyptian gods as well as regional gods, including a lion god, which is commonly found in African cultures.

Archeological evidence indicates the Kushites were a mix of Mediterranean and Negroid peoples. Kush was conquered by Nubia in 800 BCE.

Minoan civilization

The Minoans lived on the island of Crete, just off the coast of Greece. This civilization reigned from 2700 to 1450 BCE. The Minoans developed writing systems known to linguists as Linear A and Linear B. Linear A has not yet been translated; Linear B evolved into classical Greek script. "Minoans" is not the name they used for themselves, but is instead a variation on the name of King Minos, a king in Greek mythology believed by some to have been a denizen of Crete. The Minoan civilization subsisted on trade, and their way of life was often disrupted by earthquakes and volcanoes. Much is still unknown about the Minoans, and archeologists continue to study their architecture and archeological remains. The Minoan culture eventually fell to Greek invaders and was supplanted by the Mycenaean civilization.

Influences of ancient Indian civilization

The civilizations of ancient India gave rise to both Hinduism and Buddhism, major world religions that have found their way to countries far away from their place of origin. Practices such as yoga, increasingly popular in the West, can trace their roots to these earliest Indian civilizations. Literature from ancient India includes the *Mahabharata* containing the *Bhagavad Gita,* the *Ramayana*, *Arthashastra*, and the *Vedas*, a collection of sacred texts. Indo-European languages, including English, find their beginnings in these ancient cultures. Ancient Indo-Aryan languages such as Sanskrit are still used in some formal Hindu practices. Yoga poses are still formally referred to by Sanskrit names.

Earliest civilizations in China

Many historians believe Chinese civilization is the oldest uninterrupted civilization in the world. The Neolithic age in China goes back 10,000 years, with agriculture in China beginning as early as 7,000 years ago. Their system of writing dates to 1,500 BCE. The Yellow River served as the center for the earliest Chinese settlements. In Ningxia, in northwest China, there are carvings on cliffs that date back to the Paleolithic Period, at least 6,000 years ago, indicating the extreme antiquity of Chinese culture. Literature from ancient China includes works by Confucius, *Analects*, the *Tao Te Ching*, and a variety of poetry.

Ancient American cultures

Less is known of ancient American civilizations since less was left behind. Those we know something of include:
- The Norte Chico civilization in Peru, an agricultural society of 20 individual communities, that existed over 5,000 years ago. This culture is also known as Caral-Supe, and is the oldest known civilization in the Americas.
- The Anasazi, or Ancient Pueblo People, in what is now the southwestern United States. Emerging about 1200 BCE, the Anasazi built complex adobe dwellings, and were the forerunners of later Pueblo Indian cultures.
- The Maya emerged in southern Mexico and northern Central America as early as 2,600 BCE. They developed a written language and a complex calendar.

Mycenaean civilization

The Mycenaean civilization was the first major civilization in Europe. In contrast to the Minoans, whom they displaced, the Mycenaeans relied more on conquest than on trade. Mycenaean states included Sparta, Metropolis and Corinth. The history of this civilization, including the Trojan War, was recorded by the Greek poet, Homer. His work was largely considered mythical until archeologists discovered evidence of the city of Troy in Hisarlik, Turkey. Archeologists continue to add to the body of information about this

- 9 -

ancient culture, translating documents written in Linear B, a script derived from the Minoan Linear A. It is theorized that the Mycenaean civilization was eventually destroyed in either a Dorian invasion or an attack by Greek invaders from the north. This theory has not been proven, nor is it certain who the invaders might have been

Dorian invasion

A Dorian invasion does not refer to an invasion by a particular group of people, but rather is a hypothetical theory to explain the end of the Mycenaean civilization and the growth of classical Greece. Ancient tradition refers to these events as "the return of the Heracleidae," or the sons (descendents) of Hercules. Archeologists and historians still do not know exactly who conquered the Mycenaean, but it is believed to have occurred around 1200 BCE, contemporaneous with the destruction of the Hittite civilization in what is now modern Turkey. The Hittites speak of an attack by people of the Aegean Sea, or the "Sea People." Only Athens was left intact.

Spartans and Athenians

Both powerful city-states, the Spartans and the Athenians nurtured contrasting cultures.
- The Spartans, located in Peloponnesus, were ruled by an oligarchic military state. They practiced farming, disallowed trade for Spartan citizens, and valued military arts and strict discipline. They emerged as the strongest military force in the area, and maintained this status for many years. In one memorable encounter, a small group of Spartans held off a huge army of Persians at Thermopylae.
- The Athenians were centered in Attica, where there was little land available for farming. Like the Spartans, they descended from invaders who spoke Greek. Their government was very different from Sparta's; it was in Athens that democracy was created by Cleisthenes of Athens in 510 BCE. Athenians excelled in art, theater, architecture, and philosophy.

Athens and Sparta fought each other in the Peloponnesian War, 431-404 BCE.

Contributions of ancient Greece

Ancient Greece made numerous major contributions to cultural development, including:
- Theater—Aristophanes and other Greek playwrights laid the groundwork for modern theatrical performance.
- Alphabet—the Greek alphabet, derived from the Phoenician alphabet, developed into the Roman alphabet, and then into our modern-day alphabet.
- Geometry—Pythagoras and Euclid pioneered much of the system of geometry still taught today. Archimedes made various mathematical discoveries, including the value of pi.
- Historical writing—much of ancient history doubles as mythology or religious texts. Herodotus and Thucydides made use of research and interpretation to record historical events.
- Philosophy—Socrates, Plato, and Aristotle served as the fathers of Western philosophy. Their work is still required reading for philosophy students.

Alexander the Great

Born to Philip II of Macedon and tutored by Aristotle, Alexander the Great is considered one of the greatest conquerors in history. He conquered Egypt, the Achaemenid/Persian Empire, a powerful empire founded by Cyrus the Great that spanned three continents, and he traveled as far as India and the Iberian

Peninsula. Though Alexander died at the early age of 32, his conquering efforts spread Greek culture into the east. This cultural diffusion left a greater mark on history than did his empire, which fell apart due to internal conflict not long after his death. Trade between the East and West increased, as did an exchange of ideas and beliefs that influenced both regions greatly. The Hellenistic traditions his conquest spread were prevalent in Byzantine culture until as late as the 15th century.

Hittite Empire

The Hittites were centered in what is now Turkey, but their empire extended into Palestine and Syria. They conquered the Babylonian civilization, but adopted their religion and their system of laws. Overall, the Hittites tended to tolerate other religions, unlike many other contemporary cultures, and absorbed foreign gods into their own belief systems rather than forcing their religion onto peoples they conquered. The Hittite Empire reached its peak in 1600-1200 BCE. After a war with Egypt, which weakened them severely, they were eventually conquered by the Assyrians in 700 BCE.

Persian Wars

The Persian Empire, ruled by Cyrus the Great, encompassed an area from the Black Sea to Afghanistan, and beyond into Central Asia. After the death of Cyrus, Darius became king in 522 BCE. The empire reached its zenith during his reign.
From 499-448 BCE, the Greeks and Persians fought in the Persian Wars. Battles of the Persian Wars included:
- The Battle of Marathon, in which heavily outnumbered Greek forces managed to achieve victory.
- The Battle of Thermopylae, in which a small band of Spartans held off a throng of Persian troops for several days.
- The Battle of Salamis, a naval battle that again saw outnumbered Greeks achieving victory.
- The Battle of Plataea, another Greek victory, but one in which they outnumbered the Persians.

The Persian Wars did not see the end of the Persian Empire, but discouraged additional attempts to invade Greece.

Maurya Empire

The Maurya Empire was a large, powerful empire established in India. It was one of the largest ever to rule in the Indian subcontinent, and existed from 322 to 185 BCE, ruled by Chandragupta after the withdrawal from India of Alexander the Great. The Maurya Empire was highly developed, including a standardized economic system, waterworks, and private corporations. Trade to the Greeks and others became common, with goods including silk, exotic foods, and spices. Religious development included the rise of Buddhism and Jainism. The laws of the Maurya Empire protected not only civil and social rights of the citizens, but also protected animals, establishing protected zones for economically important creatures such as elephants, lions and tigers. This period of time in Indian history was largely peaceful due to the strong Buddhist beliefs of many of its leaders. The empire finally fell after a succession of weak leaders, and was taken over by Demetrius, a Greco-Bactrian king who took advantage of this lapse in leadership to conquer southern Afghanistan and Pakistan around 180 BCE.

Chinese empires

In China, history was divided into a series of dynasties. The most famous of these, the Han Dynasty, existed from 206 BCE to 220 CE. Accomplishments of the Chinese Empires included:
- Building the Great Wall of China

- Numerous inventions, including paper, paper money, printing, and gunpowder
- High level of artistic development
- Silk production

The Chinese Empires were comparable to Rome as far as their artistic and intellectual accomplishments, as well as the size and scope of their influence.

Roman Empire and Republic

Rome began humbly, in a single town that grew out of Etruscan settlements and traditions, founded, according to legend, by twin brothers Romulus and Remus, who were raised by wolves. Romulus killed Remus, and from his legacy grew Rome. A thousand years later, the Roman Empire covered a significant portion of the known world, from what is now Scotland, across Europe, and into the Middle East. Hellenization, or the spread of Greek culture throughout the world, served as an inspiration and a model for the spread of Roman culture. Rome brought in belief systems of conquered peoples as well as their technological and scientific accomplishments, melding the disparate parts into a Roman core. Rome's overall government was autocratic, but local officials came from the provinces where they lived. This limited administrative system was probably a major factor in the long life of the empire.

> ➤ **Review Video: The Holy Roman Empire**
> *Visit **mometrix.com/academy** and enter **Code: 137655***

Byzantine Empire

In the early fourth century, the Roman Empire split, with the eastern portion becoming the Eastern Empire, or the Byzantine Empire. In 330 CE, Constantine founded the city of Constantinople, which became the center of the Byzantine Empire. Its major influences came from Mesopotamia and Persia, in contrast to the Western Empire, which maintained traditions more closely linked to Greece and Carthage. Byzantium's position gave it an advantage over invaders from the west and the east, as well as control over trade from both regions. It protected the Western empire from invasion from the Persians and the Ottomans, and practiced a more centralized rule than in the West. The Byzantines were famous for lavish art and architecture, as well as the Code of Justinian, which collected Roman law into a clear system.

Nicene Creed

The Byzantine Empire was Christian-based but incorporated Greek language, philosophy and literature and drew its law and government policies from Rome. However, there was as yet no unified doctrine of Christianity, as it was a relatively new religion that had spread rapidly and without a great deal of organization. In 325, the First Council of Nicaea addressed this issue. From this conference came the Nicene Creed, addressing the Trinity and other basic Christian beliefs. The Council of Chalcedon in 451 stated that any rejection of the Trinity was blasphemy.

Fall of the Western Roman Empire

Germanic tribes, including the Visigoths, Ostrogoths, Vandals, Saxons and Franks, controlled most of Europe. The Roman Empire faced major opposition on that front. The increasing size of the empire also made it harder to manage, leading to dissatisfaction throughout the empire as Roman government became less efficient. Germanic tribes refused to adhere to the Nicene Creed, instead following Arianism, which led the Roman Catholic Church to declare them heretics. The Franks proved a powerful military force in their defeat of the Muslims in 732. In 768, Charlemagne became king of the Franks. These tribes waged several wars against Rome, including the invasion of Britannia by the Angles and Saxons. Far-flung Rome lost control over this area of its Empire, and eventually Rome itself was invaded.

Iconoclasm and conflict between Roman Catholic and Eastern Orthodox churches

Emperor Leo III ordered the destruction of all icons throughout the Byzantine Empire. Images of Jesus were replaced with a cross, and images of Jesus, Mary or other religious figures were considered blasphemy on grounds of idolatry. The current Pope, Gregory II, called a synod to discuss the issue. The synod declared that destroying these images was heretical, and that strong disciplinary measures would result for anyone who took this step. Leo's response was an attempt to kidnap Pope Gregory, but this plan ended in failure when his ships were destroyed by a storm.

Viking invasions

Vikings invaded Northern France in the tenth century, eventually becoming the Normans. Originating in Scandinavia, the Vikings were accomplished seafarers with advanced knowledge of trade routes. With overpopulation plaguing their native lands, they began to travel. From the eighth to the eleventh centuries, they spread throughout Europe, conquering and colonizing. Vikings invaded and colonized England through several waves, including the Anglo-Saxon invasions that displaced Roman control. Their influence remained significant in England, affecting everything from the language of the country to place names and even the government and social structure. By 900, Vikings had settled in Iceland. They proceeded then to Greenland and eventually to North America, arriving in the New World even before the Spanish and British who claimed the lands several centuries later. They also traded with the Byzantine Empire until the eleventh century when their significant level of activity came to an end.

Tenth century events in the West and the East

In Europe, the tenth century is largely known as the Dark Ages, as numerous Viking invasions disrupted societies that had been more settled under Roman rule. Vikings settled in Northern France, eventually becoming the Normans. By the eleventh century, Europe would rise again into the High Middle Ages with the beginning of the Crusades.
In China, wars also raged. This led the Chinese to make use of gunpowder for the first time in warfare.

In the Americas, the Mayan Empire was winding down while the Toltec became more prominent. Pueblo Indian culture was also at its zenith.

In the East, the Muslims and the Byzantine Empire were experiencing a significant period of growth and development.

European feudalism in the Middle Ages

A major element of the social and economic life of Europe, feudalism developed as a way to ensure European rulers would have the wherewithal to quickly raise an army when necessary. Vassals swore loyalty and promised to provide military service for lords, who in return offered a fief, or a parcel of land, for them to use to generate their livelihood. Vassals could work the land themselves, have it worked by peasants or serfs—workers who had few rights and were little more than slaves—or grant the fief to someone else. The king legally owned all the land, but in return promised to protect the vassals from invasion and war. Vassals returned a certain percentage of their income to the lords, who in turn passed a portion of their income on to the king. A similar practice was manorialism, in which the feudal system was applied to a self-contained manor. These manors were often owned by the lords who ran them, but were usually included in the same system of loyalty and promises of military service that drove feudalism.

> **Review Video:** **The Middle Ages: Feudalism**
*Visit **mometrix.com/academy** and enter **Code: 165907**

Influence of the Roman Catholic Church over medieval society

The Roman Catholic Church extended significant influence both politically and economically throughout medieval society. The church supplied education, as there were no established schools or universities. To a large extent, the church had filled a power void left by various invasions throughout the former Roman Empire, leading it to exercise a role that was far more political than religious. Kings were heavily influenced by the Pope and other church officials, and churches controlled large amounts of land throughout Europe.

Black Death

The Black Death, believed to be bubonic plague, came to Europe probably brought by fleas carried on rats that were regular passengers on sailing vessels. It killed in excess of a third of the entire population of Europe and effectively ended feudalism as a political system. Many who had formerly served as peasants or serfs found different work, as a demand for skilled labor grew. Nation-states grew in power, and in the face of the pandemic, many began to turn away from faith in God and toward the ideals of ancient Greece and Rome for government and other beliefs.

Crusades

The Crusades began in the eleventh century and progressed well into the twelfth. The major goal of these various military ventures was to slow the progression of Muslim forces into Europe and to expel them from the Holy Land, where they had taken control of Jerusalem and Palestine. Alexius I, the Eastern emperor, called for helped from Pope Urban II when Palestine was taken. In 1095, the Pope, hoping to reunite Eastern and Western Christian influences, encouraged all Christians to help the cause. Amidst great bloodshed, this Crusade recaptured Jerusalem, but over the next centuries, Jerusalem and other areas of the Holy Land changed hands numerous times. The Second Crusade, in 1145, consisted of an unsuccessful attempt to retake Damascus. The Third Crusade, under Pope Gregory VIII, attempted to recapture Jerusalem, but failed. The Fourth Crusade, under Pope Innocent III, attempted to come into the Holy Land via Egypt. The Crusades led to greater power for the Pope and the Catholic Church in general and also opened numerous trading and cultural routes between Europe and the East.

Developments through the eleventh century

Politics in India
After the Mauryan dynasty, the Guptas ruled India, maintaining a long period of peace and prosperity in the area. During this time, the Indian people invented the decimal system as well as the concept of zero. They produced cotton and calico, as well as other products in high demand in Europe and Asia, and developed a complex system of medicine.

The Gupta Dynasty ended in the eleventh century with a Muslim invasion of the region. These sultans ruled for several centuries. Tamerlane, one of the most famous, expanded India's borders and founded the Mogul Dynasty. His grandson Akbar promoted freedom of religion and built a wide-spread number of mosques, forts, and other buildings throughout the country.

Chinese and Japanese governments
After the Mongols, led by Genghis Khan and his grandson Kublai Khan, unified the Mongol Empire, China was led by the Ming and Manchu Dynasties. Both these Dynasties were isolationist, ending China's interaction with other countries until the eighteenth century. The Ming Dynasty was known for its porcelain, while the Manchus focused on farming and road construction as the population grew.

Japan developed independent of China, but borrowed the Buddhist religion, the Chinese writing system, and other elements of Chinese society. Ruled by the divine emperor, Japan basically functioned on a feudal system led by Daimyos, or lords, and soldiers known as samurai. Japan remained isolationist, not interacting significantly with the rest of the world until the 1800s.

Africa
Only a few areas of Africa were amenable to habitation, due to the large amount of desert and other inhospitable terrain. Egypt remained important, though most of the northern coast became Muslim as their armies spread through the area. Ghana rose as a trade center in the ninth century, lasting into the twelfth century, primarily trading in gold, which it exchange for Saharan salt. Mali rose somewhat later, with the trade center Timbuktu becoming an important exporter of goods such as iron, leather and tin. Mali also dealt in agricultural trade, becoming one of the most significant trading centers in West Africa. The Muslim religion dominated, and technological advancement was sparse.

African culture was largely defined through migration, as Arab merchants and others settled on the continent, particularly along the east coast. Scholars from the Muslim nations gravitated to Timbuktu, which in addition to its importance in trade, had also become a magnet for those seeking knowledge and education.

Islam

Born in 570 CE, Mohammed became prominent in 610, leading his followers in a new religion called Islam, which means submission to God's will. Before this time, the Arabian Peninsula was inhabited largely by Bedouins, nomads who battled amongst each other and lived in tribal organizations. But by the time Mohammed died in 632, most of Arabia had become Muslim to some extent.

Mohammed conquered Mecca, where a temple called the Kaaba had long served as a center of the nomadic religions. He declared this temple the most sacred of Islam, and Mecca as the holy city. His writings became the Koran, or Qur'an, divine revelations he said had been delivered to him by the angel Gabriel.

Mohammed's teachings gave the formerly tribal Arabian people a sense of unity that had not existed in the area before. After his death, the converted Muslims of Arabia conquered a vast territory, creating an empire and bringing advances in literature, technology, science and art just as Europe was declining under the scourge of the Black Death. Literature from this period includes the *Arabian Nights* and the *Rubaiyat* of Omar Khayyam.

Later in its development, Islam split into two factions, the Shiite and the Sunni Muslims. Conflict continues today between these groups.

> ➤ **Review Video:** Islam
> *Visit **mometrix.com/academy** and enter **Code: 359164***

- 15 -

Ottoman Empire

By 1400, the Ottomans had grown in power in Anatolia and had begun attempts to take Constantinople. In 1453 they finally conquered the Byzantine capital and renamed it Istanbul. The Ottoman Empire's major strength, much like Rome before it, lay in its ability to unite widely disparate people through religious tolerance. This tolerance, which stemmed from the idea that Muslims, Christians, and Jews were fundamentally related and could coexist, enabled the Ottomans to develop a widely varied culture. They also believed in just laws and just government, with government centered in a monarch, known as the sultan.

Renaissance

Renaissance literally means "rebirth." After the darkness of the Dark Ages and the Black Plague, interest rose again in the beliefs and politics of ancient Greece and Rome. Art, literature, music, science, and philosophy all burgeoned during the Renaissance.

Many of the ideas of the Renaissance began in Florence, Italy, spurred by the Medici family. Education for the upper classes expanded to include law, math, reading, writing, and classical Greek and Roman works. As the Renaissance progressed, the world was presented through art and literature in a realistic way that had never been explored before. This realism drove culture to new heights.

Artists, authors and scientists

Artists of the Renaissance included Leonardo da Vinci, also an inventor, Michelangelo, also an architect, and others who focused on realism in their work. In literature, major contributions came from the humanist, authors like Petrarch, Erasmus, Sir Thomas More, and Boccaccio, who believed man should focus on reality rather than on the ethereal. Shakespeare, Cervantes and Dante followed in their footsteps, and their works found a wide audience thanks to Gutenberg's development of the printing press.

Scientific developments of the Renaissance included the work of Copernicus, Galileo and Kepler, who challenged the geocentric philosophies of the church by proving the earth was not the center of the solar system.

> ➤ **Review Video: Renaissance**
> *Visit mometrix.com/academy and enter Code:* **123100**

Reformation

The Reformation consisted of the Protestant Revolution and the Catholic Reformation. The Protestant Revolution rose in Germany when Martin Luther protested abuses of the Catholic Church. John Calvin led the movement in Switzerland, while in England King Henry VIII made use of the Revolution's ideas to further his own political goals. The Catholic Reformation occurred in response to the Protestant Revolution, leading to various changes in the Catholic Church. Some provided wider tolerance of different religious viewpoints, but others actually increased the persecution of those deemed to be heretics.

> ➤ **Review Video: The Protestants**
> *Visit mometrix.com/academy and enter Code:* **583582**

From a religious standpoint, the Reformation occurred due to abuses by the Catholic Church such as indulgences and dispensations, religious offices being offered up for sale, and an increasingly dissolute clergy. Politically, the Reformation was driven by increased power of various ruling monarchs, who wished to take all power to themselves rather than allowing power to remain with the church. They also had begun to chafe at papal taxes and the church's increasing wealth. The ideas of the Protestant Revolution removed power from the Catholic Church and the Pope himself, playing nicely into the hands of those monarchs, such as Henry VIII, who wanted out from under the church's control.

Scientific Revolution

In addition to holding power in the political realm, church doctrine also governed scientific belief. During the Scientific Revolution, astronomers and other scientists began to amass evidence that challenged the church's scientific doctrine. Major figures of the Scientific Revolution included:

- Nicolaus Copernicus—wrote *Revolutions of the Celestial Spheres*, arguing that the Earth revolved around the sun.
- Tycho Brahe—catalogued astronomical observations.
- Johannes Kepler—developed Laws of Planetary Motions.
- Galileo Galilei—defended the heliocentric theories of Copernicus and Kepler, discovered four moons of Jupiter, and died under house arrest by the Church, charged with heresy.
- Isaac Newton—discovered gravity, studied optics, calculus and physics, and believed the workings of nature could be observed, studied, and proven through observation.

Enlightenment

During the Enlightenment, philosophers and scientists began to rely more and more on observation to support their ideas, rather than building on past beliefs, particularly those held by the church. A focus on ethics and logic drove their work. Major philosophers of the Enlightenment included:

- Rene Descartes—"I think, therefore I am." He believed strongly in logic and rules of observation.
- David Hume—pioneered empiricism and skepticism, believing that truth could only be found through direct experience, and that what others said to be true was always suspect.
- Immanuel Kant—believed in self-examination and observation, and that the root of morality lay within human beings.
- Jean-Jacques Rousseau—developed the idea of the social contract, that government existed by the agreement of the people, and that the government was obligated to protect the people and their basic rights. His ideas influenced John Locke and Thomas Jefferson.

> ➤ **Review Video:** <u>Age of Enlightenment</u>
> *Visit **mometrix.com/academy** and enter **Code:** 143022*

American Revolution and French Revolution

Both the American and French Revolution came about as a protest against the excesses and overly controlling nature of their respective monarchs. In America, the British colonies had been left mostly self-governing until the British monarchs began to increase control, leading the colonies to revolt. In France, the nobility's excesses had led to increasingly difficult economic conditions, with inflation, heavy taxation and food shortages creating horrible burdens on the people. Both revolutions led to the development of republics to replace the monarchies that were displaced. However, the French Revolution eventually led to the rise of the dictator Napoleon Bonaparte, while the American Revolution produced a working republic from the beginning.

In 1789, King Louis XVI, faced with a huge national debt, convened parliament. The Third Estate, or Commons, a division of the French parliament, then claimed power, and the king's resistance led to the storming of the Bastille, the royal prison. The people established a constitutional monarchy. When King Louis XVI and Marie Antoinette attempted to leave the country, they were executed on the guillotine. From 1793 to 1794, Robespierre and extreme radicals, the Jacobins, instituted a Reign of Terror, executing thousands of nobles as well as anyone considered an enemy of the Revolution. Robespierre was then executed, as well, and the Directory came into power. This governing body proved incompetent and corrupt, allowing Napoleon Bonaparte to come to power in 1799, first as a dictator, then as emperor. While the French Revolution threw off the power of a corrupt monarchy, its immediate results were likely not what the original perpetrators of the revolt had intended.

> **Review Video: <u>Revolutionary War</u>**
> *Visit **mometrix.com/academy** and enter **Code: 935282***

Russian Revolution of 1905

In Russia, rule lay in the hands of the Czars, and the overall structure was feudalistic. Beneath the Czars was a group of rich nobles, landowners whose lands were worked by peasants and serfs. The Russo-Japanese War (1904-1905) made conditions much worse for the lower classes. When peasants demonstrated outside the Czar's Winter Palace, the palace guard fired upon the crowd. The demonstration had been organized by a trade union leader, and after the violent response, many unions as well as political parties blossomed and began to lead numerous strikes. When the economy ground to a halt, Czar Nicholas II signed a document known as the October Manifesto, which established a constitutional monarchy and gave legislative power to parliament. However, he violated the Manifesto shortly thereafter, disbanding parliament and ignoring the civil liberties granted by the Manifesto. This eventually led to the Bolshevik Revolution of 1917.

Bolshevik Revolution of 1917

Throughout its modern history, Russia had lagged behind other countries in development. The continued existence of a feudal system, combined with harsh conditions and the overall size of the country, led to massive food shortages and increasingly harsh conditions for the majority of the population. The tyrannical rule favored by the Czars only made this worse, as did repeated losses in various military conflicts. Increasing poverty, decreasing supplies, and the Czar's violation of the October Manifesto which had given some political power and civil rights to the people finally came to a head with the Bolshevik Revolution.

<u>Major events</u>
A workers' strike in Petrograd in 1917 set the revolutionary wheels in motion when the army sided with the workers. While parliament set up a provisional government made up of nobles, the workers and military joined to form their own governmental system known as soviets, which consisted of local councils elected by the people. The ensuing chaos opened the doors for formerly exiled leaders Vladimir Lenin, Joseph Stalin and Leon Trotsky to move in and gain popular support as well as the support of the Red Guard. Overthrowing parliament, they took power, creating a communist state in Russia. This development led to the spread of Communism throughout Eastern Europe and elsewhere, greatly affecting diplomatic policies throughout the world for several decades.

Industrial Revolution

The Industrial Revolution began in Great Britain, bringing coal- and steam-powered machinery into widespread use. Industry began a period of rapid growth with these developments. Goods that had previously been produced in small workshops or even in homes were produced more efficiently and in much larger quantities in factories. Where society had been largely agrarian based, the focus swiftly shifted to an industrial outlook. As electricity and internal combustion engines replaced coal and steam as energy sources, even more drastic and rapid changes occurred. Western European countries in particular turned to colonialism, taking control of portions of Africa and Asia to assure access to the raw materials needed to produce factory goods. Specialized labor became very much in demand, and businesses grew rapidly, creating monopolies, increasing world trade, and creating large urban centers. Even agriculture changed fundamentally as the Industrial Revolution led to a second Agricultural Revolution as the addition of the new technologies advanced agricultural production.

First and second phases

The first phase of the Industrial Revolution took place from roughly 1750 to 1830. The textile industry experienced major changes as more and more elements of the process became mechanized. Mining benefited from the steam engine. Transportation became easier and more widely available as waterways were improved and the railroad came into prominence. In the second phase, from 1830 to 1910, industries further improved in efficiency and new industries were introduced as photography, various chemical processes, and electricity became more widely available to produce new goods or new, improved versions of old goods. Petroleum and hydroelectric became major sources of power. During this time, the industrial revolution spread out of Western Europe and into the US and Japan.

Political, social and economic side effects

The Industrial Revolution led to widespread education, a wider franchise, and the development of mass communication in the political arena. Economically, conflicts arose between companies and their employees, as struggles for fair treatment and fair wages increased. Unions gained power and became more active. Government regulation over industries increased, but at the same time, growing businesses fought for the right to free enterprise. In the social sphere, populations increased and began to concentrate around centers of industry. Cities became larger and more densely populated. Scientific advancements led to more efficient agriculture, greater supply of goods, and increased knowledge of medicine and sanitation, leading to better overall health.

> ➤ **Review Video: <u>The Industrial Revolution</u>**
> *Visit* ***mometrix.com/academy*** *and enter* ***Code: 372796***

Nationalism in the eighteenth and nineteenth centuries

Nationalism, put simply, is a strong belief in, identification with, and allegiance to a particular nation and people. Nationalistic belief unified various areas that had previously seen themselves as fragmented which led to patriotism and, in some cases, imperialism. As nationalism grew, individual nations sought to grow, bringing in other, smaller states that shared similar characteristics such as language and cultural beliefs. Unfortunately, a major side effect of these growing nationalistic beliefs was often conflict and outright war.

In Europe, imperialism led countries to spread their influence into Africa and Asia. Africa was eventually divided among several European countries that needed the raw materials to be found there. Asia also came under European control, with the exception of China, Japan and Siam (now Thailand). In the US, Manifest Destiny became the rallying cry as the country expanded west. Italy and Germany formed larger nations from a variety of smaller states.

> ➤ **Review Video: <u>Nationalism</u>**
> *Visit* ***mometrix.com/academy*** *and enter* ***Code: 865693***

WWI

Europe

WW I began in 1914 with the assassination of Archduke Franz Ferdinand, heir to the throne of Austria-Hungary, by a Serbian national. This led to a conflict between Austria-Hungary and Serbia that quickly escalated into the First World War. Europe split into the Allies—Britain, France and Russia, and later Italy, Japan and the US, against the Central Powers—Austria-Hungary, Germany and Turkey. As the war spread, countries beyond Europe became involved. The war left Europe deeply in debt, and particularly devastated the German economy. The ensuing Great Depression made matters worse, and economic devastation opened the door for Communist, Fascist and Socialist governments to gain power.

Trench warfare

Fighting during WW I took place largely in a series of trenches built along the Eastern and Western Fronts. These trenches added up to about 24,000 miles, each side having dug at least 12,000 miles' worth during the course of the war. This produced fronts that stretched nearly 400 miles, from the coast of Belgium to the border of Switzerland. The Allies made use of straightforward open-air trenches with a front line, supporting lines, and communications lines. By contrast, the German trenches sometimes included well-equipped underground living quarters.

Communism and Socialism

At their roots, socialism and communism both focus on public ownership and distribution of goods and services. However, communism works toward revolution by drawing on what it sees to be inevitable class antagonism, eventually overthrowing the upper classes and the systems of capitalism. Socialism makes use of democratic procedures, building on the existing order. This was particularly true of the Utopian-Socialists, who saw industrial capitalism as oppressive, not allowing workers to prosper. While socialism struggled between the World Wars, communism took hold, especially in Eastern Europe. After WW II, democratic socialism became more common. Later, capitalism took a stronger hold again, and today most industrialized countries in the world function under an economy that mixes elements of capitalism and socialism.

> ➤ **Review Video:** <u>Socialism</u>
> *Visit **mometrix.com/academy** and enter **Code: 917677***

Rise of the Nazi party

The Great Depression had a particularly devastating effect on Germany's economy, especially after the US was no longer able to supply reconstruction loans to help the country regain its footing. With unemployment rising rapidly, dissatisfaction with the government grew. Fascist and Communist parties rose, promising change and improvement.

Led by Adolf Hitler, the Fascist, Nazi Party eventually gained power in Parliament based on these promises and the votes of desperate German workers. When Hitler became Chancellor, he launched numerous expansionist policies, violating the peace treaties that had ended WW I. His military buildup and conquering of neighboring countries sparked the aggression that soon led to WW II.

Blitzkrieg

The blitzkrieg, or "lightning war," consisted of fast, powerful surprise attacks that disrupted communications, made it difficult if not impossible for the victims to retaliate, and demoralized

Germany's foes. The "blitz," or the aerial bombing of England in 1940, was one example, with bombings occurring in London and other cities 57 nights in a row. The Battle of Britain, from 1940 to 1941, also brought intense raids by Germany's air force, the Luftwaffe, mostly targeting ports and British air force bases. Eventually, Britain's Royal Air Force blocked the Luftwaffe, ending Germany's hopes for conquering Britain.

Battle of the Bulge

Following the D-Day Invasion, Allied forces gained considerable ground, and began a major campaign to push through Europe. In December of 1944, Hitler launched a counteroffensive, attempting to retake Antwerp, an important port. The ensuing battle became the largest land battle on the war's Western Front, and was known as the Battle of the Ardennes, or the Battle of the Bulge. The battle lasted from December 16, 1944 to January 28, 1945. The Germans pushed forward, making inroads into Allied lines, but in the end the Allies brought the advance to a halt. The Germans were pushed back, with massive losses on both sides. However, those losses proved crippling to the German army.

Holocaust

As Germany sank deeper and deeper into dire economic straits, the tendency was to look for a person or group of people to blame for the problems of the country. With distrust of the Jewish people already ingrained, it was easy for German authorities to set up the Jews as scapegoats for Germany's problems. Under the rule of Hitler and the Nazi party, the "Final Solution" for the supposed Jewish problem was devised. Millions of Jews, as well as Gypsies, homosexuals, Communists, Catholics, the mentally ill and others, simply named as criminals, were transported to concentration camps during the course of the war. At least six million were slaughtered in death camps such as Auschwitz, where horrible conditions and torture of prisoners were commonplace.   The Allies were aware of rumors of mass slaughter throughout the war, but many discounted the reports. Only when troops went in to liberate the prisoners was the true horror of the concentration camps brought to light.
The Holocaust resulted in massive loss of human life, but also in the loss and destruction of cultures. Because the genocide focused on specific ethnic groups, many traditions, histories, knowledge, and other cultural elements were lost, particularly among the Jewish and Gypsy populations. After World War II, the United Nations recognized genocide as a "crime against humanity." The UN passed the Universal Declaration of Human Rights in order to further specify what rights the organization protected. Nazi war criminals faced justice during the Nuremberg Trials. There individuals, rather than their governments, were held accountable for war crimes.

> ➤ **Review Video:** <u>The Holocaust</u>
> *Visit **mometrix.com/academy** and enter **Code: 350695***

Cold War

With millions of military and civilian deaths and over 12 million persons displaced, WW II left large regions of Europe and Asia in disarray. Communist governments moved in with promises of renewed prosperity and economic stability. The Soviet Union backed Communist regimes in much of Eastern Europe. In China, Mao Zedong led communist forces in the overthrow of the Chinese Nationalist Party and instituted a Communist government in 1949.   While the new Communist governments restored a measure of stability to much of Eastern Europe, it brought its own problems, with dictatorial governments and an oppressive police force. The spread of Communism also led to several years of tension between Communist countries and the democratic west, as the west fought to slow the spread of oppressive regimes throughout the world. With both sides in possession of nuclear weapons, tensions rose. Each side feared the other would resort to nuclear attack. This standoff lasted until 1989, when the Berlin Wall fell. The Soviet Union was dissolved two years later.

United Nations

The United Nations (UN) came into being toward the end of World War II. A successor to the less-than-successful League of Nations, formed after World War I, the UN built and improved on those ideas. Since its inception, the UN has worked to bring the countries of the world together for diplomatic solutions to international problems, including sanctions and other restrictions. It has also initiated military action, calling for peacekeeping troops from member countries to move against countries violating UN policies.

One example of UN involvement in an international conflict is the Korean War, the first war in which an international alliance of this kind was actively involved.

Decolonization

A rise of nationalism among European colonies led to many of them declaring independence. India and Pakistan became independent of Britain at this time, and numerous African and Asian colonies declared independence, as well. This period of decolonization lasted into the 1960s. Some colonies moved successfully into independence but many, especially in Africa and Asia, struggled to create stable governments and economies, and suffered from ethnic and religious conflicts. Some of those countries still struggle today.

Korean War

In 1910, Japan annexed Korea and maintained this control until 1945, when Soviet and US troops occupied the country. The Soviet Union controlled North Korea, while the US controlled South Korea. In 1947, the UN ordered elections in Korea to unify the country but the Soviet Union refused to allow them to take place, instead setting up a communist government in North Korea. In 1950, the US withdrew troops, and the North Korean troops moved to invade South Korea. The Korean War was the first war in which the UN—or any international organization—played a major role. The US, Australia, Canada, France, Netherlands, Great Britain, Turkey, China, USSR and other countries sent troops at various times, for both sides, throughout the war. In 1953, the war ended in a truce, but no peace agreement was ever achieved, and Korea remains divided.

Vietnam War and involvement of France

Vietnam had previously been part of a French colony called French Indochina.
The Vietnam War began with the French Indochina War from 1946-1954, in which France battled with the Democratic Republic of Vietnam, ruled by Ho Chi Minh.

In 1954, a siege at Dien Bien Phu ended in a Vietnamese victory. Vietnam was then divided into North and South, much like Korea. Communist forces controlled the North and the South was controlled by South Vietnamese forces, supported by the US. Conflict ensued, leading to a war. US troops eventually lead the fight, in support of South Vietnam. The war became a major political issue in the US, with many citizens protesting American involvement. In 1976, South Vietnam surrendered, and Vietnam became the Socialist Republic of Vietnam.

Globalism

In the modern era, globalism has emerged as a popular political ideology. Globalism is based in the idea that all people and all nations are interdependent. Each nation is dependent on one or more other nations for production of and markets for goods, and for income generation. Today's ease of international travel and communication, including technological advances such as the airplane, has heightened this sense of interdependence. The global economy, and the general idea of globalism, has shaped many economic and political choices since the beginning of the twentieth century. Many of today's issues, including environmental awareness, economic struggles, and continued warfare, often require the cooperation of many countries if they are to be dealt with effectively.

Effects of globalization

With countries worldwide often seeking the same resources, some, particularly nonrenewable resources, have experienced high demand. At times this has resulted in wild price fluctuations. One major example is the demand for petroleum products such as oil and natural gas. Increased travel and communication make it possible to deal with diseases in remote locations; however, it also allows diseases to be spread via travelers, as well.

A major factor contributing to increased globalization over the past few decades has been the Internet. By allowing instantaneous communication with anyone nearly anywhere on the globe, the Internet has led to interaction between far-flung individuals and countries, and an ever increasing awareness of happenings all over the world.

Middle East in international relations and economics

Its location on the globe, with ease of access to Europe and Asia, and its preponderance of oil deposits, makes the middle eastern countries a crucial factor in many international issues both diplomatic and economic. Because of its central location, the Middle East has been a hotbed for violence since before the beginning of recorded history. Conflicts over land, resources, religious and political power continue in the area today, spurred by conflict over control of the area's vast oil fields as well as over territories that have been disputed for literally hundreds—and even thousands—of years.

Genocide

The three major occurrences of genocide in modern history other than the Holocaust are as follows:
- Armenian genocide—occurred in the 1900s when the Young Turks, heirs to the Ottoman Empire, slaughtered over a million Armenians between 1915 and 1917. This constituted nearly half the Armenian population at the time.
- Russian purges under Stalin—Scholars have attributed deaths between 3 and 60 million, both directly and indirectly, to the policies and edicts of Joseph Stalin's regime. The deaths took place from 1921 to 1953, when Stalin died. In recent years, many scholars have settled on a number of deaths near 20 million but this is still disputed today.
- Rwandan Genocide—in 1994, hundreds of thousands of Tutsi and Hutu sympathizers were slaughtered during the Rwandan Civil War. The UN did not act or authorize intervention during these atrocities.

United States History

Well-known Native Americans

The following are five well-known Native Americans and their roles in early U.S. history:
- Squanto, an Algonquian, helped early English settlers survive the hard winter by teaching them the native methods of planting corn, squash, and pumpkins.
- Pocahontas, also Algonquian, became famous as a liaison with John Smith's Jamestown colony in 1607.
- Sacagawea, a Shoshone, served a vital role in the Lewis and Clark expedition when the two explorers hired her as their guide in 1805.
- Crazy Horse and Sitting Bull led Sioux and Cheyenne troops in the Battle of the Little Bighorn in 1876, soundly defeating George Armstrong Custer.
- Chief Joseph, a leader of the Nez Perce who supported peaceful interaction with white settlers, attempted to relocate his tribe to Canada rather than move them to a reservation.

Native American groups

The major regional Native American groups and the major traits of each one are as follows:
- The Algonquians in the eastern part of the United States lived in wigwams. The northern tribes subsisted on hunting and gathering, while those who were farther south grew crops such as corn.
- The Iroquois, also an east coast tribe, spoke a different language from the Algonquians, and lived in rectangular longhouses.
- The Plains tribes lived between the Mississippi River and the Rocky Mountains. Nomadic tribes, they lived in teepees and followed the buffalo herds. Plains tribes included the Sioux, Cheyenne, Comanche and Blackfoot.
- Pueblo tribes included the Zuni, Hope, and Acoma. They lived in the Southwest deserts in homes made of stone or adobe. They domesticated animals and cultivated corn and beans.
- On the Pacific coast, tribes such as the Tlingit, Chinook and Salish lived on fish as well as deer, native berries and roots. Their rectangular homes housed large family groups, and they used totem poles.
- In the far north, the Aleuts and Inuit lived in skin tents or igloos. Talented fishermen, they built kayaks and umiaks and also hunted caribou, seals, whales and walrus.

Age of Exploration

The Age of Exploration is also called the Age of Discovery. It is generally considered to have begun in the early fifteenth century, and continued into the seventeenth century. Major developments of the Age of Exploration included technological advances in navigation, mapmaking and shipbuilding. These advances led to expanded European exploration of the rest of the world. Explorers set out from several European countries, including Portuguese, Spain, France and England, seeking new routes to Asia. These efforts led to the discovery of new lands, as well as colonization in India, Asia, Africa, and North America.

> ➤ **Review Video:** Age of Exploration
> *Visit **mometrix.com/academy** and enter **Code: 612972***

Advancements in navigation and seafaring tools

For long ocean journeys, it was important for sailors to be able to find their way home even when their vessels sailed far out to sea, well out of sight of land. A variety of navigational tools enabled them to launch ambitious journeys over long distances. The compass and astrolabe were particularly important advancements. The magnetic compass had been used by Chinese navigators for some time, and knowledge of the astrolabe came to Europe from Arab navigators and traders who had refined designs developed by the ancient Greeks. The Portuguese developed a ship called a caravel in the 1400s that incorporated navigational advancements with the ability to make long sea journeys. Equipped with this advanced vessel, the Portuguese achieved a major goal of the Age of Exploration by discovering a sea route from Europe to Asia in 1498.

Voyage of Christopher Columbus

In 1492, Columbus, a Genoan explorer, obtained financial backing from King Ferdinand and Queen Isabella of Spain to seek a sea route to Asia. He sought a trade route with the Asian Indies to the west. With three ships, the *Niña*, the *Pinta* and the *Santa Maria*, he eventually landed in the West Indies. While Columbus failed in his effort to discover a western route to Asia, he is credited with the discovery of the Americas.

> ➤ **Review Video:** <u>Christopher Columbus</u>
> *Visit **mometrix.com/academy** and enter **Code: 496598***

Colonization of the Americas

The following are the various goals of the French, Spanish, Dutch and British in the colonization of the Americas:
- Initial French colonies were focused on expanding the fur trade. Later, French colonization led to the growth of plantations in Louisiana which brought numerous African slaves to the New World.
- Spanish colonists came to look for wealth, and to converting the natives to Christianity. For some, the desire for gold led to mining in the New World, while others established large ranches.
- The Dutch were also involved in the fur trade, and also imported slaves as the need for laborers increased.
- British colonists arrived with various goals. Some were simply looking for additional income, while others were fleeing Britain to escape religious persecution.

> ➤ **Review Video:** <u>Colonization of the Americas</u>
> *Visit **mometrix.com/academy** and enter **Code: 438412***

New England colonies
The New England colonies were: New Hampshire, Connecticut, Rhode Island and Massachusetts. The colonies in New England were founded largely to escape religious persecution in England. The beliefs of the Puritans, who migrated to America in the 1600s, significantly influenced the development of these colonies. Situated in the northeast coastal areas of America, the New England colonies featured numerous harbors as well as dense forest. The soil, however, is rocky and, with a very short growing season, was not well suited for agriculture. The economy of New England during the colonial period centered around fishing, shipbuilding and trade along with some small farms and lumber mills. Although some groups congregated in small farms, life centered largely on towns and cities where merchants largely controlled the trade economy. Coastal cities such as Boston grew and thrived.

Middle or Middle Atlantic Colonies

The Middle or Middle Atlantic Colonies were: New York, New Jersey, Pennsylvania and Delaware. Unlike the New England colonies, where most colonists were from England and Scotland, the Middle Colonies founders were from various countries including the Netherlands, Holland and Sweden. Various factors led these colonists to America. More fertile than New England, the Middle Colonies became major producers of crops included rye, oats, potatoes, wheat, and barley. Some particularly wealthy inhabitants owned large farms and/or businesses. Farmers in general were able to produce enough to have a surplus to sell. Tenant farmers also rented land from larger land owners.

Southern Colonies

The Southern Colonies were Maryland, Virginia, North Carolina, South Carolina and Georgia.
Of the Southern Colonies, Virginia was the first permanent English colony and Georgia the last. The warm climate and rich soil of the south encouraged agriculture, and the growing season was long. As a result, economy in the south was based largely on labor-intensive plantations. Crops included tobacco, rice and indigo, all of which became valuable cash crops. Most land in the south was controlled by wealthy plantation owners and farmers. Labor on the farms came in the form of indentured servants and African slaves. The first of these African slaves arrived in Virginia in 1619, starting a long, unpleasant history of slavery in the American colonies.

French and Indian Wars

The British defeat of the Spanish Armada in 1588 led to the decline of Spanish power in Europe. This in turn led the British and French into battle over several wars between 1689 and 1748. These wars were:
- King William's War, or the Nine Years War, 1689-1697. This war was fought largely in Flanders.
- The War of Spanish Succession, or Queen Anne's War, 1702-1713
- War of Austrian Succession, or King George's War, 1740-1748

The fourth and final, the French and Indian War, was fought largely in the North American territory, and resulted in the end of France's reign as a colonial power in North America. Although the French held many advantages, including more cooperative colonists and numerous Indian allies, the strong leadership of William Pitt eventually led the British to victory. Costs incurred during the wars eventually led to discontent in the colonies. This helped spark the American Revolution

> **Review Video: French and Indian War**
> *Visit **mometrix.com/academy** and enter **Code: 502183***

Navigation Acts

Enacted in 1651, the Navigation Acts were an attempt by Britain to dominate international trade. Aimed largely at the Dutch, the Acts banned foreign ships from transporting goods to the British colonies, and from transporting goods to Britain from elsewhere in Europe. While the restrictions on trade angered some colonists, these Acts were helpful to other American colonists who, as members of the British Empire, were legally able to provide ships for Britain's growing trade interests and use the ships for their own trading ventures. By the time the French and Indian War had ended, one-third of British merchant ships were built in the American colonies. Many colonists amassed fortunes in the shipbuilding trade.

Higher taxes after the French and Indian War

The French and Indian War created circumstances for which the British desperately needed more revenue. These included:
- The need to pay off the war debt.
- The need for funds to defend the expanding empire
- The need for funds to govern Britain's thirty-three far-flung colonies, including the American colonies

These needs led the British to pass additional laws to increase revenues from the colonies. Because they had spent so much money to defend the American colonies, the British felt it was appropriate to collect considerably higher taxes from them. The colonists felt this was unfair, and many were led to protest the increasing taxes. Eventually, protest led to violence.

Triangular trade

Triangular trade began in the Colonies with ships setting off for Africa carrying rum. In Africa, the rum was traded for gold or slaves. Ships then went from Africa to the West Indies, trading slaves for sugar, molasses, or money. To complete the triangle, the ships returned to the colonies with sugar or molasses to make more rum, as well as stores of gold and silver. This trade triangle violated the Molasses Act of 1733, which required the colonists to pay high duties to Britain on molasses acquired from French, Dutch, and Spanish colonies. The colonists ignored these duties, and the British government adopted a policy of salutary neglect by not enforcing them.

> ➢ **Review Video: Triangular Trade**
> *Visit **mometrix.com/academy** and enter **Code: 415470***

Effects of new laws on British-Colonial relations

While earlier revenue-generating acts such as the Navigation Acts brought money to the colonists, the new laws after 1763 required colonists to pay money back to Britain. The British felt this was fair since the colonists were British subjects and since they had incurred debt protecting the Colonies. The colonists felt it was not only unfair, but illegal.

The development of local government in America had given the colonists a different view of the structure and role of government. This made it difficult for the British to understand colonist's protests against what the British felt was a fair and reasonable solution to the mother country's financial problems.

Increasing discontent in the American colonies

More and more colonists had been born on American soil, decreasing any sense of kinship with the far away British rulers. Their new environment had led to new ideas of government and a strong view of the colonies as a separate entity from Britain. Colonists were allowed to self-govern in domestic issues, but Britain controlled international issues. In fact, the American colonies were largely left to form their own local government bodies, giving them more freedom than any other colonial territory. This gave the colonists a sense of independence which led them to resent control from Britain. Threats during the French and Indian War led the colonists to call for unification in order to protect themselves.

Difference between colonial government and British government

As new towns and other legislative districts developed in America, the colonists began to practice representative government. Colonial legislative bodies were made up of elected representatives chosen by male property owners in the districts. These individuals represented interests of the districts from which they had been elected.

By contrast, in Britain the Parliament represented the entire country. Parliament was not elected to represent individual districts. Instead, they represented specific classes. Because of this drastically different approach to government, the British did not understand the colonists' statement that they had no representation in the British Parliament.

Acts of British Parliament

Four major Acts of British Parliament that occurred after the French and Indian Wars and what they governed are:
- The Quartering Act, 1765. This act required colonists to provide accommodations and supplies for British troops. In addition, colonists were prohibited from settling west of the Appalachians until given permission by Britain.
- The Sugar Act, 1764. This act not only required taxes to be collected on molasses brought into the colonies, but gave British officials the right to search the homes of anyone suspected of violating it.
- The Stamp Act, 1765. The Stamp Act taxed printed materials such as newspapers and legal documents. Protests led the Stamp Act to be repealed in 1766, but the repeal also included the Declaratory Act, which stated that Parliament had the right to govern the colonies.
- The Townshend Acts, 1767. These acts taxed paper, paint, lead and tea that came into the colonies. Colonists led boycotts in protest, and in Massachusetts leaders like Samuel and John Adams began to organize resistance against British rule.

Boston Massacre

With the passage of the Stamp Act, nine colonies met in New York to demand its repeal. Elsewhere, protest arose in New York City, Philadelphia, Boston and other cities. These protests sometimes escalated into violence, often targeting ruling British officials. The passage of the Townshend Acts in 1767 led to additional tension in the colonies. The British sent troops to New York City and Boston. On March 5, 1770, protesters began to taunt the British troops, throwing snowballs. The soldiers responded by firing into the crowd. This clash between protesters and soldiers led to five deaths and eight injuries, and was christened the Boston Massacre. Shortly thereafter, Britain repealed the majority of the Townshend Acts.

Tea Act and the Boston Tea Party

The majority of the Townshend Acts were repealed after the Boston Massacre in 1770, but Britain kept the tax on tea. In 1773, the Tea Act was passed. This allowed the East India Company to sell tea for much lower prices, and also allowed them to bypass American distributors, selling directly to shopkeepers instead. Colonial tea merchants saw this as a direct assault on their business. In December of 1773, 150 merchants boarded ships in Boston Harbor and dumped 342 chests of tea into the sea in protest of the new laws. This act of protest came to be known as the Boston Tea Party.

Coercive Acts

The Coercive Acts passed by Britain in 1774 were meant to punish Massachusetts for defying British authority. The four Coercive Acts:
- Shut down ports in Boston until the city paid back the value of the tea destroyed during the Boston Tea Party.
- Required that local government officials in Massachusetts be appointed by the governor rather than being elected by the people.
- Allowed trials of British soldiers to be transferred to Britain rather than being held in Massachusetts.
- Required locals to provide lodging for British soldiers any time there was a disturbance, even if lodging required them to stay in private homes.

These Acts led to the assembly of the First Continental Congress in Philadelphia on September 5, 1774. Fifty-five delegates met, representing 12 of the American colonies. They sought compromise with England over England's increasingly harsh efforts to control the colonies.

First Continental Congress

The First Continental Congress met in Philadelphia on September 5, 1774. Their goal was to achieve a peaceful agreement with Britain. Made up of delegates from 12 of the 13 colonies, the Congress affirmed loyalty to Britain and the power of Parliament to dictate foreign affairs in the colonies. However, they demanded that the Intolerable Acts be repealed, and instituted a trade embargo with Britain until this came to pass.

In response, George III of Britain declared that the American colonies must submit or face military action. The British sought to end assemblies opposing their policies. These assemblies gathered weapons and began to form militias. On April 19, 1775, the British military was ordered to disperse a meeting of the Massachusetts Assembly. A battle ensued on Lexington Common as the armed colonists resisted. The resulting battles became the Battle of Lexington and Concord—the first battles of the American Revolution.

Second Continental Congress

The Second Continental Congress met in Philadelphia on May 10, 1775, a month after Lexington and Concord. Their discussions centered on defense of the American colonies and how to conduct the growing war, as well as local government. The delegates also discussed declaring independence from Britain, with many members in favor of this drastic move. They established an army, and on June 15, named George Washington as its commander in chief.   By 1776, it was obvious that there was no turning back from full-scale war with Britain. The colonial delegates of the Continental Congress drafted the Declaration of Independence on July 4, 1776.

> ➤ **Review Video: <u>The First and Second Continental Congress</u>**
> *Visit **mometrix.com/academy** and enter **Code: 835211***

Battles of the Revolutionary War

The following are five battles of the Revolutionary War and their significance:
- The Battle of Lexington and Concord (April, 1775) is considered the first engagement of the Revolutionary War.
- The Battle of Bunker Hill, in June of 1775, was one of the bloodiest of the entire war. Although American troops withdrew, about half the British army was lost. The colonists proved they could stand against professional British soldiers. In August, Britain declared that the American colonies were officially in a state of rebellion.
- The first colonial victory occurred in Trenton, New Jersey, when Washington and his troops crossed the Delaware River on Christmas Day, 1776 for a December 26, surprise attack on British and Hessian troops.
- The Battle of Saratoga effectively ended a plan to separate the New England colonies from their Southern counterparts. The surrender of British general John Burgoyne led to France joining the war as allies of the Americans, and is generally considered a turning point of the war.
- On October 19, 1781, General Cornwallis surrendered after a defeat in the Battle of Yorktown, Virginia, ending the Revolutionary War.

Declaration of Independence

Penned by Thomas Jefferson and signed on July 4, 1776, the Declaration of Independence stated that King George III had violated the rights of the colonists and was establishing a tyrannical reign over them. Many of Jefferson's ideas of natural rights and property rights were shaped by seventeenth century philosopher John Locke. Jefferson focused on natural rights, as demonstrated by the assertion of people's rights to "life, liberty and the pursuit of happiness." Locke's comparable idea asserted "life, liberty, and private property." Both felt that the purpose of government was to protect the rights of the people, and that individual rights were more important than individuals' obligations to the state.

> ➤ **Review Video: <u>Declaration of Independence</u>**
> *Visit **mometrix.com/academy** and enter **Code: 256838***

Treaty of Paris

The Treaty of Paris was signed on September 3, 1783, bringing an official end to the Revolutionary War. In this document, Britain officially recognized the United States of America as an independent nation. The treaty established the Mississippi River as the country's western border. The treaty also restored Florida to Spain, while France reclaimed African and Caribbean colonies seized by the British in 1763. On November 24, 1783, the last British troops departed from the newly born United States of America.

Articles of Confederation

A precursor to the Constitution, the Articles of Confederation represented the first attempt of the newly independent colonies to establish the basics of independent government. The Continental Congress passed the Articles on November 15, 1777. They went into effect on March 1, 1781, following ratification by the thirteen states. The Articles prevented a central government from gaining too much power, instead giving power to a Congressional body made up of delegates from all thirteen states. However, the individual states retained final authority.

Without a strong central executive, though, this weak alliance among the new states proved ineffective in settling disputes or enforcing laws. The idea of a weak central government needed to be revised. Recognition of these weaknesses eventually led to the drafting of a new document, the Constitution.

> ➢ **Review Video: Articles of Confederation**
> *Visit mometrix.com/academy and enter Code:* **927401**

Constitution

Delegates from twelve of the thirteen states (Rhode Island was not represented) met in Philadelphia in May of 1787, initially intending to revise the Articles of Confederation. However, it quickly became apparent that a simple revision would not provide the workable governmental structure the newly formed country needed. After vowing to keep all the proceedings secret until the final document was completed, the delegates set out to draft what would eventually become the Constitution of the United States of America. By keeping the negotiations secret, the delegates were able to present a completed document to the country for ratification, rather than having every small detail hammered out by the general public.

> ➢ **Review Video: Drafting the Constitution**
> *Visit mometrix.com/academy and enter Code:* **662451**

Structure of proposed government

The delegates agreed that the new nation required a strong central government, but that its overall power should be limited. The various branches of the government should have balanced power, so that no one group could control the others. Final power belonged with the citizens who voted officials into office based on who would provide the best representation.

Virginia Plan, New Jersey Plan, and the Great Compromise

Disagreement immediately occurred between delegates from large states and those from smaller states. The governor of Virginia, Edmond Randolph, felt that representation in Congress should be based on state population. This was the Virginia Plan. The New Jersey Plan, presented by William Paterson, from New Jersey, proposed each state have equal representation. Finally, Roger Sherman from Connecticut formulated the Connecticut Compromise, also called the Great Compromise. The result was the familiar structure we have today. Each state has the equal representation of two Senators in the Senate, with the number of representatives in the House of Representatives based on population. This is called a bicameral Congress. Both houses may draft bills, but financial matters must originate in the House of Representatives.

Three-fifths compromise

During debate on the U.S. Constitution, a disagreement arose between the Northern and Southern states involving how slaves should be counted when determining a state's quota of representatives. In the South large numbers of slaves were commonly used to run plantations. Delegates wanted slaves to be counted to determine the number of representatives, but not counted to determine the amount of taxes the states would pay. The Northern states wanted exactly the opposite arrangement. The final decision was to count three-fifths of the slave population both for tax purposes and to determine representation. This was called the three-fifths compromise.

Commerce Compromise

The Commerce Compromise also resulted from a North/South disagreement. In the North the economy was centered on industry and trade. The Southern economy was largely agricultural. The Northern states wanted to give the new government the ability to regulate exports as well as trade between the states. The South opposed this plan. Another compromise was in order. In the end, Congress received regulatory power over all trade, including the ability to collect tariffs on exported goods. In the South, this raised another red flag regarding the slave trade, as they were concerned about the effect on their economy if tariffs were levied on slaves. The final agreement allowed importing slaves to continue for twenty years without government intervention. Import taxes on slaves were limited, and after the year 1808, Congress could decide whether to allow continued imports of slaves.

Objections against the Constitution

Once the Constitution was drafted, it was presented for approval by the states. Nine states needed to approve the document for it to become official. However, debate and discussion continued. Major concerns included:
- The lack of a bill of rights to protect individual freedoms.
- States felt too much power was being handed over to the central government.
- Voters wanted more control over their elected representatives.

Discussion about necessary changes to the Constitution divided roughly into two camps: Federalists and Anti-Federalists. Federalists wanted a strong central government. Anti-Federalists wanted to prevent a tyrannical government from developing if a central government held too much power.

Federalist and Anti-Federalist camps

Major Federalist leaders included Alexander Hamilton, John Jay and James Madison. They wrote a series of letters, called the Federalist Papers, aimed at convincing the states to ratify the Constitution. These were published in New York papers.

Anti-Federalists included Thomas Jefferson and Patrick Henry. They argued against the Constitution as it was originally drafted in arguments called the Anti-Federalist Papers.
The final compromise produced a strong central government controlled by checks and balances. A Bill of Rights was also added, becoming the first ten amendments to the Constitution. These amendments protected rights such as freedom of speech, freedom of religion, and other basic rights. Aside from various amendments added throughout the years, the United States Constitution has remained unchanged.

Administration of the new government

The individuals who formed the first administration of the new government are as follows:
- George Washington was elected as the first President of the United States in 1789.
- John Adams, who finished second in the election, became the first Vice President.
- Thomas Jefferson was appointed by Washington as Secretary of State.
- Alexander Hamilton was also appointed Secretary of the Treasury.

FREE Study Skills DVD Offer

Dear Customer,

Thank you for your purchase from Mometrix! We consider it an honor and privilege that you have purchased our product and want to ensure your satisfaction.

As a way of showing our appreciation and to help us better serve you, we have developed a Study Skills DVD that we would like to give you for <u>FREE</u>. **This DVD covers our "best practices" for studying for your exam, from using our study guide and flashcards to preparing for the day of the test.**

All that we ask is that you email us your feedback that would describe your experience so far with our product. Good, bad or indifferent, we want to know what you think!

To get your **FREE Study Skills DVD**, email <u>freedvd@mometrix.com</u> with "FREE STUDY SKILLS DVD" in the subject line and the following information in the body of the email:

    a.   The name of the product you purchased.

    b.   Your product rating on a scale of 1-5, with 5 being the highest rating.

    c.   Your feedback. It can be long, short, or anything in-between, just your impressions and experience so far with our product. Good feedback might include how our study material met your needs and will highlight features of the product that you found helpful.

    d.   Your full name and shipping address where you would like us to send your free DVD.

If you have any questions or concerns, please don't hesitate to contact me directly.

Thanks again!

Sincerely,

Jay Willis
Vice President
<u>jay.willis@mometrix.com</u>
1-800-673-8175

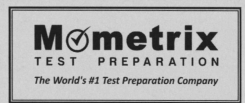

Alien and Sedition Acts

When John Adams became president, a war was raging between Britain and France. While Adams and the Federalists backed the British, Thomas Jefferson and the Republican Party supported the French. The United States nearly went to war with France during this time period, while France worked to spread its international standing and influence under the leadership of Napoleon Bonaparte. The Alien and Sedition Acts grew out of this conflict, and made it illegal to speak in a hostile fashion against the existing government. They also allowed the president to deport anyone in the U.S. who was not a citizen and who was suspected of treason or treasonous activity.

When Jefferson became the third president in 1800, he repealed these four laws and pardoned anyone who had been convicted under them.

Political parties

Many in the U.S. were against political parties after seeing the way parties, or factions, functioned in Britain. The factions in Britain were more interested in personal profit than the overall good of the country, and they did not want this to happen in the U.S.

However, the differences of opinion between Thomas Jefferson and Alexander Hamilton led to formation of political parties. Hamilton favored a stronger central government, while Jefferson felt more power should remain with the states. Jefferson was in favor of strict Constitutional interpretation, while Hamilton believed in a more flexible approach. As various others joined the separate camps, Hamilton backers began to term themselves Federalists while those supporting Jefferson became identified as Democratic-Republicans.

Whig Party, Democratic Party, and Republican Party

Thomas Jefferson was elected president in 1800 and again in 1804. The Federalist Party began a decline, and its major figure, Alexander Hamilton, died in a duel with Aaron Burr in 1804. By 1816, the Federalist Party virtually disappeared.

New parties sprang up to take its place. After 1824, the Democratic-Republican Party suffered a split. The Whigs arose, backing John Quincy Adams and industrial growth. The new Democratic Party formed, in opposition to the Whigs, and their candidate, Andrew Jackson, was elected as president in 1828.

By the 1850s, issues regarding slavery led to the formation of the Republican Party, which was anti-slavery, while the Democratic Party of the time, with a larger interest in the South, favored slavery. This Republican/Democrat division formed the basis of today's two-party system.

Marbury v. Madison

The main duty of the Supreme Court today is judicial review. This power was largely established by Marbury v. Madison. When John Adams was voted out of office in 1800, he worked, during his final days in office, to appoint Federalist judges to Supreme Court positions, knowing Jefferson, his replacement, held opposing views. As late as March 3, the day before Jefferson was to take office, Adams made last-minute appointments referred to as "Midnight Judges." One of the late appointments was William Marbury. The next day, March 4, Jefferson ordered his Secretary of State, James Madison, not to deliver Marbury's commission. This decision was backed by Chief Justice Marshall, who determined that the Judiciary Act of 1789, which granted the power to deliver commissions, was illegal in that it gave the

Judicial Branch powers not granted in the Constitution. This case set precedent for the Supreme Court to nullify laws it found to be unconstitutional.

> ➤ **Review Video:** <u>Marbury v. Madison</u>
> *Visit **mometrix.com/academy** and enter **Code: 573964***

McCulloch v Maryland

Judicial review was further exercised by the Supreme Court in McCulloch v Maryland. When Congress chartered a national bank, the Second Bank of the United States, Maryland voted to tax any bank business dealing with banks chartered outside the state, including the federally chartered bank. Andrew McCulloch, an employee of the Second Bank of the US in Baltimore, refused to pay this tax. The resulting lawsuit from the State of Maryland went to the Supreme Court for judgment.

John Marshall, Chief Justice of the Supreme Court, stated that Congress was within its rights to charter a national bank. In addition, the State of Maryland did not have the power to levy a tax on the federal bank or on the federal government in general. In cases where state and federal government collided, precedent was set for the federal government to prevail.

Effects of the Treaty of Paris on Native Americans

After the Revolutionary War, the Treaty of Paris, which outlined the terms of surrender of the British to the Americans, granted large parcels of land to the U.S. that were occupied by Native Americans. The new government attempted to claim the land, treating the natives as a conquered people. This approached proved unenforceable.

Next, the government tried purchasing the land from the Indians via a series of treaties as the country expanded westward. In practice, however, these treaties were not honored, and Native Americans were simply dislocated and forced to move farther and farther west as American expansion continued, often with military action.

Indian Removal Act of 1830 and the Treaty of New

The Indian Removal Act of 1830 gave the new American government power to form treaties with Native Americans. In theory, America would claim land east of the Mississippi in exchange for land west of the Mississippi, to which the natives would relocate voluntarily. In practice, many tribal leaders were forced into signing the treaties, and relocation at times occurred by force.

The Treaty of New Echota was supposedly a treaty between the US government and Cherokee tribes in Georgia. However, the treaty was not signed by tribal leaders, but rather by a small portion of the represented people. The leaders protested by refusing to be removed, but President, Martin Van Buren, enforced the treaty by sending soldiers. During their forced relocation, more than 4,000 Cherokee Indians died on what became known as the Trail of Tears.

Early economic trends by region

In the Northeast, the economy mostly depended on manufacturing, industry and industrial development. This led to a dichotomy between rich business owners and industrial leaders and the much poorer workers who supported their businesses. The South continued to depend on agriculture, especially large-scale farms or plantations worked mostly by slaves and indentured servants. In the West, where new

- 34 -

settlement had begun to develop, the land was largely wild. Growing communities were essentially agricultural; growing crops and raising livestock. The differences between regions led each to support different interests both politically and economically.

Louisiana Purchase

With tension still high between France and Britain, Napoleon was in need of money to support his continuing war efforts. To secure necessary funds, he decided to sell the Louisiana Territory to the U.S. At the same time President Thomas Jefferson wanted to buy New Orleans, feeling U.S. trade was made vulnerable to both Spain and France at that port. Instead, Napoleon sold him the entire territory for the bargain price of fifteen million dollars. The Louisiana Territory was larger than all the rest of the United States put together, and it eventually became fifteen additional states.

Federalists in Congress were opposed to the purchase. They feared that the Louisiana Purchase would extend slavery, and that further western growth would weaken the power of the northern states.

> ➢ **Review Video: The Louisiana Purchase**
> *Visit* **mometrix.com/academy** *and enter* **Code: 920513**

Early foreign policy

The three major ideas driving American foreign policy during its early years are described below:
- Isolationism – the early US government did not intend to establish colonies, though they did plan to grow larger within the bounds of North America.
- No entangling alliances – both George Washington and Thomas Jefferson were opposed to forming any permanent alliances with other countries or becoming involved in other countries' internal issues.
- Nationalism – a positive patriotic feeling about the United States blossomed quickly among its citizens, particularly after the War of 1812, when the U.S. once again defeated Britain. The Industrial Revolution also sparked increased nationalism by allowing even the most far-flung areas of the U.S. to communicate with each other via telegraph and the expanding railroad.

War of 1812

The War of 1812 grew out of the continuing tension between France and Great Britain. Napoleon continued to strive to conquer Britain, while the U.S. continued trade with both countries, but favoring France and the French colonies. Because of what Britain saw as an alliance between America and France, they determined to bring an end to trade between the two nations.

With the British preventing U.S. trade with the French and the French preventing trade with the British, James Madison's presidency introduced acts to regulate international trade. If either Britain or France removed their restrictions, America would not trade with the other. Napoleon acted first, and Madison prohibited trade with England. England saw this as the U.S. formally siding with the French, and war ensued in 1812.

The War of 1812 has been called the Second American Revolution. It established the superiority of the U.S. naval forces and reestablished U.S. independence from Britain and Europe.

The British had two major objections to America's continued trade with France. First, they saw the US as helping France's war effort by providing supplies and goods. Second, the United States had grown into a competitor, taking trade and money away from British ships and tradesmen. In its attempts to end American trade with France, the British put into effect the Orders in Council, which made any and all French-owned ports off-limits to American ships. They also began to seize American ships and conscript their crews, a practice greatly offensive to the U.S.

Military events

Two major naval battles, at Lake Erie and Lake Champlain, kept the British from invading the U.S. via Canada. American attempts to conquer Canadian lands were not successful.

In another memorable British attack, the British invaded Washington DC and burned the White House. Legend has it that Dolly Madison, the First Lady, salvaged the American flag from the fire. On Christmas Eve, 1814, the Treaty of Ghent officially ended the war. However, Andrew Jackson, unaware that the war was over, managed another victory at New Orleans on January 8, 1815. This victory upped American morale and led to a new wave of nationalism and national pride known as the "Era of Good Feelings."

Monroe Doctrine

On December 2, 1823, President Monroe delivered a message to Congress in which he introduced the Monroe Doctrine. In this address, he stated that any attempts by European powers to establish new colonies on the North American continent would be considered interference in American politics. The U.S. would stay out of European matters, and expected Europe to offer America the same courtesy. This approach to foreign policy stated in no uncertain terms that America would not tolerate any new European colonies in the New World, and that events occurring in Europe would no longer influence the policies and doctrines of the U.S.

> ➤ **Review Video: Monroe Doctrine**
> *Visit* ***mometrix.com/academy*** *and enter* ***Code: 953021***

Lewis and Clark Expedition

The purchase of the Louisiana Territory from France in 1803 more than doubled the size of the United States. President Thomas Jefferson wanted to have the area mapped and explored, since much of the territory was wilderness. He chose Meriwether Lewis and William Clark to head an expedition into the Louisiana Territory. After two years, Lewis and Clark returned, having traveled all the way to the Pacific Ocean. They brought maps, detailed journals, and various types of knowledge and information about the wide expanse of land they had traversed. The Lewis and Clark Expedition opened up the west in the Louisiana Territory and beyond for further exploration and settlement.

> ➤ **Review Video: The Lewis and Clark Expedition**
> *Visit* ***mometrix.com/academy*** *and enter* ***Code: 570657***

Manifest Destiny

In the 1800's, many believed America was destined by God to expand west, bringing as much of the North American continent as possible under the umbrella of U.S. government. With the Northwest Ordinance and the Louisiana Purchase, over half of the continent became American. However, the rapid and relentless expansion brought conflict with the Native Americans, Great Britain, Mexico and Spain. One result of "Manifest Destiny" was the Mexican-American War, which occurred in 1846-1848. By the end of

- 36 -

the war, Texas, California and a large portion of what is now the American Southwest joined the growing nation. Conflict also arose over the Oregon country, shared by the US and Britain. In 1846, President James Polk resolved this problem by compromising with Britain, establishing a U.S. boundary south of the 49th parallel.

> ➤ **Review Video: <u>Manifest Destiny</u>**
> *Visit mometrix.com/academy and enter **Code: 957409***

Mexican-American War

Spain had held colonial interests in America since the 1540s—earlier even than Great Britain. In 1821, Mexico revolted against Spain and became a free nation. Likewise, this was followed by Texas, who after an 1836 revolution declared its independence. In 1844, the Democrats pressed President Tyler to annex Texas. Unlike his predecessor, Andrew Jackson, Tyler agreed to admit Texas into the Union. In 1845, Texas became a state.

During Mexico's war for independence, they had incurred $4.5 million in war debts to the U.S. Polk offered to forgive the debts in return for New Mexico and Upper California, but Mexico refused. In 1846, war was declared in response to a Mexican attack on American troops along the southern border of Texas. Additional conflict arose in Congress over the Wilmot Proviso, which stated that any territory the U.S. acquired from Mexico should be legally open to slavery. The war ended in 1848.

> ➤ **Review Video: <u>The Mexican-American War</u>**
> *Visit mometrix.com/academy and enter **Code: 271216***

Gadsden Purchase and the 1853 post-war treaty with Mexico

After the Mexican-American war, a second treaty in 1853 determined hundreds of miles of America's southwest borders. In 1854, the Gadsden Purchase was finalized, providing even more territory to aid in the building of the transcontinental railroad. This purchase added what would eventually become the southernmost regions of Arizona and New Mexico to the growing nation. The modern outline of the United States was by this time nearly complete.

American System

Spurred by the trade conflicts of the War of 1812, and supported by Henry Clay and others, the American System set up tariffs to help protect American interests from competition with products from overseas. Reducing competition led to growth in employment and an overall increase in American industry. The higher tariffs also provided funds for the government to pay for various improvements. Congress passed high tariffs in 1816 and also chartered a federal bank. The Second Bank of the United States was given the job of regulating America's money supply.

Jacksonian Democracy

Jacksonian Democracy is largely seen as a shift from politics favoring the wealthy to politics favoring the common man. All free white males were given the right to vote, not just property owners, as had been the case previously. Jackson's approach favored the patronage system, Laissez faire economics, and relocation of the Indian tribes from the Southeast portion of the country. Jackson opposed the formation of a federal bank and allowed the Second Band of the United States to collapse by vetoing a bill to renew the charter. Jackson also faced the challenge of the "null and void" or nullification theory when South

Carolina claimed that it could ignore or nullify any federal law it considered unconstitutional. Jackson sent troops to the state to enforce the protested tariff laws, and a compromise engineered by Henry Clay in 1833 settled the matter for the time being.

Conflict between North and South

The conflict between North and South coalesced around the issue of slavery, but other elements contributed to the growing disagreement. Though most farmers in the South worked small farms with little or no slave labor, the huge plantations run by the South's rich depended on slaves or indentured servants to remain profitable. They had also become more dependent on cotton, with slave populations growing in concert with the rapid increase in cotton production. In the North, a more diverse agricultural economy and the growth of industry made slaves rarer. The abolitionist movement grew steadily, with Harriet Beecher Stowe's *Uncle Tom's Cabin* giving many an idea to rally around. A collection of anti-slavery organizations formed, with many actively working to free slaves in the South, often bringing them North.

Anti-slavery organizations

Five anti-slavery organizations and their significance are:
- American Colonization Society—protestant churches formed this group, aimed at returning black slaves to Africa. Former slaves subsequently formed Liberia, but the colony did not do well, as the region was not well-suited for agriculture.
- American Anti-Slavery Society—William Lloyd Garrison, a Quaker, was the major force behind this group and its newspaper, *The Liberator.*
- Female Anti-Slavery Society—a women-only group formed by Margaretta Forten because women were not allowed to join the Anti-Slavery Society formed by her father.
- Anti-Slavery Convention of American Women—This group continued meeting even after pro-slavery factions burned down their original meeting place.
- Female Vigilant Society—an organization that raised funds to help the Underground Railroad, as well as slave refugees.

Attitudes toward education

Horace Mann, among others, felt that public schooling could help children become better citizens, keep them away from crime, prevent poverty, and help American society become more unified. His *Common School Journal* brought his ideas of the importance of education into the public consciousness. Increased literacy led to increased awareness of current events, Western expansion, and other major developments of the time period. Public interest and participation in the arts and literature also increased. By the end of the 19th century, all children had access to a free public elementary education.

Transportation

As America expanded its borders, it also developed new technology to travel the rapidly growing country. Roads and railroads traversed the nation, with the Transcontinental Railroad eventually allowing travel from one coast to the other. Canals and steamboats simplified water travel and made shipping easier and less expensive. The Erie Canal (1825) connected the Great Lakes with the Hudson River. Other canals connected other major water ways, further facilitating transportation and the shipment of goods.

With growing numbers of settlers moving into the West, wagon trails developed, including the Oregon Trail, California Trail and the Santa Fe Trail. The most common vehicles seen along these westbound trails were covered wagons, also known as prairie schooners.

Industrial activity and major inventions

During the eighteenth century, goods were often manufactured in houses or small shops. With increased technology allowing for the use of machines, factories began to develop. In factories a large volume of salable goods could be produced in a much shorter amount of time. Many Americans, including increasing numbers of immigrants, found jobs in these factories, which were in constant need of labor. Another major invention was the cotton gin, which significantly decreased the processing time of cotton and was a major factor in the rapid expansion of cotton production in the South.

Labor movements in the 1800s

In 1751, a group of bakers held a protest in which they stopped baking bread. This was technically the first American labor strike. In the 1830s and 1840s, labor movements began in earnest. Boston's masons, carpenters and stoneworkers protested the length of the workday, fighting to reduce it to ten hours. In 1844, a group of women in the textile industry also fought to reduce their workday to ten hours, forming the Lowell Female Labor Reform Association. Many other protests occurred and organizations developed through this time period with the same goal in mind.

Second Great Awakening

Led by Protestant evangelical leaders, the Second Great Awakening occurred between 1800 and 1830. Several missionary groups grew out of the movement, including the American Home Missionary Society, which formed in 1826. The ideas behind the Second Great Awakening focused on personal responsibility, both as an individual and in response to injustice and suffering. The American Bible Society and the American Tract Society provided literature, while various traveling preachers spread the word. New denominations arose, including the Latter Day Saints and Seventh-Day Adventists.

Another movement associated with the Second Great Awakening was the temperance movement, focused on ending the production and use of alcohol. One major organization behind the temperance movement was the Society for the Promotion of Temperance, formed in 1826 in Boston, Massachusetts.

Women's rights movement

The women's rights movement began in the 1840s with leaders including Elizabeth Cady Stanton, Ernestine Rose and Lucretia Mott. Later, in 1869, the National Woman Suffrage Association, fighting for women's right to vote, came into being. It was led by Susan B. Anthony, Ernestine Rose and Elizabeth Cady Stanton.

In 1848 in Seneca Falls, the first women's rights convention was held, with about three hundred attendees. The Seneca Falls Convention brought to the floor the issue that women could not vote or run for office. The convention produced a "Declaration of Sentiments" which outlined a plan for women to attain the rights they deserved. Frederick Douglass supported the women's rights movement, as well as the abolition movement. In fact, women's rights and abolition movements often went hand-in-hand through this time period.

Missouri Compromise

By 1819, the United States had developed a tenuous balance between slave and free states, with exactly twenty-two senators in Congress from each faction. However, Missouri was ready to join the union as a state. As a slave state, it would tip the balance in Congress. To prevent this imbalance, the Missouri Compromise brought the northern part of Massachusetts into the union as Maine, established as a free state. Maine's admission balanced the admission of Missouri as a slave state, maintaining the status quo. In addition, the remaining portion of the Louisiana Purchase was to remain free north of latitude 36° 30'. Since cotton did not grow well this far north, this limitation was acceptable to congressmen representing the slave states.

However, the proposed Missouri constitution presented a problem, as it outlawed immigration of free blacks into the state. Another compromise was in order, this time proposed by Henry Clay. Clay earned his title of the Great Compromiser by stating that the U.S. Constitution overruled Missouri's.

> ➢ **Review Video:** **The Missouri Compromise**
> *Visit mometrix.com/academy and enter Code:* **848091**

Popular sovereignty and the Compromise of 1850

In addition to the pro-slavery and anti-slavery factions, a third group rose who felt that each individual state should decide whether to allow or permit slavery within its borders. This idea was referred to as popular sovereignty.

When California applied to join the union in 1849, the balance of congressional power was again threatened. The Compromise of 1850 introduced a group of laws meant to bring an end to the conflict. These laws included:
- California being admitted as a free state.
- Slave trade in Washington, D.C. being outlawed.
- An increase in efforts to capture escaped slaves.
- New Mexico and Utah territories would decide individually whether or not to allow slavery.

In spite of these measures, debate raged each time a new state prepared to enter the union.

Kansas-Nebraska Act

With the creation of the Kansas and Nebraska territories in 1854, another debate began. Congress allowed popular sovereignty in these territories, but slavery opponents argued that the Missouri Compromise had already made slavery illegal in this region. In Kansas, two separate governments arose, one pro- and one anti-slavery. Conflict between the two factions rose to violence, leading Kansas to gain the nickname of "Bleeding Kansas."

Dred Scott Decision

Abolitionist factions coalesced around the case of Dred Scott, using his case to test the country's laws regarding slavery. Scott, a slave, had been taken by his owner from Missouri, which was a slave state. He then traveled to Illinois, a free state, then on to the Minnesota Territory, also free based on the Missouri Compromise. Then, he returned to Missouri. The owner subsequently died. Abolitionists took Scott's case to court, stating that Scott was no longer a slave but free, since he had lived in free territory. The case went to the Supreme Court.

The Supreme Court stated that, because Scott, as a slave, was not a U.S. citizen, his time in free states did not change his status. He also did not have the right to sue. In addition, the Court determined that the Missouri Compromise was unconstitutional, saying Congress had overstepped its bounds by outlawing slavery in the territories.

> ➤ **Review Video:** Dred Scott
> *Visit **mometrix.com/academy** and enter **Code:** 364838*

Harper's Ferry and John Brown

John Brown, an abolitionist, had participated in several anti-slavery actions, including killing five pro-slavery men in retaliation, after Lawrence, Kansas, an anti-slavery town, was sacked. He and other abolitionists also banded together to pool their funds and build a runaway slave colony.
In 1859, Brown seized a federal arsenal in Harper's Ferry, located in what is now West Virginia. Brown intended to seize guns and ammunition and lead a slave rebellion. Robert E. Lee captured Brown and 22 followers, who were subsequently tried and hanged. While Northerners took the executions as an indication that the government supported slavery, Southerners were of the opinion that most of the North supported Brown and were, in general, anti-slavery.

1860 election candidates

The 1860 Presidential candidates represented four different parties, each with a different opinion on slavery.
- John Breckenridge, representing the Southern Democrats, was pro-slavery.
- Abraham Lincoln, of the Republican Party, was anti-slavery.
- Stephen Douglas, of the Northern Democrats, felt that the issue should be determined locally, on a state-by-state basis.
- John Bell, of the Constitutional Union Party, focused primarily on keeping the Union intact.

In the end, Abraham Lincoln won both the popular and electoral election. Southern states, who had sworn to secede from the Union if Lincoln was elected did so, led by South Carolina. Shortly thereafter, the Civil War began when shots were fired on Fort Sumter in Charleston.

Advantages of the North and South in the Civil War

The Northern states had significant advantages, including:
- Larger population. The North consisted of 24 states to the South's 11.
- Better transportation and finances. With railroads primarily in the North, supply chains were much more dependable, as was trade coming from overseas.
- More raw materials. The North held the majority of America's gold, as well as iron, copper and other minerals vital to wartime.

The South's advantages included:
- Better-trained military officers. Many of the Southern officers were West Point trained and had commanded in the Mexican and Indian wars.
- More familiar with weapons. The climate and lifestyle of the South meant most of the people were well versed in both guns and horses. The industrial North had less extensive experience

- Defensive position. The South felt victory was guaranteed, since they were protecting their own lands, while the North would be invading.
- Well-defined goals. The South was fighting an ideological war to be allowed to govern themselves and preserve their way of life.

> ➤ **Review Video: Civil War**
> *Visit mometrix.com/academy and enter Code: 239557*

Emancipation Proclamation

The Emancipation Proclamation, issued by President Lincoln in 1862, freed all slaves in Confederate States that did not return to the Union by the beginning of the year. While the original proclamation did not free any slaves actually under Union control, it did set a precedent for the emancipation of slaves as the war progressed.

The Emancipation Proclamation worked in the Union's favor as many freed slaves and other black troops joined the Union Army. Almost 200,000 blacks fought in the Union army, and over 10,000 served in the navy. By the end of the war, over 4 million slaves had been freed, and in 1865 slavery was banned by Constitutional amendment.

> ➤ **Review Video: Emancipation Proclamation**
> *Visit mometrix.com/academy and enter Code: 181778*

Civil War events

Six major events of the Civil War and their outcomes or significance are as follows:
- The Battle of Bull Run, July 21, 1861. The First Battle of Bull Run, was the first major land battle of the war. Observers, expecting to enjoy an entertaining skirmish, set up picnics nearby. Instead, they found themselves witness to a bloodbath. Union forces were defeated, and the battle set the course of the Civil War as long, bloody and costly.
- The Capture of Fort Henry by Ulysses S. Grant. This battle in February of 1862 marked the Union's first major victory.
- The Battle of Gettysburg, July 1-3, 1863. Often seen as the turning point of the war, Gettysburg also saw the largest number of casualties of the war, with over 50,000 dead. Robert E. Lee was defeated, and the Confederate army, significantly crippled, withdrew.
- The Overland Campaign, 1864. Grant, now in command of all the Union armies, led this high casualty campaign that eventually positioned the Union for victory.
- Sherman's March to the Sea. William Tecumseh Sherman, in May of 1864, conquered Atlanta. He then continued to Savannah, destroying indiscriminately as he went.
- Following Lee's defeat at the Appomattox Courthouse, General Grant accepted Lee's surrender in the home of Wilmer McLean, Appomattox, Virginia on April 9, 1865.

Lincoln's assassination

The Civil War ended with the surrender of the South on April 9, 1865. Five days later, Lincoln and his wife, Mary, attended the play *Our American Cousin* at the Ford Theater. John Wilkes Booth, unaware that the war was over, performed his part in a conspiracy to aid the Confederacy by shooting Lincoln in the back of the head. Booth was tracked down and killed by Union soldiers 12 days later. Lincoln, carried from the theater to a nearby house, died the next morning.

Reconstruction and the Freedmen's Bureau

In the aftermath of the Civil War, the South was left in chaos. From 1865 to 1877, government on all levels worked to help restore order to the South, ensure civil rights to the freed slaves, and bring the Confederate states back into the Union.
In 1866, Congress passed the Reconstruction Acts, putting former Confederate states under military rule.

The Freedmen's Bureau was formed to help freedmen and give assistance to whites in the South who needed basic necessities like food and clothing. Many in the South felt the Freedmen's Bureau worked to set freed slaves against their former owners. The Bureau was intended to help former slaves become self-sufficient, and to keep them from falling prey to those who would take advantage of them.

Radical and Moderate Republicans

The Radical Republicans wished to treat the South quite harshly after the war. Thaddeus Stephens, the House Leader, suggested that the Confederate States be treated as if they were territories again, with ten years of military rule and territorial government before they would be readmitted. They also wanted to give all black men the right to vote. Former Confederate soldiers would be required to swear they had not fought against the Union in order to be granted full rights as American citizens.

By contrast, the moderate Republicans wanted only black men who were literate or who had served as Union troops to be able to vote. All Confederate soldiers except troop leaders would also be able to vote. Before his death, Lincoln had favored a more moderate approach to Reconstruction, hoping this approach might bring some states back into the Union before the end of the war.

Black Codes and the Civil Rights bill

The Black Codes were proposed to control freed slaves. They would not be allowed to bear arms, assemble, serve on juries, or testify against whites. Schools would be segregated, and unemployed blacks could be arrested and forced to work.

The Civil Rights bill countered these codes, providing much wider rights for the freed slaves.

Andrew Johnson, who became president after Lincoln's death, supported the Black Codes, and vetoed the Civil Rights bill. Congress overrode his veto and impeached Johnson, the culmination of tensions between Congress and the president. He came within a single vote of being convicted.

Thirteenth, Fourteenth and Fifteenth Amendments

The Thirteenth, Fourteenth and Fifteenth Amendments, all passed shortly after the end of the Civil War, are described below:
- The Thirteenth Amendment was passed on December 18, 1865. This amendment prohibited slavery in the United States.
- The Fourteenth Amendment overturned the Dred Scott decision, and was ratified July 9, 1868. American citizenship was redefined, with all citizens guaranteed equal legal protection by all states. It also guaranteed citizens the right to file a lawsuit or serve on a jury.
- The Fifteenth Amendment was ratified February 3, 1870. It states that no citizen of the United States can be denied the right to vote based on race, color, or previous status as a slave.

Reconstruction

The three phases of Reconstruction are:
- Presidential Reconstruction – largely driven by President Andrew Johnson's policies, the Presidential phase of Reconstruction was lenient on the South and allowed continued discrimination against and control over blacks.
- Congressional Reconstruction – Congress, controlled largely by Radical Republicans, took a different stance, providing a wider range of civil rights for blacks and greater control over Southern government. Congressional Reconstruction is marked by military control of the former Confederate States.
- Redemption – Gradually, the Confederate states were readmitted into the union. During this time, white Democrats took over the government of most of the South. Troops finally departed the South in 1877.

> ➢ **Review Video: Reconstruction Era**
> *Visit* ***mometrix.com/academy*** *and enter **Code: 435458***

Carpetbaggers and Scalawags

The chaos in the south attracted a number of people seeking to fill the power vacuums and take advantage of the economic disruption. Scalawags were southern Whites who aligned with Freedmen to take over local governments. Many in the South who could have filled political offices refused to take the necessary oath required to grant them the right to vote, leaving many opportunities for Scalawags and others. Carpetbaggers were northerners who traveled to the South for various reasons. Some provided assistance, while others sought to make money or to acquire political power during this chaotic period.

Transcontinental railroad

In 1869, the Union Pacific Railroad completed the first section of a planned transcontinental railroad. This section went from Omaha, Nebraska to Sacramento, California. With the rise of the railroad, products were much more easily transported across country. While this was positive overall for industry throughout the country, it was often damaging to family farmers, who found themselves paying high shipping costs for smaller supply orders while larger companies received major discounts. Ninety percent of the workers constructing the railroad were Chinese, working in very dangerous conditions for very low pay.

Measures taken to limit immigration

In 1870, the Naturalization Act put limits on U.S. citizenship, allowing full citizenship only to whites and those of African descent. The Chinese Exclusion Act of 1882 put limits on Chinese immigration. The Immigration Act of 1882 taxed immigrants, charging fifty cents per person. These funds helped pay administrative costs for regulating immigration. Ellis Island opened in 1892 as a processing center those arriving in New York. 1921 saw the Emergency Quota Act passed, also known as the Johnson Quota Act, which severely limited the number of immigrants allowed into the country.

Nineteenth century changes in agriculture

Technological advancements
During the mid 1800s, irrigation techniques improved significantly. Advances occurred in cultivation and breeding, as well as fertilizer use and crop rotation. In the Great Plains, also known as the Great American Desert, the dense soil was finally cultivated with steel plows. In 1892, gasoline-powered tractors arrived, and were widely used by 1900. Other advancements in agriculture's tool set included barbed wire fences, combines, silos, deep-water wells, and the cream separator.

Government actions
Four major actions by the government that helped improve agriculture for the U.S. in the nineteenth century are as follows;
- The Department of Agriculture came into being in 1862, working for the interests of farmers and ranchers across the country.
- The Morrill Land-Grant Acts were passed in 1862, allowing land-grant colleges.
- In conjunction with land-grant colleges, the Hatch Act of 1887 brought agriculture experimental stations into the picture, helping discover new farming techniques.
- In 1914, the Smith-Lever Act provided cooperative programs to help educate people about food, home economics, community development and agriculture. Related agriculture extension programs helped farmers increase crop production to feed the rapidly growing nation.

Inventors and inventions

Major inventors from the 1800s and their inventions are:
- Alexander Graham Bell—the telephone
- Orville and Wilbur Wright—the airplane
- Richard Gatling—the machine gun
- Walter Hunt, Elias Howe and Isaac Singer—the sewing machine
- Nikola Tesla—alternating current
- George Eastman—the camera
- Thomas Edison—light bulbs, motion pictures, the phonograph
- Samuel Morse—the telegraph
- Charles Goodyear—vulcanized rubber
- Cyrus McCormick—the reaper
- George Westinghouse—the transformer, the air brake

This was an active period for invention, with about 700,000 patents registered between 1860 and 1900.

Gilded Age

The time period from the end of the Civil War to the beginning of the First World War is often referred to as the Gilded Age, or the Second Industrial Revolution. The U.S. was changing from an agriculturally based economy to an industrial economy, with rapid growth accompanying the shift. In addition, the country itself was expanding, spreading into the seemingly unlimited West.

This time period saw the beginning of banks, department stores, chain stores, and trusts—all familiar features of our modern-day landscape. Cities also grew rapidly, and large numbers of immigrants arrived in the country, swelling the urban ranks.

Populist Party

A major recession struck the United States during the 1890s, with crop prices falling dramatically. Drought compounded the problems, leaving many American farmers in crippling debt. The Farmers Alliance formed, drawing the rural poor into a single political entity.

Recession also affected the more industrial parts of the country. The Knights of Labor, formed in 1869 by Uriah Stephens, was able to unite workers into a union to protect their rights. Dissatisfied by views espoused by industrialists, these two groups, the Farmers Alliance and the Knights of Labor, joined to form the Populist Party. Some of the elements of the party's platform included:
- National currency
- Income tax
- Government ownership of railroads, telegraph and telephone systems
- Secret ballot for voting
- Immigration restriction
- Term limits for President and Vice-President

The Populist Party was in favor of decreasing elitism and making the voice of the common man more easily heard in the political process.

Labor movement

The first large, well-organized strike occurred in 1892. Called the Homestead Strike, it occurred when the Amalgamated Association of Iron and Steel Works struck against the Carnegie Steel Company. Gunfire ensued, and Carnegie was able to eliminate the plant's union. In 1894, workers, led by Eugene Debs, initiated the Pullman Strike after the Pullman Palace Car Co. cut their wages by 28 percent. President Grover Cleveland called in troops to break up the strike on the grounds that it interfered with mail delivery. Mary Harris Jones, also known as Mother Jones, organized the Children's Crusade to protest child labor. A protest march proceeded to the home of President Theodore Roosevelt in 1902. Jones also worked with the United Mine Workers of America, and helped found the Industrial Workers of the World.

Panic of 1893

Far from a U.S.-centric event, the Panic of 1893 was an economic crisis that affected most of the globe. As a response to the Panic, President Grover Cleveland repealed the Sherman Silver Purchase Act, afraid it had caused the downturn rather than boosting the economy as intended. The Panic led to bankruptcies, with railroads going under and factory unemployment rising as high as 25 percent. In the end, the Republican Party regained power due to the economic crisis.

Progressive Era

From the 1890s to the end of the First World War, Progressives set forth an ideology that drove many levels of society and politics. The Progressives were in favor of workers' rights and safety, and wanted measures taken against waste and corruption. They felt science could help improve society, and that the government could—and should—provide answers to a variety of social problems. Progressives came from a wide variety of backgrounds, but were united in their desire to improve society.

> ➢ **Review Video: Progressive Era**
> *Visit* **mometrix.com/academy** *and enter* **Code: 722394**

Muckrakers

"Muckrakers" was a term used to identify aggressive investigative journalists who brought to light scandals, corruption, and many other wrongs being perpetrated in late nineteenth century society. Among these intrepid writers were:

- Ida Tarbell—he exposed the Standard Oil Trust.
- Jacob Riis—a photographer, he helped improve the lot of the poor in New York.
- Lincoln Steffens—he worked to expose political corruption.
- Upton Sinclair—his book *The Jungle* led to reforms in the meat packing industry.

Through the work of these journalists, many new policies came into being, including workmen's compensation, child labor laws, and trust-busting.

Sixteenth, Seventeenth, Eighteenth and Nineteenth Amendments

The early twentieth century saw several amendments made to the U.S. Constitution. These included:

- Sixteenth Amendment, 1913 established a graduated income tax.
- Seventeenth Amendment, 1913 allowed direct election of Senators.
- Eighteenth Amendment, 1919 prohibited the sale, production and importation of alcohol. This amendment was later repealed by the Twenty-first Amendment.
- Nineteenth Amendment, 1920 gave women the right to vote.

These amendments largely grew out of the Progressive Era, as many citizens worked to improve American society.

Federal Trade Commission and elimination of trusts

Muckrakers such as Ida Tarbell and Lincoln Steffens brought to light the damaging trend of trusts—huge corporations working to monopolize areas of commerce and so control prices and distribution. The Sherman Act and the Clayton Antitrust Act set out guidelines for competition among corporations and set out to eliminate these trusts. The Federal Trade Commission was formed in order to enforce antitrust measures and ensure companies were operated fairly and did not create controlling monopolies.

Government dealings with Native Americans

America's westward expansion led to conflict and violent confrontations with Native Americans such as the Battle of Little Bighorn. In 1876, the American government ordered all Indians to relocate to reservations. Lack of compliance led to the Dawes Act in 1887, which ordered assimilation rather than separation. This act remained in effect until 1934. Reformers also forced Indian children to attend Indian Boarding Schools, where they were not allowed to speak their native language and were forced to accept Christianity. Children were often abused in these schools, and were indoctrinated to abandon their identity as Native Americans.

In 1890, the massacre at Wounded Knee, accompanied by Geronimo's surrender, led the Native Americans to work to preserve their culture rather than fight for their lands.

Native Americans in wartime

The Spanish-American war, 1898-1902, saw a number of Native Americans serving with Teddy Roosevelt in the Rough Riders. Apache scouts accompanied General John J. Pershing to Mexico, hoping to find Pancho Villa. More than 17,000 Native Americans were drafted into service for World War I, though at the time they were not considered as legal citizens. In 1924, Indians were finally granted official citizenship by the Indian Citizenship Act. After decades of relocation, forced assimilation and outright genocide the number of Native Americans in the U.S. has greatly declined. Though many Native Americans have chosen—or have been forced—to assimilate, about 300 reservations exist today, with most of their inhabitants living in abject poverty.

Spanish-American War

Spain had controlled Cuba since the fifteenth century. Over the centuries, the Spanish had quashed a variety of revolts. In 1886, slavery ended in Cuba, and another revolt was rising.

In the meantime, the US had expressed interest in Cuba, offering Spain $130 million for the island in 1853, during Franklin Pierce's presidency. In 1898, the Cuban revolt was underway. In spite of various factions supporting the Cubans, the US President, William McKinley, refused to recognize the rebellion, preferring negotiation over involvement in war. Then The Maine, a US battleship in Havana Harbor, was blown up, costing nearly 300 lives. The US declared war two months later, and the war ended four months later with a Spanish surrender.

Panama Canal

Initial work began on the Panama Canal in 1880, though the idea had been discussed since the 1500s. The Canal greatly reduces the length and time needed to sail from one ocean to the other by connecting the Atlantic to the Pacific through the Isthmus of Panama, which joins South America to North America. Before the Canal was built, travelers had to sail all the way around South America to reach the West Coast of the US. The French began the work in 1880, after successfully completing the Suez Canal, connecting the Mediterranean Sea to the Red Sea. However, their efforts quickly fell apart. The US moved in to take over, completing the complex canal in 1914. The Panama Canal was constructed as a lock-and-lake canal, with ships actually lifted on locks to travel from one lake to another over the rugged, mountainous terrain. In order to maintain control of the Canal Zone, the US assisted Panama in its battle for independence from Columbia.

Roosevelt's "Big Stick Diplomacy" and foreign policy in Latin America

Theodore Roosevelt's famous quote, "Speak softly and carry a big stick," is supposedly of African origins, at least according to Roosevelt. He used this proverb to justify expanded involvement in foreign affairs during his tenure as President. The US military was deployed to protect American interests in Latin America. Roosevelt also worked to maintain an equal or greater influence in Latin America than those held by European interests. As a result, the US Navy grew larger, and the US generally became more involved in foreign affairs. Roosevelt felt that if any country was left vulnerable to control by Europe, due to economic issues or political instability, the US had not only a right to intervene, but was obligated to do so. This led to US involvement in Cuba, Nicaragua, Haiti and the Dominican Republic over several decades leading into the First and Second World Wars.

William Howard Taft's "Dollar Diplomacy" approach

During William Howard Taft's presidency, Taft instituted "Dollar Diplomacy." This approach was used as a description of American efforts to influence Latin America and East Asia through economic rather than military means. Taft saw past efforts in these areas to be political and warlike, while his efforts focused on peaceful economic goals. His justification of the policy was to protect the Panama Canal, which was vital to US trade interests.

In spite of Taft's assurance that Dollar Diplomacy was a peaceful approach, many interventions proved violent. During Latin American revolts, such as those in Nicaragua, the US sent troops to settle the revolutions. Afterwards, bankers moved in to help support the new leaders through loans. Dollar Diplomacy continued until 1913, when Woodrow Wilson was elected President.

Woodrow Wilson's approach to international diplomacy

Turning away from Taft's "Dollar Diplomacy", Wilson instituted a foreign policy he referred to as "moral diplomacy." This approach still influences American foreign policy today.

Wilson felt that representative government and democracy in all countries would lead to worldwide stability. Democratic governments, he felt, would be less likely to threaten American interests. He also saw the US and Great Britain as the great role models in this area, as well as champions of world peace and self-government. Free trade and international commerce would allow the US to speak out regarding world events.

Main elements of Wilson's policies included:
- Maintaining a strong military
- Promoting democracy throughout the world
- Expanding international trade to boost the American economy

First World War

The First World War occurred from 1914 to 1918 and was fought largely in Europe. Triggered by the assassination of Austrian Archduke Francis Ferdinand, the war rapidly escalated. At the beginning of the conflict, Woodrow Wilson declared the US neutral. Major events influencing US involvement included:
- Sinking of the Lusitania - The British passenger liner RMS Lusitania was sunk by a German U-boat in 1915. Among the 1,000 civilian victims were 100 Americans. Outraged by this act, many Americans began to push for US involvement in the war, using the Lusitania as a rallying cry.
- German U-boat aggression - Wilson continued to keep the US out of the war, with his 1916 reelection slogan, "He kept us out of war." While he continued to work toward an end of the war, German U-boats began to indiscriminately attack American and Canadian merchant ships carrying supplies to Germany's enemies in Europe.
- Zimmerman Note - The final event that brought the US into World War I was the interception of the Zimmerman Note. In this telegram, Germany communicated with the Mexican government its intentions to invade the US with Mexico's assistance.

US efforts during World War I

American railroads came under government control in December 1917. The widespread system was consolidated into a single system, with each region assigned a director. This greatly increased the efficiency of the railroad system, allowing the railroads to supply both domestic and military needs. Control returned to private ownership in 1920. In 1918, telegraph, telephone and cable services also came under Federal control, to be returned to private management the next year. The American Red Cross supported the war effort by knitting clothes for Army and Navy troops. They also helped supply hospital and refugee clothing and surgical dressings. Over eight million people participated in this effort. To generate wartime funds, the US government sold Liberty Bonds. In four issues, they sold nearly $25 billion—more than one fifth of Americans purchased them. After the war, Liberty Bonds were replaced with Victory Bonds.

> **Review Video:** World War I
> *Visit **mometrix.com/academy** and enter Code: **947845***

Wilson's Fourteen Points

President Woodrow Wilson proposed Fourteen Points as the basis for a peace settlement to end the war. Presented to the US Congress in January 1918, the Fourteen Points included:
- Five points outlining general ideals
- Eight points to resolve immediate problems of political and territorial nature
- One point proposing an organization of nations with the intent of maintaining world peace

In November of that same year, Germany agreed to an armistice, assuming the final treaty would be based on the Fourteen Points. However, during the peace conference in Paris 1919, there was much disagreement, leading to a final agreement that punished Germany and the other Central Powers much more than originally intended. Henry Cabot Lodge, who had become the Foreign Relations Committee chairman in 1918, wanted an unconditional surrender from Germany. A League of Nations was included in the Treaty of Versailles at Wilson's insistence. The Senate rejected the Treaty of Versailles, and in the end Wilson refused to concede to Lodge's demands. As a result, the US did not join the League of Nations.

America during the 1920s

The post-war '20s saw many Americans moving from the farm to the city, with growing prosperity in the US. The Roaring Twenties, or the Jazz Age, was driven largely by growth in the automobile and entertainment industries. Individuals like Charles Lindbergh, the first aviator to make a solo flight cross the Atlantic Ocean, added to the American admiration of individual accomplishment. Telephone lines, distribution of electricity, highways, the radio, and other inventions brought great changes to everyday life.

<u>Cultural movements influenced or driven by African Americans</u>
The Harlem Renaissance saw a number of African American artists settling in Harlem, New York City. This community produced a number of well-known artists and writers, including Langston Hughes, Nella Larson, Zora Neale Hurston, Claude McKay, Countee Cullen and Jean Toomer. The growth of jazz, also largely driven by African Americans, defined the Jazz Age. Its unconventional, improvisational style matched the growing sense of optimism and exploration of the decade. Originating as an offshoot of the blues, jazz began in New Orleans. Some significant jazz musicians were Duke Ellington, Louis Armstrong and Jelly Roll Morton. Big Band and Swing Jazz also developed in the 1920s. Well-known musicians of this movement included Bing Crosby, Frank Sinatra, Count Basie, Benny Goodman, Billie Holiday, Ella Fitzgerald and The Dorsey Brothers.

National Origins Act of 1924

The National Origins Act (Johnson-Reed Act) placed limitations on immigration. The number of immigrants allowed into the US was based on the population of each nationality of immigrants who were living in the country in 1890. Only two percent of each nationality's 1890 population numbers were allowed to immigrate. This led to great disparities between immigrants from various nations, and Asian immigration was not allowed at all. Some of the impetus behind the Johnson-Reed Act came as a result of paranoia following the Russian Revolution. Fear of communist influences in the US led to a general fear of immigrants.

Red Scare

World War I created many jobs, but after the war ended these jobs disappeared, leaving many unemployed. In the wake of these employment changes the International Workers of the World and the

- 50 -

Socialist Party, headed by Eugene Debs, became more and more visible. Workers initiated strikes in an attempt to regain the favorable working conditions that had been put into place before the war. Unfortunately, many of these strikes became violent, and the actions were blamed on "Reds," or Communists, for trying to spread their views into America. With the Bolshevik Revolution being recent news in Russia, many Americans feared a similar revolution might occur here. The Red Scare ensued, with many individuals jailed for supposedly holding communist, anarchist or socialist beliefs.

Growth of civil rights for African Americans

Marcus Garvey founded the Universal Negro Improvement Association, which became a large and active organization focused on building black nationalism. In 1911, the National Association for the Advancement of Colored People (NAACP) came into being, working to defeat Jim Crow laws. The NAACP also helped prevent racial segregation from becoming federal law, fought against lynchings, helped black soldiers in WWI become officers, and helped defend the Scottsboro Boys, who were unjustly accused of rape.

Ku Klux Klan

In 1866, Confederate Army veterans came together to fight against Reconstruction in the South, forming a group called the Ku Klux Klan (KKK). With white supremacist beliefs, including anti-Semitism, nativism, anti-Catholicism, and overt racism, this organization relied heavily on violence to get its message across. In 1915, they grew again in power, using a film called *The Birth of a Nation*, by D.W. Griffith, to spread their ideas. In the 1920s, the reach of the KKK spread far into the North and Midwest, and members controlled a number of state governments. Its membership and power began to decline during the Great Depression, but experienced a major resurgence later.

American Civil Liberties Union

The American Civil Liberties Union (ACLU), founded in 1920, grew from the American Union Against Militarism. This former organization helped conscientious objectors avoid going to war during WWI, and also helped those being prosecuted under the Espionage Act (1917) and the Sedition Act (1918), many of whom were immigrants. Their major goals were to protect immigrants and other citizens who were threatened with prosecution for their political beliefs, and to support labor unions, which were also under threat by the government during the Red Scare.

Anti-Defamation League

In 1913, the Anti-Defamation League was formed to prevent anti-Semitic behavior and practices. Its actions also worked to prevent all forms of racism, and to prevent individuals from being discriminated against for any reason involving their race. They spoke against the Ku Klux Klan, as well as other racist or anti-Semitic organizations. This organization still exists, and still works to fight discrimination against minorities of all kinds.

Great Depression

The Great Depression, which began in 1929 with the Stock Market Crash, grew out of several factors that had developed over the previous years including:
- Growing economic disparity between the rich and middle-class, with the rich amassing wealth much more quickly than the lower classes
- Disparity in economic distribution in industries

- Growing use of credit, leading to an inflated demand for some goods
- Government support of new industries rather than providing additional support for agriculture
- Risky stock market investments, leading to the stock market crash

Additional factors contributing to the Depression also included the Labor Day Hurricane in the Florida Keys (1935) and the Great Hurricane of 1938, in Long Island, along with the Dust Bowl in the Great Plains, which destroyed crops and resulted in the displacement of as many as 2.5 million people.

> **Review Video: The Great Depression**
> Visit **mometrix.com/academy** and enter **Code: 635912**

Roosevelt administration

Roosevelt's "New Deal"
Franklin D. Roosevelt was elected president in 1932 with his promise of a "New Deal" for Americans. His goals were to provide government work programs to provide jobs, wages and relief to numerous workers throughout the beleaguered US. Congress gave Roosevelt almost free rein to produce relief legislation. The goals of this legislation were:
- Relief: Accomplished largely by creating jobs
- Recovery: Stimulate the economy through the National Recovery Administration
- Reform: Pass legislation to prevent future similar economic crashes

The Roosevelt Administration also passed legislation regarding ecological issues, including the Soil Conservation Service, aimed at preventing another Dust Bowl.

Roosevelt's "alphabet organizations"
So-called alphabet organizations set up during Roosevelt's administration included:
- Civilian Conservation Corps (CCC)—provided jobs in the forestry service
- Agricultural Adjustment Administration (AAA)—increased agricultural income by adjusting both production and prices.
- Tennessee Valley Authority (TVA)—organized projects to build dams in the Tennessee River for flood control and production of electricity, resulting in increased productivity for industries in the area, and easier navigation of the Tennessee River
- Public Works Administration (PWA) and Civil Works Administration (CWA)—initiated over 34,000 projects, providing employment
- Works Progress Administration (WPA)—helped unemployed persons to secure employment on government work projects or elsewhere

Actions taken to prevent future crashes and stabilize the economy
The Roosevelt administration passed several laws and established several institutions to initiate the "reform" portion of the New Deal, including:
- Glass-Steagall Act—separated investment from the business of banking
- Securities Exchange Commission (SEC)—helped regulate Wall Street investment practices, making them less dangerous to the overall economy
- Wagner Act—provided worker and union rights to improve relations between employees and employers.
- Social Security Act of 1935—provided pensions as well as unemployment insurance

Other actions focused on insuring bank deposits and adjusting the value of American currency. Most of these regulatory agencies and government policies and programs still exist today.

- 52 -

Labor regulations

Three major regulations regarding labor that were passed after the Great Depression are:
- The Wagner Act—established that unions were legal, protected members of unions, and required collective bargaining. This act was later amended by the Taft-Hartley Act of 1947 and the Landrum Griffin Act of 1959, which further clarified certain elements.
- Davis-Bacon Act (1931)—provided fair compensation for contractors and subcontractors.
- Walsh-Healey Act (1936)—established a minimum wage, child labor laws, safety standards, and overtime pay.

World War II

Interventionist and Isolationist approaches to involvement
When war broke out in Europe in 1939, President Roosevelt stated that the US would remain neutral. However, his overall approach was considered "interventionist," as he was willing to provide any necessary aid to the Allies short of actually entering the conflict. Thus the US supplied a wide variety of war materials to the Allied nations.

Isolationists believed the US should not provide any aid to the Allies, including supplies. They felt Roosevelt, by assisting the Allies, was leading the US into a war for which it was not prepared. Led by Charles A. Lindbergh, the Isolationists believed any involvement in the European conflict endangered the US by weakening its national defense.

U.S. entry into the war
In 1937, Japan invaded China, prompting the US to halt all exports to Japan. Roosevelt also did not allow Japanese interests to withdraw money held in US banks. In 1941, General Tojo rose to power as the Japanese Premier. Recognizing America's ability to bring a halt to Japan's expansion, he authorized the bombing of Pearl Harbor on December 7, of that year. The US responded by declaring war on Japan. Because of the Tipartite Pact among the Axis Powers, Germany and Italy then declared war on the US, followed by Bulgaria and Hungary.

Surrender of Germany
In 1941, Hitler violated the non-aggression pact he had signed with Stalin in 1939 by invading the USSR. Stalin then joined the Allies. Stalin, Roosevelt and Winston Churchill planned to defeat Germany first, then Japan, bringing the war to an end. Starting in 1942 through 1943, the Allies drove Axis forces out of Africa. In addition, the Germans were soundly defeated at Stalingrad. Between July 1943 and May 1945, Allied troops liberated Italy. June 6, 1944, known as D-Day, the Allies invaded France at Normandy. Soviet troops moved on the eastern front at the same time, driving German forces back. April 25, 1945, Berlin was surrounded by Soviet troops. On May 7, Germany surrendered.

Surrender of Japan
War continued with Japan after Germany's surrender. Japanese forces had taken a large portion of Southeast Asia and the Western Pacific, all the way to the Aleutian Islands in Alaska. General Doolittle bombed several Japanese cities while American troops scored a victory at Midway. Additional fighting in the Battle of the Coral Sea further weakened Japan's position. As a final blow, the US dropped two atomic bombs, one on Hiroshima and the other on Nagasaki, Japan. This was the first time atomic bombs had ever been used in warfare, and the devastation was horrific and demoralizing. Japan surrendered on September 2, 1945.

<u>442ⁿᵈ Regimental Combat Team, the Tuskegee Airmen, and the Navajo Code Talkers</u>
The 442nd Regimental Combat Team consisted of Japanese Americans fighting in Europe for the US. The most highly decorated unit per member in US history, they suffered a 93 percent casualty rate during the war. The Tuskegee Airmen were African American aviators, the first black Americans allowed to fly for the military. In spite of not being eligible to become official navy pilots, they flew over 15,000 missions and were highly decorated. The Navajo Code Talkers were native Navajo who used their traditional language to transmit information among Allied forces. Because Navajo is a language and not simply a code, the Axis powers were never able to translate it. Use of Navajo Code Talkers to transmit information was instrumental in the taking of Iwo Jima and other major victories of the war.

<u>Women during World War II</u>
Women served widely in the military during WWII, working in numerous positions, including the Flight Nurses Corps. Women also moved into the workforce while men were overseas, leading to over 19 million women in the US workforce by 1944. Rosie the Riveter stood as a symbol of these women and a means of recruiting others to take needed positions. Women, as well as their families left behind during wartime, also grew Victory Gardens to help provide food.

<u>Atomic bomb</u>
The atomic bomb, developed during WWII, was the most powerful bomb ever invented. A single bomb, carried by a single plane, held enough power to destroy an entire city. This devastating effect was demonstrated with the bombing of Hiroshima and Nagasaki in 1945 in what later became a controversial move, but ended the war. The bombings resulted in as many as 200,000 immediate deaths and many more as time passed after the bombings, mostly due to radiation poisoning. Whatever the arguments against the use of "The Bomb", the post WWII era saw many countries develop similar weapons to match the newly expanded military power of the US. The impact of those developments and use of nuclear weapons continues to haunt international relations today.

> **Review Video:** <u>World War II</u>
*Visit **mometrix.com/academy** and enter **Code: 759402***

Yalta Conference and the Potsdam Conference

In February 1945, Joseph Stalin, Franklin D. Roosevelt and Winston Churchill met in Yalta to discuss the post-war treatment of Europe, particularly Germany. Though Germany had not yet surrendered, its defeat was imminent. After Germany's official surrender, Clement Attlee, Harry Truman and Joseph Stalin met to formalize those plans. This meeting was called the Potsdam Conference.

Basic provisions of these agreements included:
- Dividing Germany and Berlin into four zones of occupation
- Demilitarization of Germany
- Poland remaining under Soviet control
- Outlawing the Nazi Party
- Trials for Nazi leaders
- Relocation of numerous German citizens
- The USSR joined the United Nations, established in 1945
- Establishment of the United Nations Security Council, consisting of the US, the UK, the USSR, China and France

Agreements made with post-war Japan

General Douglas MacArthur directed the American military occupation of Japan after the country surrendered. The goals the US occupation included removing Japan's military and making the country a democracy. A 1947 constitution removed power from the emperor and gave it to the people, as well as granting voting rights to women. Japan was no longer allowed to declare war, and a group of 25 government officials were tried for war crimes. In 1951, the US finally signed a peace treaty with Japan. This treaty allowed Japan to rearm itself for purposes of self-defense, but stripped the country of the empire it had built overseas.

Alien Registration Act and treatment of Japanese immigrants

In 1940, the US passed the Alien Registration Act, which required all aliens older than fourteen to be fingerprinted and registered. They were also required to report changes of address within five days.

Tension between whites and Japanese immigrants in California, which had been building since the beginning of the century, came to a head with the bombing of Pearl Harbor in 1941. Believing that even those Japanese living in the US were likely to be loyal to their native country, the president ordered numerous Japanese to be arrested on suspicion of subversive action isolated in exclusion zones known as War Relocation Camps. Over 120,000 Japanese Americans, two thirds of them citizens of the US, were sent to these camps during the war.

General state of the US after World War II

Following WWII, the US became the strongest political power in the world, becoming a major player in world affairs and foreign policies. The US determined to stop the spread of Communism, naming itself the "arsenal of democracy." In addition, America had emerged with a greater sense of itself as a single, integrated nation, with many regional and economic differences diminished. The government worked for greater equality and the growth of communications increased contact among different areas of the country. Both the aftermath of the Great Depression and the necessities of WWII had given the government greater control over various institutions as well as the economy. This also meant the American government took on greater responsibility for the well being of its citizens, both in the domestic arena, such as providing basic needs, and in protecting them from foreign threats. This increased role of providing basic necessities for all Americans has been criticized by some as "the welfare state."

Harry S. Truman

Harry S. Truman took over the presidency from Franklin D. Roosevelt near the end of WW II. He made the final decision to drop atomic bombs on Japan, and he played a major role in the final decisions regarding treatment of post-war Germany. On the domestic front, Truman initiated a 21-point plan known as the Fair Deal. This plan expanded Social Security, provided public housing, and made the Fair Employment Practices Act permanent. Truman helped support Greece and Turkey, under threat from the USSR, supported South Korea against communist North Korea, and helped with recovery in Western Europe. He also participated in the formation of NATO, the North Atlantic Treaty Organization.

Korean War

The Korean War began in 1950 and ended in 1953. For the first time in history, a world organization—the United Nations—played a military role in a war. North Korea sent Communist troops into South Korea, seeking to bring the entire country under Communist control. The UN sent out a call to member nations, asking them to support South Korea. Truman sent troops, as did many other UN member nations. The war ended three years later with a truce rather than a peace treaty, and Korea remains divided at 38 degrees North Latitude, with Communist rule remaining in the North and a democratic government ruling the South.

Dwight D. Eisenhower

Eisenhower carried out a middle-of-the-road foreign policy and brought about several steps forward in equal rights. He worked to minimize tensions during the Cold War, and negotiated a peace treaty with Russia after the death of Stalin. He enforced desegregation by sending troops to Little Rock, Arkansas when the schools there were desegregated, and also ordered the desegregation of the military. Organizations formed during his administration included the Department of Health, Education and Welfare, and the National Aeronautics and Space Administration (NASA).

John F. Kennedy

Although cut short by his assassination, during his term JFK instituted economic programs that led to a period of continuous expansion in the US unmatched since before WW II. He formed the Alliance for Progress and the Peace Corps, organizations intended to help developing nations. He also oversaw the passage of new civil rights legislation, and drafted plans to attack poverty and its causes, along with support of the arts. Kennedy's presidency ended when he was assassinated by Lee Harvey Oswald in 1963.

Cuban Missile Crisis

The Cuban Missile Crisis occurred in 1962, during John F. Kennedy's presidency. Russian Premier Nikita Khrushchev decided to place nuclear missiles in Cuba to protect the island from invasion by the US. American U-2 planes flying over the island photographed the missile bases as they were being built. Tensions rose, with the US concerned about nuclear missiles so close to its shores, and the USSR concerned about American missiles that had been placed in Turkey. Eventually, the missile sites were removed, and a US naval blockade turned back Soviet ships carrying missiles to Cuba. During negotiations, the US agreed to remove their missiles from Turkey and agreed to sell surplus wheat to the USSR. A telephone hot line between Moscow and Washington was set up to allow instant communication between the two heads of state to prevent similar incidents in the future.

Lyndon B. Johnson

Kennedy's Vice President, Lyndon Johnson, assumed the presidency after Kennedy's assassination. He supported civil rights bills, tax cuts, and other wide-reaching legislation that Kennedy had also supported. Johnson saw America as a "Great Society," and enacted legislation to fight disease and poverty, renew urban areas, support education and environmental conservation. Medicare was instituted under his administration. He continued Kennedy's supported of space exploration, and he is also known, although less positively, for his handling of the Vietnam War.

Civil Rights Movement

In the 1950s, post-war America was experiencing a rapid growth in prosperity. However, African Americans found themselves left behind. Following the lead of Mahatma Gandhi, who lead similar class struggles in India; African Americans began to demand equal rights. Major figures in this struggle included:

- Rosa Parks—often called the "mother of the Civil Rights Movement," her refusal to give up her seat on the bus to a white man served as a seed from which the movement grew.
- Martin Luther King, Jr.—the best-known leader of the movement, King drew on Gandhi's beliefs and encouraged non-violent opposition. He led a march on Washington in 1963, received the Nobel Peace Prize in 1968, and was assassinated in 1968.
- Malcolm X—espousing less peaceful means of change, Malcolm X became a Black Muslim, and supported black nationalism.
- Stokely Carmichael—Carmichael invented the term "Black Power" and served as head of the Student Nonviolent Coordinating Committee. He believed in black pride and black culture, and felt separate political and social institutions should be developed for blacks.
- Adam Clayton Powell—chairman of the Coordinating Committee for Employment, he led rent strikes and other actions, as well as a bus boycott, to increase the hiring of blacks.
- Jesse Jackson—Jackson was selected to head the Chicago Operation Breadbasket in 1966 by Martin Luther King, Jr., and went on to organize boycotts and other actions. He also had an unsuccessful run for President.

Three major events of the Civil Rights Movement are:

- Montgomery Bus Boycott—in 1955, Rosa Parks refused to give her seat on the bus to a white man. As a result, she was tried and convicted of disorderly conduct and of violating local ordinances. A 381-day boycott ensued, protesting segregation on public buses.
- Desegregation of Little Rock—In 1957, after the Supreme Court decision on Brown vs. Board of Education, which declared "separate but equal" unconstitutional, the Arkansas school board voted to desegregate their schools. Even though Arkansas was considered progressive, its governor brought in the National Guard to prevent nine black students from entering Central High School in Little Rock. President Eisenhower responded by federalizing the National Guard and ordering them to stand down.
- Birmingham Campaign—Protestors organized a variety of actions such as sit-ins and an organized march to launch a voting campaign. When the City of Birmingham declared the protests illegal, the protestors, including Martin Luther King, Jr., persisted and were arrested and jailed.

Three major pieces of legislation passed as a result of the Civil Rights movement are:

- Brown vs. Board of Education (1954)—the Supreme Court declared that "separate but equal" accommodations and services were unconstitutional.
- Civil Rights Act of 1964—declared discrimination illegal in employment, education, or public accommodation.
- Voting Rights Act of 1965—ended various activities practiced, mostly in the South, to bar blacks from exercising their voting rights. These included poll taxes and literacy tests.

Vietnam War

After World War II, the US pledged, as part of its foreign policy, to come to the assistance of any country threatened by Communism. When Vietnam was divided into a Communist North and democratic South, much like Korea before it, the eventual attempts by the North to unify the country under Communist rule led to intervention by the US. On the home front, the Vietnam War became more and more unpopular politically, with Americans growing increasingly discontent with the inability of the US to achieve the goals it had set for the Asian country. When President Richard Nixon took office in 1969, his escalation of the war led to protests at Kent State in Ohio, during which several students were killed by National Guard troops.

Protests continued, eventually resulting in the end of the compulsory draft in 1973. In that same year, the US departed Vietnam. In 1975, the south surrendered, and Vietnam became a unified country under Communist rule.

US Cold War foreign policy acts

The following are US Cold War foreign policy acts and how they affected international relationships, especially between the US and the Soviet Union:
- Marshall Plan—sent aid to war-torn Europe after WW II, largely focusing on preventing the spread of communism.
- Containment—proposed by George F. Kennan, Containment focused on containing the spread of Soviet communism.
- Truman Doctrine—Harry S. Truman stated that the US would provide both economic and military support to any country threatened by Soviet takeover.
- National Security Act—passed in 1947, this act created the Department of Defense, the Central Intelligence Agency, and the National Security Council.

The combination of these acts led to the cold war, with Soviet communists attempting to spread their influence and the US and other countries trying to contain or stop this spread.

NATO, the Warsaw Pact, and the Berlin Wall

NATO, the North Atlantic Treaty Organization, came into being in 1949. It essentially amounted to an agreement among the US and Western European countries that an attack on any one of these countries was to be considered an attack against the entire group.

Under the influence of the Soviet Union, the Eastern European countries of USSR, Bulgaria, East Germany, Poland, Romania, Albania, Poland and Czechoslovakia responded with the Warsaw Pact, which created a similar agreement among those nations.
In 1961, a wall was built to separate Communist East Berlin from democratic West Berlin. A similar, though metaphorical, wall lay between east and west, as well, and was referred to as the Iron Curtain.

Arms race

After the World War II, major nations, particularly the US and USSR, rushed to develop the atomic bomb, and later the hydrogen bomb, as well as many other highly advanced weapons systems. These countries seemed determined to outpace each other with the development of numerous, deadly weapons. These weapons were expensive and extremely dangerous, and it is possible that the war between US and Soviet interests remained "cold" due to the fear that one side or the other would use these terrifyingly powerful weapons.

End of the cold war

In the late 1980s, Mikhail Gorbachev ruled the Soviet Union. He introduced a series of reform programs. Also during this period, the Berlin Wall came down, ending the separation of East and West Germany. The Soviet Union relinquished its power over the various republics in Eastern Europe, and they became independent nations with their own individual governments. With the end of the USSR, the cold war also came to an end.

> ➢ **Review Video: The Cold War Resolution**
> *Visit **mometrix.com/academy** and enter **Code: 278032***

Technological advances after WWII

Numerous technological advances after the Second World War led to more effective treatment of diseases, more efficient communication and transportation, and new means of generating power. Advances in medicine increased the lifespan of people in developed countries, and near-instantaneous communication began to make the world a much smaller place.
- Discovery of penicillin (1945)
- Supersonic air travel (1947)
- First commercial airline flight (1948)
- Nuclear power (1951)
- Orbital leading to manned space flight (Sputnik—1957)
- First man on the moon (1969)

US policy toward immigrants after World War II

Prior to WW II, the US had been limiting immigration for several decades. After WW II, policy shifted slightly to accommodate political refugees from Europe and elsewhere. So many people were displaced by the war that in 1946, The UN formed the International Refugee Organization to deal with the problem. In 1948, the US Congress passed the Displaced Persons Act, which allowed over 400,000 European refugees to enter the US, most of them concentration camp survivors and refugees from Eastern Europe.

In 1952, the President's Escapee Program allowed refugees from Communist Europe to enter the US, as did the Refugee Relief Act, passed in 1953. At the same time, however, the Internal Security Act of 1950 allowed deportation of declared Communists, and Asians were subjected to a quota based on race, rather than country of origin. Later changes included:
- 1962—Migration and Refugee Assistance Act—helped assist refugees in need.
- 1965—Immigration Act—ended quotas based on nation of origin.
- 1986—Immigration Reform and Control Act—prohibited the hiring of illegal immigrants, but also granted amnesty to about three million illegals already in the country.

Richard Nixon

Richard Nixon is best known for illegal activities during his presidency, but other important events marked his tenure as president, including:
- Vietnam War comes to an end
- Improved diplomatic relations between the US and China, and the US and the USSR
- National Environmental Policy Act passed, providing for environmental protection

- Compulsory draft ended
- Supreme Court legalizes abortion in Roe v Wade
- Watergate

The Watergate scandal of 1972 ended Nixon's presidency, when he resigned rather than face impeachment and removal from office.

Gerald Ford

Gerald Ford was appointed to the vice presidency after Nixon's vice president Spiro Agnew resigned under charges of tax evasion. With Nixon's resignation, Ford became president.

Ford's presidency saw negotiations with Russia to limit nuclear arms, as well as struggles to deal with inflation, economic downturn, and energy shortages. Ford's policies sought to reduce governmental control of various businesses and reduce the role of government overall. He also worked to prevent escalation of conflicts in the Middle East.

Carter administration

Jimmy Carter was elected president in 1976. Faced with a budget deficit, high unemployment, and continued inflation, Carter also dealt with numerous matters of international diplomacy including:
- Panama Canal Treaties
- Camp David Accords—negotiations between Anwar el-Sadat, the president of Egypt, and Menachem Begin, the Israeli Prime Minister, leading to a peace treaty between the two nations.
- Strategic Arms Limitation Talks (SALT) and resulting agreements and treaties
- Iran Hostage Crisis—when the Shah of Iran was deposed, an Islamic cleric, the Ayatollah Ruholla Khomeini, came into power. Fifty-three American hostages were taken and held for 444 days in the US Embassy.

Jimmy Carter was awarded the Nobel Peace Prize in 2002.

Ronald Reagan

Ronald Reagan, at 69, became the oldest American president. The two terms of his administration included notable events such as:
- Reaganomics, also known as supply-side or trickle-down economics, involving major tax cuts in the upper income brackets
- Economic Recovery Tax Act of 1981
- First female justice appointed to the Supreme Court, Sandra Day O'Connor
- Massive increase in the national debt—increased from $600 billion to $3 trillion
- Reduction of nuclear weapons via negotiations with Mikhail Gorbachev
- Iran-Contra scandal—cover-up of US involvement in revolutions in El Salvador and Nicaragua
- Deregulation of savings and loan industry
- Loss of the space shuttle Challenger

George Herbert Walker Bush

Reagan's presidency was followed by a term under his former Vice President, George H. W. Bush. His run for president included the famous "thousand points of light" speech, which was instrumental in increasing his standing in the election polls.

During Bush's presidency, numerous major international events took place, including:
- Fall of the Berlin wall and Germany's unification
- Panamanian dictator Manuel Noriega captured and tried on drug and racketeering charges
- Dissolution of the Soviet Union
- Gulf War, or Operation Desert Storm, triggered by Iraq's invasion of Kuwait
- Tiananmen Square Massacre in Beijing, China
- Ruby Ridge
- The arrival of the World Wide Web

William Clinton

William Jefferson Clinton was the second president in US history to be impeached, but he was not convicted, and maintained high approval ratings in spite of the impeachment. Major events during his presidency included:
- Family and Medical Leave Act
- Don't Ask Don't Tell, a compromise position regarding homosexuals serving in the military
- North American Free Trade Agreement, or NAFTA
- Defense of Marriage Act
- Oslo Accords
- Siege at Waco, Texas, involving the Branch Davidians led by David Koresh
- Bombing of the Murrah Federal Building in Oklahoma City, Oklahoma
- Troops sent to Haiti, Bosnia and Somalia to assist with domestic problems in those areas

Expansion of minority rights

Several major acts have been passed, particularly since WW II, to protect the rights of minorities in America. These include:
- Civil Rights Act—1964
- Voting Rights Act—1965
- Age Discrimination Act—1978
- Americans with Disabilities Act—1990

Other important movements for civil rights included a prisoner's rights movement, movements for immigrant rights, and the women's rights movement. The National Organization for Women (NOW) was established in 1966 and worked to pass the Equal Rights Amendment. The amendment was passed, but not enough states ratified it for it to become part of the Constitution.

George W. Bush

Amidst controversy, George W. Bush, son of George Herbert Walker Bush, became president after William Clinton. The election was tightly contested, and though he did not win the popular vote, he won the electoral vote. In the end a Supreme Court ruling was necessary to resolve the issue. His second term was also tightly contested. However, in the election for his second term, Bush won both the popular and the electoral vote. On 9/11/2001, during his first year in office, Bush's presidency was challenged by the first terrorist attack on American soil when al-Qaeda terrorists flew planes into the World Trade Center, destroying it, and into the Pentagon, causing major damage. This event led to major changes in security in the US, especially regarding airline travel. It also led to US troops being deployed in Afghanistan.

Later, Bush initiated war in Iraq with the claim that the country held weapons of mass destruction. On March 20, 2003, the US, along with troops from more than 20 other countries, invaded Iraq. Though no weapons were found, the war continues.

The last months of Bush's administration saw a serious economic meltdown in the US and worldwide. Dramatic increases in oil prices resulted in extreme increases of gasoline prices. This, along with the meltdown of the mortgage industry, created serious and overwhelming economic issues for the Bush administration.

Obama Presidency to date

In 2008, Barack Obama, a Senator from Illinois, became the first African-American US president. His administration has focused on improving the lot of a country suffering from a major recession. His major initiatives have included:
- Economic bailout packages
- Improvements in women's rights
- Moves to broaden gay rights
- Health care reform legislation
- Reinforcement of the war in Afghanistan

The Spanish mission system

Spain created the **mission system** in order to take over California land and use it for agricultural purposes. The Spanish lacked the population to settle on the land and outnumber the large Indian population, so they created missions. The purpose of the mission system was to encourage the Indians to abandon their lifestyle and religion and become Catholic. The Spanish hoped this would cause the Indians to become loyal to Spain and work for the country. The Indians began entering the mission system and were baptized without understanding the impact this would have on their culture. The Indians were forced to accept the Spanish culture and if they objected, they were whipped into submission. The Spanish viewed the Indian culture as inhuman, claiming that the Indians spoke, danced and carried on like animals rather than humans. Traditional aspects of the Indian culture, such as language and dress, were lost to the conversion of the Indians to Christianity through the mission system. More than half of the Indians living in California died from disease by the end of the mission system in California.

Type of land California Indians settled

California Indians chose land that provided for their basic needs. The land chosen had ample access to water that was fresh and could be used for drinking, cleaning and bathing. The Indians chose land that was on even ground so they could manage the terrain easily, which was necessary because they relied on the land for food and shelter. The Indians used aspects of their environment to maintain survival. They learned what plants were safe to eat and what animals could be used for food and clothing, such as deer and buffalo. They hunted with handmade weapons such as sticks and bows. The Indians lived off the natural resources the land provided but some tribes did not have the necessary skills to cultivate crops. When the Spanish began settling in California, the Indians found an economic opportunity in trade. Because of Spanish influence, the Indians where forced to master a system of agriculture through which they learned how to build canals and canoes to navigate waters.

Social, religious and political aspects of the early Indian culture

Early American Indians settled in small communities often referred to as tribes. The creation of a tribe was not meant to create rivalry with other tribes but rather to be a basis of community to maintain survival of the individuals within the tribe. Tribes located within a short distance from one another formed an extended community typically branching from a main tribe where a chief lived who would make group decisions if necessary. The early Indians rarely participated in violence but would protect their land if necessary. The various tribes shared religious beliefs. The environment was believed to be full of spirits, which caused the Indian population to have a unique respect for their environment. Many of their homes were built from wood cut from living trees, and the wood was thought to have Spirit Beings alive within it. Some Indian tribes, mainly located in Northwestern California, gave higher social status and leadership positions to those within the tribe that possessed coveted material items.

Causes of the Mexican-American War

The **Mexican-American War** began over land disputes between the United States and Mexico in Texas. Texas had fought with Mexico in 1836, won independence and became part of the United States in 1845. There remained some dispute over land after the separation. Land between the Nueces River and the Rio

Grande was being claimed as part of Texas territory, while Mexico claimed ownership of the land. United States President Polk wanted the land in Texas and other land in California and New Mexico to be part of the United States as part of Manifest Destiny. President Polk sent a representative, John Slidell, to buy the land, but Mexico refused to negotiate. President Polk responded by provoking the Mexican government. He sent troops led by Zachary Taylor into the disputed Texas land, which was a move perceived by the Mexicans as a step towards war. Mexico responded in 1846 by sending troops of its own, and a battle ensued. Americans were killed and President Polk used the battle as a reason for war, which was officially declared on May 13, 1846.

California in the Mexican-American War

The involvement of California in the Mexican-American War began when American Lieutenant John C. Fremont entered a largely Mexican-populated California. His intentions were to battle over the territory and eventually win the territory for the United States. Fremont went to California with a small army and was told to leave by the Mexican government. Fremont returned to California, an event that gave a group of American settlers the support they needed to make a stance against Mexico for the territory of California that became known as the Bear Flag revolt. The small group captured Mexican Colonel Mariano Guadalupe Vallejo and claimed establishment of a California Republic complete with a flag picturing a star and bear. The bear flag is the basis for the current California flag. The United States Navy arrived shortly after the revolt and battles in California ensued. The Mexican fighters were led by General Andres Pico, who was Governor of Alto California. Pico eventually surrendered to Fremont on January 13, 1847, which ended the fighting in California.

Explorers to discover California

The Spanish began exploring California in search of wealth in the form of gold and silver. The state name of California is based on a character Calafia in a book written by Garci Rodriguez Ordonez de Montalvo. The book was fiction and claimed California was a land inhabited solely by African American women and the land was filled full of gold. Another reason the Spanish searched California was that explorers, including Christopher Columbus, were trying to discover a means to travel to Asia via North America. This water source was thought to exist in California and was called the Strait of Anian. Hernan Cortes dispatched a group of explorers led by Fortun Jimenez who discovered the Bay of La Paz in 1533. Cortes traveled to the Baja Peninsula in Northern California in 1535. Cortes sent a last group of explorers in 1539 led by Francisco de Ulloa who discovered the southern part of California, which was called Baja California. Alta California was found in 1542 by Juan Rodriguez Cabrillo who was looking for the Strait of Anian.

Spanish ranchos and Spanish pueblos

Spanish ranchos were formed by land grants issued by the Spanish government in order to attract settlers to California and to encourage the growth of agriculture. The ranchos were used to breed sheep and cattle for economic use. Crops, including hay and pineapple, were cultivated on ranchos. Because the system of land grants was weak in enforcement, rancho owners had to protect their land by force. The Spanish government also issued land grants for the creation of **pueblos**, which were designated for the purpose of farming. Before the creation of pueblos, Mexico was supplying California with grains and other raw materials needed for Spanish survival. Once the pueblos and ranchos were created, the Spanish settlers no longer had to rely on imports for agriculture.

Spanish colonization of California

The Spanish colonization of California began with the creation of a San Diego mission and presidio. The numbers of presidios, missions, and pueblos grew with the exploration of the California land. Once a presidio or pueblo was created, the individual who created it was entitled by the Spanish government to grant land within its territory to other settlers. The land not covered within the territory of presidios and pueblos was divided up through rancho grants. Through an application process, an individual could request land from the Spanish government, but only around 30 of the applications were actually approved by the Spanish government. When America won the Mexican-American War, the Treaty of Guadalupe Hidalgo was signed in 1848. The treaty protected individual landowners from losing their established land through a claims process to the American-founded Board of Land Commissioners. As long as the owners could prove through witnesses or written documentation that they owned the land prior to the signing of the treaty, they were allowed to keep it.

California American Indians relationship

The California Indians were the first known people living in California. There were many different tribes living there, although they all believed they were one with the environment and most believed they were created with the land and were actually part of the landscape. Their climate dictated their way of life and the Indians adapted to heat or cold. The Indians used animal bones to create jewelry. Obsidian rock was used to create weapons, such as spears and arrowheads, mainly used for the purpose of hunting. The Indians lived near creeks, where they fished for salmon. They harvested grass, seed and acorns for food. The Indians used plants such as buck brush to create tools for gathering seeds. Twine and wicker was woven to make baskets, called burden baskets, which the Indians used to carry seeds, berries, clams or anything else that was gathered. Corn, squash, and melon were grown by the Mojave Indians and water from the Colorado River was used to keep the crops alive. Those Indians living in warm climates built homes with mud and grass to provide shelter from the heat. Shelter in the cooler climates consisted of branches and leaves from plants.

Mexican-American War impact on California

A major impact of the Mexican-American War on California was that with the signing of the Treaty of Guadalupe Hidalgo. The entire area of California was transferred to the United States, thereby ending Mexican control of the state. The existing (mainly Mexican) population, known as Californios, had to prove they owned the land on which they had established residence. While the Mexican landowners were petitioning the United States government for their land, which was a long process, people known as squatters would move onto their land and settle. The squatters would claim ownership and wait in hopes that the Spanish owners would not be granted land title. As the Spanish landowners were fighting off squatters, they were forced to pay property taxes, which they had never paid before and most could not afford. They would pay lawyers for representation and some lawyers stole money from the landowners. Because most of the income and food was produced by landowners on farms, the loss of land caused a huge increase in the number of poor people who had to perform hard labor to survive.

Gold in California

The first gold was found in California by Francisco Lopez in 1842 in San Feliciano Canyon near Los Angeles. The discovery was accidental, because Lopez was simply retrieving onions to eat from the ground when he saw flakes of gold. Word of the discovery spread and people living in California went to take part in the gold find. By 1843, Mexicans from the State of Sonora came for the gold and brought a new way to retrieve gold, called dry washing. The process of dry washing was better than the methods

- 65 -

used by California citizens, which basically consisted of washing dirt off small gold particles. Through the dry washing process, chunks of dirt were excavated and crushed, leaving small particles. The small dust particles were then tossed up and wind would remove the light dust, leaving particles of gold. The United States had never minted gold before it received a deposit from Don Abel Stearns, who lived in Los Angeles in 1843.

James Marshall's discovery of gold

The series of events that led James Marshall to discover gold in California began when John Sutter offered Marshall employment in 1847 to create and run a sawmill near the American River. Marshall and his laborers were allowed to live in homes near the site in the Coloma Valley. Within a year the mill was ready for use, but there was a problem. The water from the mill was supposed to be deposited into channels that were not built deeply enough because the base of the mill was lower than it should have been. Marshall's laborers had to keep digging to try to make the channel deeper. On January 24, 1848, Marshall saw gold in the channel and began gathering particles with his knife. Marshall told Sutter and wished to keep the discovery of gold a secret, but news quickly spread to the newspaper, *The Californian*, which wrote about the discovery on March 15, 1848. By 1849, the Gold Rush ensued.

California labor force and economy following the discovery of gold
Immediately after *The Californian* newspaper announced the discovery of gold on March 15, 1848, businesses shut down and homes stopped being built all through California. The price to employ someone to build a home or run a store tripled or quadrupled and towns were almost completely abandoned, especially by men. Companies closed, let their workers go, and everyone left in search for gold. The cost of real estate dropped and the only merchandise that was still expensive was mining materials. The Gold Rush unleashed the largest migration in United States history and drew people from a dozen countries to form a multi-ethnic society in California. Many immigrants came from China. The Treaty of Guadalupe Hidalgo, which made California part of the United States, was not signed until 1848, after gold was discovered. After the Treaty was signed, two years passed before California officially became a state. In the meantime, the U.S. military was dispatched to the area to maintain order. Some of the enlisted men wanted to be part of the Gold Rush and soldiers were lost to the discovery of gold.

The affect of the Gold Rush on San Francisco
On December 5, 1848, President Polk announced the discovery of gold in California to the American people. Not only were people migrating to California in large numbers from other states in America, international migrants from countries such as Peru, Chile and China sailed into San Francisco with supplies needed to sustain the miners. San Francisco thrived as a city with the huge international migration. Business owners came back from mining to make a living from trade because there were huge numbers of people passing through the city. House prices increased and workers were earning high salaries to service the migrants. The Pacific Mail Steamship Company in 1848 won a contract to provide mail service between New York and Panama and used the San Francisco Bay as its base. This brought more activity and migrants to San Francisco by way of three steamboats named the Oregon, Panama, and California.

Lifestyle of the '49ers
The '49ers were those migrants who came to California during 1849 in search of gold. They came from all areas of the United States, including as far as the east coast and traveled by boat or on wagons. The trip was long and grueling, taking up to nine months to complete. Upon arriving in California, the miners soon discovered how difficult collecting gold was. Heavy rain and snow during the winter months made for very difficult living and mining conditions. Sickness and colds were common from sleeping on cold, damp ground. The food was not nutritious, resulting in generally poor health. Scurvy was common from lack of

fruits and vegetables. Sanitation was poor and miners seldom bathed or washed their clothes. The migrants missed their families and many were plagued by exhaustion. Drinking alcohol and gambling were common pastimes of the '49ers. The Indians of California were forced to work for the miners and many were killed, which dramatically reduced the Indian population. As more white people entered the state, Californios and Indians were the subject of racism, and the miners abused and stole from anyone who was not white. California did not become a state until 1850, so there was no authority to enforce civil rights.

Positive and negative impacts of the Gold Rush
The Gold Rush had a lasting impact on California. The effects can be listed as follows:
- **Environmental Effects:** wide expanses of prime farmland destroyed by dredging; worsened flooding; destruction of extensive old growth forest by hydraulic mining and logging; destabilization of slopes and hillsides from hydraulic mining; and contamination of soil, groundwater, rivers and lakes by arsenic, mercury, cyanide and acids used during the mining process.
- **Sociological Effects:** the destruction and elimination of native cultures in the California Region; thousands of people dead from starvation and disease; hastening of the exploration and colonization of the American west; diverse and cosmopolitan nature of California's population began with the Gold Rush.
- **Economic Effects:** support for the Union war effort in the 1860's; increase in the national monetary supply; many people became fabulously rich; historic mining districts are now important tourist destinations.
- **Technological Effects:** expansion of the agricultural frontier by the need for a food supply in the mining areas; numerous improvements and innovations in mining technology; construction of the infra-structure for hydroelectric power development in the Sierra Nevada.

International migration to California

The Gold Rush brought international immigrants from all over the world including Chile, Ireland, Germany and Mexico. The immigrants came for gold and planned to return to their home country. After gold became less abundant, U.S. miners wanted to be rid of their foreign competition. The Foreign Miners Tax from the California legislature in 1850 was the solution and the tax caused many immigrants to leave California.

The Chinese were a large group of immigrants who came to California in the 19th century and stayed. Because of the mining tax, the Chinese established an income through service industries such as laundry and fishing. With the popularity of the railroad growing in the 1860's, more Chinese came to California to work. The Chinese established communities that were typically separated from other races and became an integral part of California's landscape. African American slaves were another group of people left behind to live in California when miners did not want to share gold with foreigners. To this day, California is one of the most diverse states due to international migration that occurred in the 19th century due to the Gold Rush.

With the construction of the railroad and the stories of riches due to the Gold Rush, people from China, Germany, Chile, Mexico, Ireland, Turkey, and France traveled to California ready to mine gold. The Chinese were more prominent than the other foreigners. Americans were disgruntled by the fact the influx of immigrants meant more people mining for "their" gold. They soon passed the Foreign Miners tax, hoping to discourage the immigrants from taking part in "their" treasure hunt.

Economic effects California felt during and after the international migration in the 19th century
The Chinese immigrants gave Americans access to cheap labor, which was welcomed while constructing the Central Pacific Railroad, but soon Americans were claiming that cheap labor lowered the standard of living. The railroads brought another boost to the economy, due to the unsung efforts of the immigrants. Between 1850 and 1870, one county collected over $100,000 in Foreign Miners Tax, almost exclusively from the Chinese. The Chinese brought more labor, more work, and more money by moving to California. Though the Americans did not like the competition, the immigrants helped the economy.

California Constitutional reform in 1879

The California constitutional reform of 1879 was influenced by a variety of factors. Between 1849 and 1879, California's population changed dramatically due to immigration caused by the Gold Rush. Although it was a period of prosperity as the state's agricultural and manufacturing industries grew, the 1870s saw widespread unemployment, homelessness, foreclosures and business and bank closures. Local governments had no power under the 1949 constitution, and thus the state legislature had unchecked power. Railroads, corporate ranchers and other business interests unduly influenced many legislators, to the detriment of the state's citizens. The people of California banded together and started protesting for change. They wanted the California government to control corporations and make rules that would stop the formation of monopolies. A new constitution was produced in 1879.

Major revisions to the California Constitution

On February 9, 1911, California governor Hiram Johnson and other Progressives were able to add initiative, referendum, and recall to state government, viewing them as good influences for citizen participation against the historic influence of large corporations. **Initiative** provides a means by which a petition signed by a certain minimum number of registered voters can force a public vote. **Referendum** is a direct vote in which an entire electorate is asked to either accept or reject a particular proposal. **Recall** is a procedure by which voters can remove an elected official from office. Reformers of the Progressive Era wanted a truly direct democracy where the citizens could control and maintain a voice in certain areas of government.

California vs. United States Constitutions

The Constitutions of the United States and California have many similarities. The legislatures of the United States and California are defined by their respective Constitutions as being bicameral. Bicameral means they consist of two groups: the U.S. legislature, consisting of the House of Representatives and the Senate, and the California legislature, consisting of a Senate and Assembly detailed in Article 4 of the California Constitution. The President of the United States and the Governor of California run every 4 years and are both limited to two terms. The U.S. and California Constitutions both contain a detailed Bill of Rights. Both Constitutions provide a system of checks and balances among the three branches of their respective governments: the Judicial, Executive and Legislative. Both Constitutions require members of the Legislature to be United States citizens for a designated period of time.

The term limits for the California and U.S. legislatures are different. California Senators can hold office for no more than two four-year terms while the assembly can hold office for no more than three two-year terms. United States Senators hold office for six years at a time, while House members can hold office for two years; neither is limited on the number of terms they can serve. The California Constitution requires elections for the Lieutenant Governor and other various offices in the executive branch while the U.S. Constitution allows for Presidential appointment of these equivalent offices. Both Supreme Court and district judges are elected per the California Constitution and both have term limits, but the U.S.

Constitution allows for presidential appointment of Supreme Court justices and they serve life terms. The California Constitution allows for referendum, initiative and recall, which are all components of a direct democracy and are not included in the United States Constitution. The California Constitution is lengthier and discusses in more detail specific state issues and responsibilities, while the U.S. Constitution provides a less-specific government framework.

Intrastate migration to California

The creation of major highway systems in California in the 20th century led to a massive migration of people from other states. The first highway allowing travelers from the east coast to travel to the west coast and vice versa was the Lincoln Highway, created in the early 1900s. Another major highway called Route 66 brought people from as far away as Chicago to California. The population of California grew by more than 50% in the 20th century. The Dust Bowl of the 1930s led to a large intrastate migration of people from Oklahoma to California. World War II brought more migrants from other states because California was a state of industry and employment could be found easily. Many soldiers remained in California after the war ended, adding to the population. The population increase has caused transportation problems such as overcrowded freeways and highway systems. The cost of housing and cost of living are dramatically high, making it difficult for many to afford to live in the state.

Mexican and Asian migration to California

Mexicans are a large source of international migration to California and make up a large portion of the population. California agriculture has become a main economic source for the state in the 20th century and many Mexicans were brought to America legally to provide labor for the California farms and crops. Because California is so close to the Mexican border, illegal Mexicans have flooded the state and posed an economic strain on the tax paying citizens there. Most illegal Mexicans come to work in California and send money back to their families in Mexico. Politically, the large Mexican population has made a huge impact. Politicians are less likely to fight for immigration reform because they do not want to be seen by voting Mexicans as tough on the Mexican population.

The **Japanese and Chinese** population greatly increased in California in the 20th century and most migrated looking for employment Most found it in migratory labor, working the farms, mines, canneries, and railroads. The effects of international migration on the state include the necessity for classes teaching English because many immigrants do not know the language. Overcrowding has become a problem but international immigrants are more willing to live in these crowded situations.

Air pollution

Air pollution has been a problem for California since the state experienced a huge increase in population after World War II. The increase in population meant a great increase in the number of cars in the state. Smog, or fog combined with smoke, became present in California in 1943 due to the output from vehicles. The smog problem in California was unique to the state and in response, the Governor of California in 1947 established the Air Pollution Control Act, which created districts within California that would be responsible for air quality. The Federal Air Quality Act passed in 1967 had different provisions for California because of the emissions issues. In 1959 California reacted to the state's emissions problems by making the Department of Public Safety responsible for finding ways to protect the environment from vehicle emissions. Positive Crankcase Ventilation and the Smog Check Program are among the improvements made to emissions standards. The pollution problem in California continues to get worse and the state government has continued to create legislation and develop ways to improve the environmental problem. Millions of dollars have been spent attempting to fix the pollution problem.

Water supply and delivery in California

Water supply and delivery in California is a problem in times of drought. The water supply in California comes from the northern part of the state but the highest demand for water comes from the central and southern parts of the state. The Delta is an estuary that provides water to most of the state of California and protection of the Delta has become an important issue. To make delivery possible, California has created systems such as dams and reservoirs called the Central Valley Project, the creation of which has led to environmental concerns and conflicts between state territories. Because agriculture is a huge market in California, a great deal of water is required to enable the crops to grow. Lawmakers want to create more dams to increase water supply but are met with social opposition from environmentalists who want nature to remain undisturbed. Politically, the water problem resulted in the creation of the State Department of Water Resources. The Department's role is to find ways of maintaining and handling the current and future water issues in the state.

Marbury v. Madison

Marbury v. Madison is a landmark case in United States law that forms the basis for judicial review under Article III of the Constitution. This case resulted from a petition to the Supreme Court by William Marbury, who had been appointed by President John Adams as Justice of the Peace in the District of Columbia but whose commission was not subsequently delivered. Marbury petitioned the Supreme Court to force Secretary of State James Madison to deliver the documents, but the court, with John Marshall as Chief Justice, denied Marbury's petition, holding that the statute upon which he based his claim, the Judiciary Act of 1789, was unconstitutional. It was the first time the Supreme Court had declared any act "unconstitutional" and led to the concept of judicial review in the United States.

Water wars

The California Water Wars refers to a long-running struggle between the city of Los Angeles and the residents of Owens Valley over water rights. In 1913, the 223-mile long Los Angeles Aqueduct was completed, which diverted water from the Owens River. Much of the water rights were acquired through deception and neighbors were pitted against each other. The purchases led to anger among local farmers, which erupted in violence in 1924, when parts of the water system were sabotaged by farmers. Eventually Los Angeles acquired a large fraction of the water rights in the valley, diverting water for Owens Lake to such an extent that the lake dried up completely, leaving an alkali flat and causing alkali dust storms. In 1970, Los Angeles completed a second aqueduct from Owens Valley. More surface water was diverted and groundwater was pumped to feed the aqueduct. Owens Valley springs disappeared, and groundwater-dependent vegetation began to die. Years of litigation followed until finally Los Angeles promised to rewater the lower Owens River.

California water rights scandal

Fred Eaton is best known as the driving force behind the Los Angeles Aqueduct. In 1875, Eaton became head of the Los Angeles City Water Company. Later, when Eaton became Mayor of Los Angeles, he created the Los Angeles Department of Water and, and appointed his friend, **William Mulholland**, as superintendent. Together, they planned and organized the Aqueduct, which was completed in 1913. In the early 1900s, the United States Bureau of Reclamation was preparing to support an irrigation system to assist the farmers in the Owens Valley. Eatonhad received inside information about water rights in the Owens Valley and had purchased land there as a private citizen allegedly planning to sell it to Los Angeles for profit. The aqueduct was advertised as being vital to the growth of the city. However, the public was not informed that the initial water would be used to irrigate the San Fernando Valley to the north, which was not at the time a part of the city. So much water was diverted from Owens Lake that it was entirely dry by 1924.

20th century migration

California's culture was greatly impacted by the discovery of oil in 1920, the Dust Bowl migration of the 1930s and the war boom influx of the 1940s. California was perceived by many as a place of unlimited opportunity. The movie industry continued to expand and prosper, with Hollywood as its core. Steinbeck wrote *Grapes of Wrath* inspired by the migrant workers traveling from Oklahoma to California in search for work during the Great Depression. In 1955 Disneyland opened and in 1958 the Dodgers and Giants baseball teams arrived in California. People held on to a dream of a better tomorrow in California—after all, they did discover gold and oil there! Lyrics were written capturing the hope of the utopian society: "California Girls", "California Dreamin'", and "Hotel California." Most recently, substantial increases in immigration from Mexico and Central America have affected California's culture in terms of such things as food, music, and language.

California Constitution

The California Constitutional Convention commenced on September 1, 1849 and within three days the attendees had elected officers. Forty-eight delegates represented ten districts and after only forty-three days, the people of California stamped their approval by voting "yes" to the new Constitution on November 13, 1849. This was all accomplished before California became the 31st state in the United States. The Progressives began amending the document to rescue California from the powerful monopolies. By 1962 the Constitution had over 75, 000 words and the California Constitution Revision Commission was established; over 40,000 words were removed. The document, over one hundred pages in length, is filled mostly with amendments. Unlike other states, the California Constitution protects the individual and lists clauses broader than the United States Bill of Rights.

Economic impact of 20th century migration

The migrant workers of the Great Depression resulted in a strain on the California economy. State officials asked the Federal Government for assistance when it was estimated that over 100,000 people migrated to California in a single year. They asked for funding to assist in food, shelter, and education for these homeless migrant workers. In the 1970s the pay scale lowered for high school graduates and high school dropouts. Most immigrants moving to California did not have a high school diploma and employers could pay them less than the native-Californians. This led to a large influx of laborers willing do more work for less money, thus giving businesses a competitive edge. During this period, high school dropouts were paid at rates between 10 to 16 percent lower than the national average. This competition did not seem carry over to higher-paid jobs, because most immigrants did not have higher education.

Air quality issues in California

With the great success of transportation and big business in California, air pollution grew to be a serious problem for the state. By the 1970s, "smog days" instead of "snow days" caused students to miss school when visibility was low and students could not safely attend school. Carpool lanes were implemented as one solution in order to help save the air. Motorists who operated electric vehicles also had use of the carpool lane with no passengers in an effort to persuade others to choose less pollution. California has the strictest air regulations in the United States. Thanks to these efforts, the amount of smog has drastically lowered but is still monitored by the Air Quality Management Districts.

Reasons of overall migration to California

With the discovery of oil in 1920, California saw a natural rise in migration. Oil was the most lucrative industry at that time. Movie studios set up shop in California because the state offered various terrain, thereby allowing the movie industry the ability to capture aspects of different parts of the world within hours (versus days) and cheaply. This produced aspiring actors and people dreaming of being a part of that business. The 1930s brought 300,000 migrants from the Dust Bowl who were looking for work during the Great Depression. During World War II, California housed military bases, factories, and shipyards—expanding many cities. Soon, developers bought cheap land and sold it for a big profit. Technology took off in 1950, with computers and subsequently, video games. Education was the focus in 1960s as California developed professional universities through a Master Plan for Higher Education. This contributed an even more educated workforce. Between 1940 and 1990, twelve million people migrated to California in search of a better life.

Aspects of initiative, referendum, and recall

Initiative: Initiative, a means by which a petition signed by a certain minimum number of registered voters can force a public vote, was part of the reforms initiated during the Progressive Era in 1911. That year, the people of California used initiative to print an unbiased newspaper because they wanted an even playing field for all political parties. This newspaper failed due to a boycott led by their competition who printed a more slanted view. 1914 was the first time a statewide initiative was implemented; their efforts eliminated the poll tax.

Referendum: Referendum is a direct vote in which an entire electorate is asked to either accept or reject a particular proposal. Many Californians like having referendum when they want to object to government policy. The downfall of referendum is that if it is used too frequently, it may lead to 'voter fatigue' and disappointing turnout.

Recall: Recall is the ability to remove elected officials. The recall process became available to Californians in 1911 during the Progressive Era. Before the successful recall of Gray Davis in 2003, no California statewide official had ever been recalled, though there had been 117 previous attempts. Only seven of those even made it onto the ballot, all for state legislators.

Transportation monopoly in California

By 1900 the Southern Pacific railway overshadowed the other railways in California by 85% and owned many other forms of transportation as well, thus effectively creating a monopoly. Tension rose and reformers objected to the supremacy of the railroad, giving rise to the Progressive Movement aimed at changing the corrupt political environment that allowed the railroad to use political and economic authority to avoid government control. Many authority figures owned part of the railroad, making it difficult to change the monopoly. Railroad authorities would arrange nominations of pro-railroad candidates for election. The monopoly affected everything, including prices, availability of goods, farmers, and families.

Hiram Johnson and political development

Opposed to waste and corruption, Hiram Johnson found a voice in politics for the Progressive movement. In 1910 he won the Republican seat for Governor of California. Between 1911 and 1917 he served two terms in the Governor's office, established the railroad commission in order to oversee the power of the

Southern Pacific Railroad, assisted in seeing to it that many reforms were pushed through the legislature, and left a four-million dollar surplus. The reforms gave the power back to the people through initiative, referendum, and recall, established public utilities and conservation commissions, focused on women's suffrage, set up laws for worker's compensation, placed restrictions on child labor, and assisted in breaking up monopolies. Johnson followed Roosevelt to the Progressive Party and was a nominee for Vice President under Roosevelt in 1912. In 1917 he was elected as a U.S. Senator. Interestingly enough, Johnson chose to complete his term as Governor and was late claiming his seat as a senator in Washington, D.C. Hecontinued to serve until his death in 1945.

The Anti-Saloon Act

The Progressives longed for more churches and less saloons in order to "save" California. Morality was their top priority. The Anti-Saloon Act banned slot machines, betting on horse racing, and attempted to clear the streets of "ladies of the night." This was not an easy undertaking. Surprisingly, the Anti-Saloon Act did not ban alcohol—that remained legal until the United States deemed it illegal with the 18th amendment in 1919. The 18th amendment devastated California's wine industry and forced many vineyards out of business. Overall, the Progressives were attempting to create a better and safer environment.

Women's movement in California

Women in California began organizing and joining clubs in the late 1800s/early 1900s. These organizations included clubs advocating kindergarten, pure milk laws, and self-control. Most women were seeking fellowship and friendship, but found a voice of freedom, too. The women in the clubs encouraged each other to have political knowledge and involvement. These organizations were the first steps toward women's suffrage and a brick in the foundation of progressivism. While running for office, Hiram Johnson knew he had to recognize these women who had built progressive organizations, so he listened to their dream of having a national voice. Hiram Johnson followed through to help make women's suffrage a reality. Many feared that this voice would give women too much power and the amendment barely passed.

Contributions made by the Chinese

Twenty-five thousand Chinese migrated to California seeking opportunity. They had developed mining throughout Southeast Asia and felt confident of their skills. They soon found that they were unwanted, and so to protect their goods, they would melt the gold, making pots and pans to conceal their success. After the Foreign Miners tax was passed, many Chinese left the mines and moved to San Francisco, thus began "Chinatown." While some set up shop in the city, more than 10,000 Chinese worked in the construction of the Central Pacific Railroad. They worked harder and faster than the Americans. They were described as resourceful while demonstrating physical courage. When the railroad was completed, the Chinese turned to farming. The Chinese brought ancient building techniques and herbal remedies to America.

Social reaction projected onto the Chinese

The Chinese immigrants preserved the values and attitudes of their culture, which was foreign to the American way of life. When Chinese miners took over mines that Americans had claimed worthless and made them profitable, the acceptance gap widened. At first, they were welcomed for their cheap labor and hard work, but as land became scarce and more people came in search for gold, the foreigners became targets for prejudice. Tensions rose as more Chinese immigrated to California, creating competition in the workforce. Anti-Chinese feelings spread throughout the state, as publications were printed mocking the efforts of the immigrants.

Impact the Gold Rush had on California Indians

The Native Americans could not fathom the excitement surrounding the minerals found; they had only viewed the land as a means of survival, not wealth. Many tribes were pushed out of their territories by miners seeking gold. Some began to understand the value, and the entire family would join in by digging and washing their treasures extracted from the ground. At first, many were cheated as they began spending their gold, but quickly learned how to be educated consumers. Laws were passed to prohibit American Indians working in the mines. Newspapers instructed the majority to eradicate the Indians. American Indians fought for land rights and were defeated by superior weaponry and manpower. In 1850 California passed the Act for the Government and Protection of the Indians, which granted the white man the right to enslave any unemployed American Indian. In 1853 the government moved the American Indians to reservations to clear the land for the white settlers who came to search of wealth. By 1870, California was left with less than 30,000 American Indians.

Gold rush on California's society

When gold was discovered in California, people began to migrate there in droves. People came by land and sea. Men traded the keys to their businesses for hard, manual labor. Women began to take on more responsibility at home by tending the farm and/or businesses while the men were searching for gold. At one point, there were over 100,000 people living in California and two-thirds were Americans. People become territorial and violent over mining for gold; they drove out foreigners and American Indians. Laws were finally set to protect the people and the land. When the gold ran out for individuals and big businesses took over, men had to go back home to work. With so many families moving to California searching for the American Dream, communities were built, along with roads, schools, and churches.

The economy's development during and after the Gold Rush

The effects of the Gold Rush on the California economy were substantial. A few people gained great wealth, while many who came to seek their fortunes returned home with little more than they started with. San Francisco grew from a small settlement to a boomtown, and roads, churches, schools and other towns were built throughout California. A system of laws and a government were created, leading to the admission of California as a state in 1850. New methods of transportation developed as steamships came into regular service and railroads were built. The business of agriculture, California's next major growth field, was started on a wide scale throughout the state. However, the Gold Rush also had negative effects: Native Americans were attacked and pushed off traditional lands, and gold mining caused environmental harm.

Regulations set by the miners and government

At first, there were no restrictions: no private property, no licensing, and no taxes. With the Treaty of Guadalupe Hidalgo, California now belonged to the United States. However, a state government was not established and Californians were uneducated on the federal laws. So with money to be made and no time to waste, the miners decided to follow Mexican law. Mining claims were implemented by the miners in camps. This gave an individual the right to take minerals from public land and was only valid if the land was actively being worked. This idea was illegal according to US law, but because California was not receiving national attention at this point, miners continued claiming the gold. At first the claims were respected, but when more people began to move to California seeking gold, miners began "claim-jumping"

- 74 -

and often led to violence. In 1866 the US government stepped in and gave miners the rights to extract minerals from the land. This was an attempt to assist in maintaining order.

Construction and completion of the Panama Railway

The **Panama Railway** is a 48-mile, double-track railroad that links the Atlantic Ocean to the Pacific Ocean via the Isthmus of Panama in Central America. In May 1850, the railroad construction began; but conditions were so difficult that work progressed slowly. Much of the route was through jungle and swamps, with stifling heat and mosquitoes everywhere. During the rainy season that lasted half the year, workers labored in water up to four feet deep. Diseases were spread by mosquitoes and it is estimated that from 5,000 to 10,000 people may have died in construction of the railroad. It is reported that a man died for every railroad tie laid. The train started running on January 28, 1855, charging $25.00 for a first-class, one-way ticket and $10.00 for second class; personal bags cost five cents per pound. Mail was 22 cents a pound, while first-class freight was 55 cents per cubic foot and was paid in gold.

Principles of American Democracy

Marbury v. Madison

Marbury v. Madison, written by John Marshall in 1803, is credited with giving the Supreme Court the power of judicial review: that is, the authority to review and decide Constitutional questions. This authority was not clear in the Constitution and may not have been intended by its authors. Marshall's court, through *Marbury v. Madison*, argued that judicial review was implied by the Constitution which the Court had the right to interpret. The decision gave the Court the final say regarding state and Congressional decisions, including the right to overturn those decisions. This decision asserted that upholding the Constitution was the most important responsibility of the Supreme Court.

<u>Supreme Court decision in *McCulloch v. Maryland*</u>
The Supreme Court decision in *McCulloch v. Maryland* was written by Chief Justice John Marshall in 1819. This decision, citing the Constitution's necessary and proper clause, established that the Supreme Court could enact federal laws for the good of the country, even if the laws violate state law. The ruling further declared that a state cannot stop or impede a federal action deemed appropriate within the Constitution or by the Supreme Court. This power is not directly stated in the Constitution, but could be inferred as an implied power of the Supreme Court. The case involved the United States creating a national bank and the state of Maryland trying to stop them through a tax. *McCulloch v. Maryland* strengthened the Supreme Court and the federal government.

Civil War amendments

The Thirteenth Amendment banned all forms of slavery. Although the Amendment was ratified, many southern states adopted Black Codes to counteract the amendment. The Fourteenth Amendment guaranteed all U.S. citizens equal protection and due process under the law. The amendment guaranteed citizenship to all freed slaves and supported the Civil Rights Act of 1866, which granted citizenship to African-Americans and gave the government the right to step in when states interfered with citizenship rights. The Fifteenth Amendment gave the right to vote to all citizens regardless of the color of their skin or ethnic background. However, it did not however mention sex, and women were still not allowed to vote because they were not considered citizens, though they were counted as part of the population.

The court's interpretation of the Bill of Rights

The Bill of Rights guarantees certain rights, such as freedom of speech and freedom of religion. The Supreme Court ruled that these rights pertained to the actions of the U.S. government and were not intended to limit the actions of the states. The addition of the Fourteenth Amendment raised the question of how much the states could be limited by the Bill of Rights. The due process clause states that certain basic rights must not be infringed upon without due process of law. A debate ensued regarding how much power that gave the federal government over the states' actions. The courts did interpret the Fifth and Fourteenth Amendments in 1897 as meaning that the states would have to prove the laws they passed were in the best interest of their people's health, welfare or public morals. The federal courts rarely interfered with state matters, and the states continuously limited people's freedom of speech when they in any way spoke against the government. Finally, the courts declared that states could not have complete freedom to limit people's speech regarding politics, since this right is protected in the Bill of Rights.

Supreme Court decision in *United States v. Nixon*

The Supreme Court Decision in *United States v. Nixon* was written in 1974 by Chief Justice Warren Earl Burger. The case involved the Watergate scandal, in which Republican President Nixon was thought to have been involved the theft of items from the Democratic Party offices. Several men were indicted, and the court wanted Nixon to submit related documentation and tapes that could be potentially damaging to the accused and the president. Nixon cited executive privilege, a power granted by the Constitution, and refused the request. With the ruling in the *United States v. Nixon*, the Supreme Court decided that Nixon did not have the right to cite executive privilege under all circumstances. Furthermore, the Court reserved the right to adjudicate executive privilege as it relates to criminal cases. This ruling further demonstrated that the Constitution binds the president by the same laws as it binds all citizens.

Plessy v. Ferguson and Brown v. Board of Education

The Supreme Court has made a number of important rulings regarding racial segregation. Questions of civil rights require the Court to interpret the Fourteenth Amendment, and the Court's interpretation has changed over time. The Supreme Court ruled in *Plessy v. Ferguson* (1896) that states were within their rights to have racially segregated railroads. The ruling led to the use of the separate but equal doctrine in other areas, such as education and the use of public facilities. The *Plessy* ruling was overturned by the Court's decision in *Brown v. Board of Education* (1954). Oliver Brown of Topeka sued and was backed by the NAACP because he believed that the public school system did not provide equal access for minorities to education. The Court agreed that separate but equal education was impossible. The decision eventually led to the desegregation of public schools.

Miranda v. Arizona and Roe v. Wade

In *Miranda v. Arizona* (1966), the Supreme Court interpreted the Constitution to include a specific individual right even though this right is not explicitly mentioned. The Court ruled that a person must be told that he or she does not have to talk to police without legal representation. As a consequence of this ruling, all states had to adopt the Miranda warnings. Controversy surrounded the ruling, as some believed that criminals did not deserve the right of representation upon arrest. *Roe v. Wade* (1973), which protected an individual's right to have an abortion, was another decision where the Supreme Court invoked the Fourteenth Amendment to allow an inferred civil right. The Court ruled that first trimester abortions could not be forbidden by the state and that the fetuses were not protected by the Constitution. Both cases were controversial because they asserted the Supreme Court's ability to create rights not defined specifically by the Constitution.

California v. Bakke and Adarand Constructors, Inc. v. Pena

Over time, Supreme Court rulings have changed the scope of controversial affirmative action programs. The Supreme Court decision in *Regents of the University of California v. Bakke* (1978) determined that ethnicity is an acceptable consideration during the college admissions process. However, many justices argued that using race at all was a form of discrimination. The decision did not allow colleges to establish a mandatory number of minorities to be admitted to the college each year. The Supreme Court limited affirmative action programs in *Adarand Constructors, Inc. v Pena* (1995). This case challenged a previous court ruling that allowed special incentives to be granted to companies who gave business to minority-owned companies. The Court decided that federal affirmative action programs have to be held up to "strict scrutiny," a phrase that means they should be reviewed by the Supreme Court in order to ensure equal treatment for all people.

United States v. Virginia and Bush v. Palm Beach County Canvassing Board

The equal protection under the law guaranteed by the Fourteenth Amendment was the basis of the decision in *United States v. Virginia* (1966). The Court deemed that it was unconstitutional for the Virginia Military Institute to enroll only men. The ruling advanced women's rights, stating that no law that limited the rights of females would be allowed. The Supreme Court decision in *Bush v. Palm Beach County Canvassing Board* (2000) effectively ended the Presidential race between Al Gore and George W. Bush. There had been a malfunction in voting procedures in Florida: since Bush was leading, Gore demanded a manual recount. Bush claimed the count could not be completed by a preset deadline established by the Constitution. The Court decided there would be no manual recount, a ruling that limited voting rights insofar as it indicated that not all of the votes would count.

Popular consent

Popular consent is a key concept in a democracy; it asserts that the government operates only with the consent of the citizens. Citizens agree to be governed by people elected by a majority. this concept is based on John Locke's social contract theory. The system relies on people actually voting; otherwise, the government may end up consenting to a limited portion of the population rather than all of the people they govern.

Social contract theory

The *social contract theory* is the idea that all citizens have the right to be governed and, alternately, must submit to being governed. Both John Locke, a major influence on the Declaration of Independence, and Thomas Hobbes theorized that the right to be governed was God-given, since at birth all people are equal and free. In Locke's social contract theory, people would consent to be governed to protect their basic rights, such as life and liberty. The only acceptable government would either honor the consent of the governed, or, failing to do that, be removed.

Direct and indirect democracy

In a *direct democracy*, the citizens can call a meeting and vote something into law with a majority. In this system, the people are directly involved in forming policies. There are few if any representatives for the people in this type of government. An *indirect democracy*, like the United States, is a representative democracy in which citizens vote for a representative to act in their best interest. This system is necessary because it is impossible to have a town hall big enough to hold every American. Before the United States became an indirect democracy, town hall meetings were common venues for popular participation in government. Many political theorists, like Plato, Aristotle, and Jean-Jacques Rousseau, argue that true democracy is not achieved unless each person gets his or her say.

Workings of the Electoral College

Each state receives one electoral vote for each of its United States senators and representatives. Typically, the electors are chosen by the political parties as recognition of loyalty. Each state certifies its electors with Certificates of Ascertainment, which must contain the following: governor's signature; the names of the electors and the number of votes they received; the names of the other candidates and the votes they received, and the state seal. The votes are divided into two lists. One contains all of the people who received a vote for President and the number of votes person received, and the other contains all of the people who received an electoral vote for Vice President and the number of votes each received. The electorate prepares six Certificates of Vote; each contains both prepared lists and is signed by each elector. The electors attach one of the Certificates of Ascertainment received by the Governor to each of the six Certificates of Vote, and these are then sealed by the electors. One is sent by registered mail to the President of the US Senate, two are sent to the Archivist of the US, two are sent to the Secretary of each state, and one is sent to the Chief Judge of the Federal District Court for the jurisdiction of the elector's meeting.

College of Electors and the election of 1800

In the original Constitution, the College of Electors was used in the selection of the President and Vice-President. Every state had a designated number of representatives and senators, and that number would equal the electoral votes each state would cast in an election. Whichever candidate had the highest number of votes would become the President, and the person with the next largest number of votes would become the Vice-President. If neither person had a majority of votes, the House of Representatives would decide the winner giving one vote to each state. The Election of 1800 between Thomas Jefferson and Aaron Burr led to a change in the College of Electors. This election ended in a tie, which the House then had to break. In 1804, the Twelfth Amendment was added to the Constitution, mandating two separate elections: one for the President and one for the Vice-President. Henceforth, the College of Electors would cast votes for two offices rather than one.

College of Electors and the 2000 election

The College of Electors represents the votes of individual citizens. In other words, a citizen does not vote directly for the President or Vice-President, but rather a for person representing each of the candidates. In almost every state, the winner of the popular vote receives all of the electoral votes. (The exceptions are Maine and Nebraska, in which the popular vote is tallied up for each congressional district.) One possible consequence of the College of Electors is that a candidate can win the popular vote and still not be elected. In the 2000 Presidential race, the popular vote was very close, with Gore leading Bush. However, since the larger states had more electoral votes and Bush won more of these state, he won the election anyway. The fact that certain states have more electoral votes means that candidates will campaign harder in those states. In some cases, smaller states are ignored and the residents do not feel represented or that their votes matter.

The earliest political parties

Differences in opinion about how the Constitution should be interpreted led to the creation of two different political parties. The two people responsible for dividing the parties, Alexander Hamilton and Thomas Jefferson, both worked under President Washington. Alexander Hamilton's group would become known as the Federalists. The Federalists believed that the central government should be powerful and that a national bank should be created. The Federalists argued that not every government right was expressly written in the Constitution, and that many powers could be inferred. Jefferson's group would become known as the Republicans. The Republicans argued that the Constitution was written clearly and should be followed to the letter. This meant no national bank should be formed and the government should intervene as little as possible, particularly in the promotion of industry. The Republicans supported the working class, while the Federalists supported the upper class. John Adams, a Federalist, won the next election, but in 1800, Jefferson was elected and the Republicans retook power.

Development of the two-party system

The Republican and Federalist parties allied from 1813 to 1824, during the Madison and Monroe administrations. This period was known as the Era of Good Feelings. Compromise and the absorption of some Federalist beliefs, like a strong central government, by the Republicans created a party that could represent all people. The next parties to form would be the Whigs and the Democrats. The Democrats argued for state rights over a powerful federal government. The Whigs wanted big government and a national bank. The Whig Party broke apart after the 1854 Kansas-Nebraska Act, which divided the party into pro- and anti-slavery groups. Republicans reemerged with the selection of President Lincoln in 1860. Both the Republican and Democratic Parties had internal conflicts over slavery. The parties would persevere, however, as the two main political parties in the United States.

Role of political parties in society

The role of political parties in a democracy is to provide each individual citizen with a choice when voting. The political parties represent different ideas and interests. Democrats and Republicans are the two main parties in the United States, but for those who do not affiliate with one or the other there are numerous other groups, including the Independent and Libertarian parties. Laws get passed through legislation supported and introduced by the two political parties. Third parties in the United States still have a voice, but in order to be heard, they must lobby one of the main parties. In close elections, candidates representing the two main parties try to woo voters from the smaller parties, which can elevate the status of these otherwise marginal parties.

Role of political parties in Congress

The majority party controls the congressional committees, which are responsible for referring bills and setting the agenda for Congress. The majority party can stop bills, hurry them through, or change them. Committee chairs hold a lot of power: they can decide if a bill is even heard, and they appoint subcommittees to work on bills. Committee chairs are selected by House leadership, and are typically a member of the majority political party. The Speaker of the House elected by the representatives from the majority party. For instance, after the 2006 elections the Democratic Party held more seats in the House than the Republicans and selected Nancy Pelosi to become Speaker of the House.

Reapportionment, redistricting and gerrymandering

The House of Representatives has 435 members. After the census every 10 years, the Constitution requires that those seats are divided among the states proportionately based upon population. This process is called *reapportionment*. Each state is divided into congressional districts, areas that are also represented by a state legislator. After the census takes place and the congressional seats are reapportioned, the congressional districts are redrawn to reflect the shift in the number of seats, to ensure that an equal number of people in each district are represented by legislature. That process is called *redistricting*. Controversy has surrounded redistricting: state representatives have been accused of creating boundaries that will favor a particular party, a maneuver known as *gerrymandering*.

The three branches of the federal government

The federal government is organized into three branches: the executive, legislative, and judicial. Checks and balances between the three branches ensure that no one branch can be too powerful. The executive branch includes the President, Vice-President, departments, and independent agencies that cooperate to make sure laws are being followed. The judicial branch consists of the Supreme Court and the federal circuit courts, and is responsible for hearing cases and interpreting laws. The legislative branch includes the Congress, which is divided between the Senate and House of Representatives, and agencies that work with the Congress. The Congress is responsible for creating currency, overseeing the military, declaring war, and regulating commerce. In extreme circumstances, the Congress can vote to end a federal official's term by impeachment. The Congress creates legislation that must be voted on and then accepted by the President, an example of checks and balances within the government.

State governments

State governments, like the federal government, have three branches: the executive, legislative, and judicial. States have governors, whose responsibilities are similar to those of the president. Each state has a unique constitution, covering issues unique to that jurisdiction. The states cannot create laws or direct citizens in any way that contradicts the United States Constitution, because the federal government holds ultimate authority. States must fund their own governments and run their own elections. Each state is responsible for creating agencies to ensure that residents are healthy and safe. Commerce within the state is controlled by the state. A state cannot create its own monetary system. State governments are not responsible for federal services, like mail service and the national military. Foreign relations are maintained through the national rather than the state government

Local governments

Within each state there are several local governments, including towns, counties, cities, municipalities, special districts, and school districts. Local governments can create their own governments with special rules, as long as they do not interfere with national or state laws. Local governments are important, because state government officials cannot know and meet all of the needs of every citizen. When a state is divided into smaller local units, local governments can represent the special interests and issues of their community. School districts elect a governing body that makes rules and budget plans, allowing each district to customize its spending on the needs of the district. Cities can create laws that apply within city limits, like a rule prohibiting smoking in public places. Special city elections are often held to approve such rules.

Tribal governments

Tribal governments have the right to organize themselves however they see fit within their own land. This is known as *tribal sovereignty*. The Commerce Clause in the Constitution has been interpreted to give jurisdiction over Indian tribes to the federal rather than state government. Most tribal governments consist of three branches similar those of the state and national governments. A principal chief usually heads the government, and tribal courts hear cases. The tribal council oversees legislative functions. The tribal government decides who can participate in the tribe, negotiates with state and local governments, and controls the educational system and health codes of the tribe. The tribe has authority over what kind of activities are legal on their property. For example, gambling may be illegal in a state but legal on tribal property. This explains the preponderance of casinos on tribal land.

Original and appellate jurisdiction

The *Original jurisdiction* is where a case is first heard. Jurisdiction is determined by the authority in the area in which the case will be heard. Whether the case will be heard at the federal or state level is determined by the type of case. Cases involving federal matters are heard by federal courts, while others are heard by state courts. *Appellate jurisdiction* is applied once a case has been decided by a lower court and the decision has been appealed. The appellate court, unlike the court of original jurisdiction, does not hear all of the facts of the case. Rather, it decides if the case was handled correctly by the previous courts. U.S. District Courts have no appellate jurisdiction, but the U.S. Court of Appeals and the U.S. Supreme Court do. The U.S Court of Appeals has no original jurisdiction, but the District Courts do and, although it is rarely used, the Supreme Court does as well.

State and federal jurisdictions on Indian reservations

Because each tribe has sovereign status over its land, the tribe carries jurisdiction over its land in most cases. When there is criminal activity, the tribe can enforce laws through the judicial branch of its government. Tribest typically have jurisdiction if the accused is a member of the tribe or a fellow Native American. If a civil infraction occurs on tribal land, the tribe has jurisdiction no matter whether the accused is part of the tribe or not. Because jurisdiction can be difficult to determine, many crimes by and against Native Americans are ignoredto the detriment of the population. Jurisdiction issues have arisen surrounding the natural resources on tribal reservations. The state and local governments want access to the resources, while the tribe wants them to be reserved for its members. The state governments have appealed to the federal government, arguing that natural resources are not part of tribal jurisdiction.

Dual federalism

In a system of *dual federalism*, federal and state governments should have clear jurisdiction over their territory. Both governments are separated into the legislative, executive and judicial branches, and each branch has specific responsibilities. The state is separated into territories, with local governments having their own responsibilities and tribal governments having jurisdiction over the land they inhabit. Because the system is set up such that each government functions independently, the governments have a tendency to avoid helping one another. The problem with this tendency is that each government has different resources at its disposal. The federal government has more resources than the state to try cases, and the state more resources than the local governments, so often the local government or tribe does not have enough money to deal with criminal problems. Jurisdiction issues also arise in cases of identity theft through mail fraud. For example, tampering with mail is a federal crime, but federal prosecutors may not go after a small-time criminal who breaks into mailboxes to steal a person's identity. The state government is left with no means of prosecution, and the citizens suffer the consequences.

Money in political races

Money and the ability to raise money have become a prime indicator a politician's potential for success. Millions of dollars are required to reach enough voters to win a national campaign. Personally wealthy individuals have an advantage since, according to the Federal Election Campaign Act, candidates can have unlimited access to their own money during a campaign. If a candidate chooses to run while only spending the amount set by the government, he or she becomes eligible for public financing. Because of campaign legislation, private contributions are limited. These limitations were imposed because large groups of extremely wealthy individuals contributed huge amounts of money to win an election. In a democracy, people are supposed to have the right to elect government representatives. It can be argued that when money becomes necessary to win an election, not every person can run for office and Americans do not have a true array of choices.

Mass media's influence on American politics

The mass media has both positive and negative influence on democracy. Positively, media gives the general public access to the world. Political and social, and state and local information can be obtained through the media. People have access to more information now than at any other time in history. However, the mass media can negatively affect a democracy as well. There are a small number of corporations who own the media, and some would argue that this leads to a narrow delivery of the news and the possibility of certain groups or politicians using the mass media to further a political agenda. If a politician is friends with the head of a media outlet, he or she may obtain unfairly positive coverage. Another area of concern is that a politician may promise favors to the corporation in exchange for positive coverage. If the information that is being broadcast by the mass media is not fair and accurate, then democratic politics can be subverted.

Economic and special interest groups

Campaign finance laws have increased the role of economic interests and special interest groups in American politics. Politicians are forced to get small donations from a large number of corporations, individuals, and groups. According to the Bipartisan Campaign Reform Act, the contributions of individuals and political committees are limited. This activity can result in the election of individuals who are not representing the interests of the public as a whole, but rather are representing special interest groups or corporations. For example, if a special interest group wants legislation that protects a woman's right to have an abortion in the third trimester, they may donate to a Democratic politician and expect the person to pursue that legislation once elected. The politician may agree to represent the agenda of the special interest group in return for non-monetary services, like canvassing and making phone calls to undecided voters.

Supreme Court ruling in Buckley v. Valeo

In *Buckley v. Valeo* (1976), the Supreme Court allowed individuals to spend as much of their own money as they want on their campaign, citing the right as a matter of free speech. However, this ruling upheld federal limits on campaign contributions. This decision is important because it gives extremely wealthy candidates to have a possible advantage in an election. A wealthy candidate can spend a great deal on media and advertising, while his or her opponent may not have access to the same amount of funds. For this reason, many commentators feel that the Bipartisan Campaigns Reform Act, upheld by the Supreme Court in 1993, negates the *Buckley v. Valeo* ruling. Some argue that by limiting how people can spend their money, such as by banning the use of unregulated funds in media advertising mentioning a candidate's name within 30 days of the election, the Court is stealing the free speech protected in *Buckley v. Valeo*. Because it is much more difficult to defeat an incumbent, a wealthy incumbent can become virtually invulnerable thanks to this legislation.

Influence of media on foreign policy

The media can influence foreign policy through reporting and investigation. When the media uncovers government lies and manipulation, they undermine support for the government's policy. If they investigate military actions too excessively, they can give away important strategy and locations, thereby endangering soldiers. On the other hand, the government can use the media to gain military advantage. In the Persian Gulf War, for instance, the government induced the media to pay heavy attention to military action near the Kuwaiti coast. Meanwhile, American troops were actually attacking farther inland. The Iraqis viewed this coverage and responded accordingly, giving the U.S. an advantage. Media can bring attention to situations, such as the abuse at the Abu Ghraib prison, thus influencing the foreign policy agenda.

Media influences on politics and public opinion

The media has become a dominating influence in politics and public opinion. Through appearances on television programs, candidates have sought to gain supporters and influence public opinion. Candidates like Bill Clinton have appeared on MTV, hoping to gain support of younger voters. Actors and actresses have become more involved in politics, frequently appearing on television to encourage people to vote. Some political groups have been successful in harming a candidate through the media. A notable example is the Swift Boat Veterans for Truth a group that claimed presidential candidate John Kerry's military record was untruthful and that his actions in Vietnam endangered other soldiers. Kerry's poll numbers plummeted, and he eventually lost the election. The media is often been accused of supporting one political party more than the other. Because so many people listen to the television and radio, the media can influence democratic politics by running positive stories about one candidate and negative stories about another.

Political websites and blogs

The internet is a powerful force in politics. Political blogs and live chats on political subjects are easy to find. The far left and the far right (that is, extremely partisan liberals and conservatives) share opinions and organize on-line. The influence of the internet is troubling to some, because not all of the information that is found there is true. The code of journalistic ethics, which is meant to keep the news organizations honest, is not always followed on the internet. Problems can arise when people form opinions based on false reports. Another problem is that internet commentary is often hateful. For example, after White House Secretary Tony Snow was diagnosed with cancer, some bloggers reacted by gleefully anticipating his death. This could be considered hate speech. Politicians must be careful before aligning themselves with writers on the web.

Internet and public opinion

The recent war in Iraq has been a clear indicator of how the internet can influence government and politics. The Arabic news organization Al Jazeera aired the beheading of a United States soldier and violent conflicts between the United States and Iraq in great detail. This footage became available on the internet, creating a public outcry against the war saw, for the first time, U.S. citizens saw actual violence. The internet has also been used to influence public opinion during presidential races. Hillary Clinton recently used the internet to post a *Sopranos* spoof encouraging people to vote for her campaign song during the Democratic prmiaries. YouTube featured live debates between the Democratic candidates for President, in which people could send in questions on-line. The use of the internet is meant to reach a generation of younger voters who historically vote in small numbers. If the internet can encourage these people to vote, the results of the election could be affected.

Media and FCC regulation

The *right of rebuttal* is a guarantee by the government that if someone is personally attacked in the media, they will have an opportunity to respond there. The significance of the right of rebuttal is that it is one of several ways the federal government can regulate what is on radio and TV. Unlike in print media, the Federal Communications Commission can regulate in some ways what is aired. Because it is not regulated by the FCC, print media is considered a better source of information and is often the source for broadcast media. The FCC regulates explicit material for the good of society, but too much FCC control, one could argue, may tamper with the freedom of speech guaranteed in the Constitution. The right of rebuttal raises questions about who should decide who and what can be said about a public figure.

Institutional advertising's influence

Institutional advertising is a way for corporations to gain favorable public opinion by placing advertisements that show the company in a positive light. Institutional advertising, social movements, and grassroots mobilization are all attempts to gain public support for a group's agenda. An advertiser can generate support for a political agenda. The public has to realize that some advertising may be deceptive and lead to a falsely positive feeling. The public should critically analyze advertising. For example, the company Beyond Petroleum runs ads claiming to help the environment. The claim may be true, or may be a response to the media attention environmental issues are getting. With the new abundance of ad campaigns, people are being paid a lot of money to influence the public. It is important not to blindly trust a company based on institutional advertising.

Political systems ruled by one person, including *monarchies, autocracies,* and *dictatorships*

In a *monarchy*, one person rules. The ruler of a monarchy (as for instance a king or queen) typically gains his or her power by dint of lineage. A monarch is supposed to act in the best interests of the citizenry. England is a contemporary example of a monarchy. An *autocracy* is ruled by one person, who has complete power over the land and uses this power for personal interests. Acting in the best interest of the people is not necessary for an autocrat. Force will be used if necessary to control the citizens and make them conform to the wishes of the autocrat. A *dictatorship*, as for example Russia when ruled by Stalin, is a form of government in which a single person uses force to rule a country. The rape and torture of citizens by government officials is common in a dictatorship.

Political systems based on social status

In an *oligarchy*, social status, wealth, military position, or achievement determines who serves in the government. An oligarchy consists of a small group of people who rule a country. Ancient Greece was ruled by oligarchies instead of monarchies. In an *aristocracy*, the government is composed of the most educated, wealthy, and prominent members of society. The theory of an aristocracy is that the smartest and most illustrious people in society should make the decisions for the rest. Aristocrats are the elite who were eligible to serve in the government. In a *plutocracy*, income is the main basis for government and the rich rule the land. Occasionally, the United States is described as a plutocracy, because the people who win big elections tend to be wealthy.

Parliamentary political system

The *parliamentary political system* is based on achieving agreement between the executive and legislative branches of government. Before one branch of government can act, the other must support the action. The leader of a parliamentary government is the prime minister, who is chosen by the legislature's passing a vote of confidence rather than by election. Typically, the leader of the state or executive part of the parliamentary government is elected, although sometimes he or she is born into the title. The parliamentary system of government requires compromise between the head of state and prime minister in order to function. Once in agreement, laws are easily passed. Some would argue that there is a lack of oversight between the legislative and executive branches, because once the two branches are in agreement, there is no longer a debate over legislation and whatever the two main heads of government decide becomes law.

Communist philosophy

Communism is the political philosophy that all people within a country should be economically equal. What a person owns is not a matter of inheritance or job title, but rather is an equal portion of the country's wealth, which is distributed evenly by the government. Property, land, and all other economic activity are owned and controlled by the government. Communism is difficult to maintain, because people generally want to be paid based on merit rather than a preset amount. People in communist societies have the tendency to produce exactly what is required of them by the government. Communist communities lack progress and innovation, and eventually fail. Karl Marx and Friedrich Engels wrote *The Communist Manifesto*, which encouraged an overthrow of the government by subjugated industry workers. According to Marx, communism would resolve the inequalities between rich and poor.

Liberalism

The ideological tenets of *liberalism* have changed over time. Originally, liberalism was about promoting individual freedom. Early liberals did not want the government interfering in the private lives of individuals. Liberalism eventually adjusted to inlcude the idea that the best way to promote individual freedom is to have the government enforce it. Modern liberalism calls for the government to create programs that will assist society. Public healthcare, a better environment, and other social programs will improve social conditions and ensure individual freedom. FDR's New Deal is a perfect example of liberal social programs, created and controlled by the government, designed to recover the economy during the Great Depression. For liberals, many of these programs come from the idea that individual freedom is an inherent right, one that each person is born with and that should be protected. Liberals put the responsibility of a flailing economy squarely on the shoulders of the government, and expect the government to act in the benefit of the welfare of society.

Conservatism

Conservatism argues that tradition, albeit flawed, should direct society, and that changes based upon the unknown are unnecessary and foolish. Conservatives believe government should play a very minimal role in the private lives of individuals. Conservatives would argue that society is best served not by government programs, but rather by the individual pursuit of economic and social success. Economic freedom is a result of hard work and opportunity, rather than an inherent right from birth. Because of these beliefs, conservatism calls for low taxes and claims that the economy will thrive when people are allowed to spend the money they have earned. At its roots, conservatism calls for less government, but because it has strong ties to Christianity, conservatism sometimes calls for government intervention in private life. These are more reactive gestures to a perceived movement to remove God from all public institutions.

Democracy

A *democracy* is a form of government in which the citizens decide how the country will be run. The American political system is a form of democracy called a *representative democracy*. In a representative democracy, a group of people are elected by the people to act on behalf of the entire state, country, or nation. Representative democracies developed because of the impossibility of making room for every voice in a populous nation. In a direct democracy, like that of the state of California, the people vote directly on important matters affecting the state. There are elected officials, but major legislation is passed or denied directly by a vote of the citizens. The philosophy behind a representative democracy is that each person has a right to be heard, and that this can only be accomplished through a system where every person votes on each issue.

Economic problems found in new democracies

Many new democracies, as for instance in Chile, inherit a huge debt and a flailing economy. Inexperienced new leaders want to gain the confidence of the people who elected them and often make unrealistic promises of economic growth. Most new democracies are capitalistic, but the leaders have a hard time making a capitalistic new democracy successful. Long-standing democratic countries do not automatically want to trade with new democracies, and the new democracies lose out on the large revenue streams associated with global economic activity. It takes many years to achieve economic success, and the citizens become impatient and wonder if their old government structure was better after all.

Security problems common in new democracies

The defense of a new democracy, including the maintenance of an armed service, has proved challenging. Protecting a country rather than a ruler requires a transition, and the new leaders are often inexperienced at creating national defense strategy. They often look to experts in the field, which can be a problem when these individuals were involved in the pre-democratic military. Even if the leaders can find a group of independent experts, they have a hard time deciphering the best advice, and may even accept conflicting advice. Military leaders are often loyal to the former regime, and do not want to be accept the new policies of the democratic government. The new government often inherits an inept police force and a broken judicial system. They rely more heavily on military, because the police cannot handle the criminal activity.

Political boundary problems in South Africa

Former political boundaries in South Africa have been a problem for the new democratic government. Historically, the boundaries were drawn to repress certain people or to give more land to one group of people. This produced inequality within the country, which became a problem the new democracy had to tackle. Many groups were fighting with each other over land rights, fighting which continued after the election of the new democratic government. South Africa's new democratic leadership has tried to resolve the disputes by dividing the land more equally. However, the African Union, a group designed to help unify African countries, suggests the political boundaries stay the same. To this point, South Africa has complied.

First Amendment and religion

The establishment clause of the First Amendment creates a separation between church and state by forbidding the government to take part in or make laws regarding the establishment of religion. The free exercise clause states that the government cannot interfere with or stop someone from exercising his or her religion. The establishment clause is absolute, meaning that all religious beliefs are protected from government interference. The free exercise clause, however, is not absolute. If the practice of religion interferes with state laws protecting the rights of society as a whole, the practice cannot be supported by the Supreme Court. For example, if a religion requires human sacrifice, this practice will not be protected by the courts. The difficulty in interpreting these two clauses lies in how religion affects public institutions, such as schools. There is a long-running debate over whether prayer in school infringes in the rights of students who do not pray. The courts have ruled against organized prayer, but also that schools must allow prayer after school, for example, as long as all religions are free to exercise their religion during the same time period.

Lemon test

The Lemon test is a set of guidelines established by the Supreme Court to assess cases related to religious establishment and the separation of church and state. In the ruling for *Lemon v. Kurtzman* (1971), the Court declared that a practice was Constitutional if it had no religious basis and did not cause the government to be involved in deciding religious issues. The Lemon Test was designed to make sure that government did not have involvement in religious issues which the First Amendment includes in the separation of church and state. Historically, instead of following the Lemon test, the courts have allowed religious practice in schools so long as school prayer was not involved and all religions were given the same rights. In other words, the courts have continued to be entangled in issues of religion.

Reynolds v. United States and Everson v. Board of Education

In *Reynolds v. United States* (1879), the Supreme Court ruled that polygamy (having more than one wife) was not covered by the First Amendment's freedom of religion clause. Reynolds argued that his Mormon religion allowed him to marry more than one woman, and that the state should not be able to prosecute the union as a crime. The Court interpreted separation of church and state to mean that although the Court could not stop anyone from being of a certain religion, the state had the right to prosecute if the religion partook in illegal activity. The Supreme Court ruling in *Everson v. Board of Education* (1947) was important for future cases. In it, the Court established that separation of church and state meant the government should stay out of all issues regarding religion. The case involved whether tax money should be used for students to get to and from private, faith-based schools. The Court decided that it is it not an issue for the federal government to decide, so long as the government is not encouraging religion in any way.

Separation of church and state

Believers in strict separation between church and state argue that the Constitution separates the government from making any decisions regarding religion and that the two entities should never intertwine. People arguing for strict separation between church and state argue that the First Amendment clearly states that the government should not support or reject religion, but instead should be completely uninvolved. Advocates of this position disagree with allowing prayer in schools or saying God in the Pledge of Allegiance during school activity. People who argue for accommodation regarding issues of separation between church and state, on the other hand, argue that the federal government has some oversight when it comes to religion, and that an absolute separation of church and state is an incorrect interpretation of the First Amendment. Believers in accommodation argue that if a community agrees on a religious practice, the federal government should allow it. Advocates of accomodation do not support removing God from public buildings.

Majority rule

Majority rule is part of a democracy. Decisions are based on voting: the position or person with the most votes wins. Compromise is necessary in a majority rule system. In such a system, there always will be some opposition or minority. The minority of voters must be represented in a democracy, so the leadership has to work on behalf of the common good of all citizens once elected. Achieving a tone of compromise is difficult, especially in a two-party system. In the United States, the two parties (Democrats and Republicans) fight for two completely different agendas. Once one party is elected, many would argue that the rights of the people in the other party are not protected or even considered by the majority party.

Regents of the University of California v. Bakke

The University of California had two separate admission paths. Minority applicants had a different list of requirements than white students. They competed for 16% of the spots. Bakke applied in 1973 and scored 468 out of 500. He was not accepted, even though 4 minority spots had not been filled. A year later he reached a score of 549 out of 600 but was again denied while minority students did not score as high. Bakke then sued the university, seeking justice for discrimination. After the California Supreme Court sided with Bakke, the university pled their case to the U.S. Supreme Court. Four years later, the Court announced that this was a form of reverse discrimination. This made them question whether affirmative action was constitutional. The Fourteenth Amendment allowed minorities to receive equality, but the University was not allowing equality by giving special privileges to them and denying the white students admission. The decision was split on whether or not universities should allow race to be a factor in admission.

Roe v. Wade controversy

This court case challenged Texas law that made abortions illegal. The attorney looked to the Griswold v. Connecticut case from 1965, in which the court upheld the right of privacy laid out in the Bill of Rights. Roe was counting on that, along with the claim that the Texas law was vague. In January of 1973, the Supreme Court ruled against Wade, finding the Texas law unconstitutional and claiming that abortions within the first trimester are legal and those after the first trimester can be legal only if the mother's health was at risk. The fetus was not found to be a citizen; therefore, the Constitution cannot protect it. Many still argue this fact, but the Court felt that mothers have the right to privacy, translating into the right to choose whether to carry the baby to term or terminate the pregnancy.

Impact Brown v. Board of Education

In the early 1950s, white and black schools were closely approaching equality in buildings and education, but black children were still denied admission to white schools. This was taken to the Supreme Court in 1952, questioning the segregation laws in comparison to the Fourteenth Amendment. The Court found it unconstitutional. Though the separate but equal idea was directly working, it was indirectly fostering inequality. The segregation had an effect on the minority, and they felt that they were not as good as the white children. Some people argued that the Court went beyond its powers by starting a new law. On the other hand, this marked the end of separate but equal idea for minorities and assisted in the expansion of the Civil Rights Movement.

Environmental issues in California's soil

Big government programs are incentives for farmers for their conservation efforts. The people of California understand the value of the land in California and feel that it is necessary to take care of it. Through the Farm Service Agency and the National Resource Conservation Service, farmers are paid to refrain from using specific land from production. This land might be susceptible to erosion, contribute to serious water issues, provide habitat for animals, or offer other benefits. Farmers are also rewarded for planting a certain crop that assists with the erosion problem. In 1985, Congress created a Soil Bank in hopes of preventing another 1930 Dust Bowl. Approximately 383 farmers participate in these efforts to conserve soil and land.

Effects of Owens Lake drying up

Salt-rich dust from what used to be Owens Lake penetrates the soils and affects vegetation and life in the surrounding area. The dry bed allows dust storms to blow the salt-rich dust for miles. This dust has traces of metals and is dangerous to inhale. The Los Angeles Department of Water and Power created a plan. The first step was to irrigate part of the lake to keep it wet, so the dust won't blow. They also decided that the best vegetation would be saltgrass. This assisted in keeping the dust under control while also contributing to the aesthetic feel of the area that Owens Lake used to offer instead of a dry lake bed.

Political science

Political science focuses on studying different governments and how they compare to each other, general political theory, ways political theory is put into action, how nations and governments interact with each other, and a general study of governmental structure and function. Other elements of political science include the study of elections, governmental administration at various levels, development and action of political parties, and how values such as freedom, power, justice and equality are expressed in different political cultures.

Political science also encompasses elements of other disciplines, including:

- History—how historical events have shaped political thought and process
- Sociology—the effects of various stages of social development on the growth and development of government and politics
- Anthropology—the effects of governmental process on the culture of an individual group and its relationships with other groups
- Economics—how government policies regulate distribution of products and how they can control and/or influence the economy in general

General political theory

1. Ensuring national security—the government protects against international, domestic and terrorist attack and also ensures ongoing security through negotiating and establishing relationships with other governments.
2. Providing public services—government should "promote the general welfare," as stated in the Preamble to the US Constitution, by providing whatever is needed to its citizens.
3. Ensure social order—the government supplies means of settling conflicts among citizens as well as making laws to govern the nation, state, or city.
4. Make decisions regarding the economy—laws help form the economic policy of the country, regarding both domestic and international trade and related issues. The government also has the ability to distribute goods and wealth among its citizens.

Theories regarding the origin of the state

Evolutionary—the state evolved from the family, with the head of state the equivalent of the family's patriarch or matriarch.

Force—one person or group of people brought everyone in an area under their control, forming the first government.

Divine Right—certain people were chosen by the prevailing deity to be the rulers of the nation, which is itself created by the deity or deities.

Social Contract—there is no natural order. The people allow themselves to be governed to maintain social order, while the state in turn promises to protect the people they govern. If the government fails to protect its people, the people have the right to seek new leaders.

Influences of philosophers

Ancient Greek philosophers Aristotle and Plato believed political science would lead to order in political matters, and that this scientifically organized order would create stable, just societies.

Thomas Aquinas adapted the ideas of Aristotle to a Christian perspective. His ideas stated that individuals should have certain rights, but also certain duties, and that these rights and duties should determine the type and extent of government rule. In stating that laws should limit the role of government, he laid the groundwork for ideas that would eventually become modern constitutionalism.

Niccolò Machiavelli, author of *The Prince*, was a proponent of politics based solely on power.

Thomas Hobbes and John Locke

Thomas Hobbes, author of *Leviathan* (1651), believed that individual's lives were focused solely on a quest for power, and that the state must work to control this urge. Hobbes felt that people were completely unable to live harmoniously without the intervention of government.

John Locke wrote *Two Treatises of Civil Government* in 1690. This work argued against the ideas of Thomas Hobbes. He put forth the theory of *tabula rasa*—that people are born with minds that are a blank slate. Experience molds individual minds, not innate knowledge or intuition. He also believed that all men are essentially good, as well as independent and equal. Many of Locke's ideas found their way into the Constitution of the United States.

Montesquieu and Rousseau

These two French philosophers heavily influenced the French Revolution (1789-1815). They believed government policies and ideas should change to alleviate existing problems, an idea referred to as "liberalism." Rousseau in particular directly influenced the Revolution with writings such as *The Social Contract* (1762), *Declaration of the Rights of Man,* and *The Citizen* (1789). Other ideas Rousseau and Montesquieu espoused included:
- Individual freedom and community welfare are of equal importance
- Man's innate goodness leads to natural harmony
- Reason develops with the rise of civilized society
- Individual citizens carry certain obligations to the existing government

Other philosophers

Hume and Bentham believed politics should have as its main goal maintaining "the greatest happiness of the greatest number." Hume also believed in empiricism, or that ideas should not be believed until the proof has been observed. He was a natural skeptic, as well, and always sought out the truth of matters himself rather than believing what he was told.
John Stuart Mill, a British philosopher as well as an economist, believed in progressive policies such as women's suffrage, emancipation, and the development of labor organizations and farming cooperatives. Fichte and Hegel were eighteenth century German philosophers who supported a form of liberalism grounded largely in socialism and a sense of nationalism.

Four main political orientations

1. Liberal—believes in working to increase equality, sometimes at the expense of some freedoms, but overall the government should not interfere with individual freedom. Focus on health, justice, and education for citizens should be a major focus.
2. Conservative—government should be limited in all cases except those of supporting longstanding moral values, often tied to religious beliefs. The government should allow its citizens to solve social issues rather. Businesses should not be regulated, allowing a free market.
3. Moderate—incorporates some liberal and some conservative values, generally falling somewhere in between in overall belief.
4. Libertarian—believes in limiting the role of government to the defense of the country and supporting social as well as economic freedom.

Six major principles of government

1. Federalism—the power of the government does not belong entirely to the national government, but is divided between national and state governments.
2. Popular sovereignty—the government is determined by the people, and gains its authority and power from the people.
3. Separation of powers—the government is divided into three branches, executive, legislative and judicial, with each branch having its own set of powers.
4. Judicial review—courts at all levels of government can declare laws invalid if they contradict the constitutions of individual states, or the US Constitution, with the Supreme Court serving as the final judicial authority on decisions of this kind.
5. Checks and balances—no single branch can act without input from another, and each branch has the power to "check" any other, as well as balance other branches' powers.
6. Limited government—governmental powers are limited and certain individual rights are defined as inviolable by the government.

National government powers

The structure of the US government divides powers between national and state governments. Powers delegated to the national government by the Constitution are:
1. Expressed powers—powers directly defined in the Constitution, including power to declare war, regulate commerce, make money, and collect taxes.
2. Implied powers—powers the national government must have in order to carry out the expressed powers.
3. Inherent powers—powers inherent to any government. These powers are not expressly defined in the constitution.

Some of these powers, such as collection and levying of taxes, are also granted to the individual state governments.

Federalism

Debate on how federalism should function in practice has gone on since the period when the Constitution was being written. There were—and still are—two main factions regarding this issue:
1. States' rights—those favoring the states' rights position feel that the state governments should take the lead in performing local actions to manage various problems.
2. Nationalist—those favoring a nationalist position feel the national government should take the lead to deal with those same matters.
The flexibility of the Constitution has allowed US government to shift and adapt as the needs of the country have changed. Power has often shifted from the state governments to the national government and back again, and both levels of government have developed various ways to influence each other.
How federalism affects policy-making and the overall balance of politics in the US

Federalism has three major effects on public policy in the US.
1. Determining whether the local, state or national government originates policy
2. Affecting how policies are made
3. Ensuring policy-making functions under a set of limitations

Federalism also influences the political balance of power in the US by:
1. making it difficult if not impossible for a single political party to seize total power.
2. ensuring that individuals can participate in the political system at various levels.
3. making it possible for individuals working within the system to be able to affect policy at some level, whether local or more widespread.

Three branches of the Federal government

1. Legislative Branch—consists of the two Houses of Congress: the House of Representatives and the Senate. All members of the Legislative Branch are elected officials.
2. Executive Branch—consists of the President, Vice President, presidential advisors, and other various cabinet members. These advisors are appointed by the President, but must be approved by Congress
3. Judicial Branch—is made up of the federal court system, headed by the Supreme Court.

Responsibilities of the three branches
1. The Legislative Branch is largely concerned with law-making. All laws must be approved by Congress before they go into effect. They are also responsible for regulating money and trade, approving presidential appointments, and establishing organizations like the postal service and federal courts. Congress can also propose amendments to the Constitution, and can impeach, or bring charges against, the president. Only Congress can declare war.
2. The Executive Branch carries out laws, treaties, and war declarations enacted by Congress. The President can also veto bills approved by Congress, and serves as commander-in-chief of the US military. The president appoints cabinet members, ambassadors to foreign countries, and federal judges.
3. The Judicial Branch makes decisions on challenges as to whether laws passed by Congress meet the requirements of the US Constitution. The Supreme Court may also choose to review decisions made by lower courts to determine their constitutionality.

> ➤ **Review Video: Three Branches of Government**
> *Visit **mometrix.com/academy** and enter **Code: 718704***

Qualifications of a US citizen, and how citizenship may be lost

Anyone born in the US, born abroad to a US citizen, or who has gone through a process of naturalization to become a citizen, is considered a citizen of the United States. It is possible to lose US citizenship as a result of conviction of certain crimes such as treason. Citizenship may also be lost if a citizen pledges an oath to another country or serves in the military of a country engaged in hostilities with the US. A US citizen can also choose to hold dual citizenship, work as an expatriate in another country without losing US citizenship, or even to renounce citizenship if he or she so chooses.

Rights, duties and responsibilities of citizens
Citizens are granted certain rights under the US government. The most important of these are defined in the Bill of Rights, and include freedom of speech, religion, assembly, and a variety of other rights the government is not allowed to remove.

Duties of a US citizen include:
1. Paying taxes
2. Loyalty to the government, though the US does not prosecute those who criticize or seek to change the government

- 93 -

3. Support and defend the Constitution
4. Serve in the Armed Forces as required by law
5. Obeying laws as set forth by the various levels of government.

Responsibilities of a US citizen include:
1. Voting in elections
2. Respecting one another's rights and not infringing upon them
3. Staying informed about various political and national issues
4. Respecting one another's beliefs

Importance of the Bill of Rights

The first ten amendments of the US Constitution are known as the Bill of Rights. These amendments prevent the government from infringing upon certain freedoms that the founding fathers felt were natural rights that already belonged to all people. These rights included freedom of speech, freedom of religion, right to bear arms, and freedom of assembly. Many of the rights were formulated in direct response to the way the colonists felt they had been mistreated by the British government.
The first ten amendments were passed by Congress in 1789. Three-fourths of the existing thirteen states had ratified them by December of 1791, making them official additions to the Constitution.

Rights granted in the Bill of Rights:

- First Amendment—grants freedom of religion, speech, freedom of the press, and the right to assemble.
- Second Amendment—right to bear arms.
- Third Amendment—Congress cannot force individuals to house troops.
- Fourth Amendment—protection from unreasonable search and seizure.
- Fifth Amendment—no individual is required to testify against himself, and no individual may be tried twice for the same crime.
- Sixth Amendment—right to criminal trial by jury, right to legal counsel.
- Seventh Amendment—right to civil trial by jury.
- Eighth Amendment—no excessive bail, no cruel and unusual punishment.
- Ninth Amendment—prevents the absence of rights not explicitly named in the Constitution from being interpreted as a reason to have them taken away.
- Tenth Amendment—any rights not directly delegated to the national government, or not directly prohibited, belong to the states or to the people

Government's restriction or regulation of First Amendment freedoms

In some cases, the government restricts certain elements of First Amendment rights. Some examples include:
- Freedom of religion—when a religion espouses activities that are otherwise illegal, the government often restricts these forms of religious expression. Examples include polygamy, animal sacrifice, and use of illicit drugs or illegal substances.
- Freedom of speech—can be restricted if exercise of free speech endangers other people.
- Freedom of the press—laws prevent the press from publishing falsehoods.

In emergency situations such as wartime, stricter restrictions are sometimes placed on these rights, especially rights to free speech and assembly, and freedom of the press, in order to protect national security.

Constitution and those accused of crimes

The US Constitution makes allowances for the rights of criminals, or anyone who has transgressed established laws. There must be laws to protect citizens from criminals, but those accused of crimes must also be protected and their basic rights as individuals preserved. In addition, the Constitution protects individuals from the power of authorities who act in case of transgressions to prevent police forces and other enforcement organizations from becoming oppressive.

The Fourth, Fifth, Sixth and Eighth amendments specifically address these issues:
- No unreasonable search and seizure (Fourth Amendment)
- No self-incrimination or double jeopardy—being tried for the same crime more than once (Fifth Amendment)
- Right to trial by jury and right to legal counsel (Sixth Amendment)
- No cruel or unusual punishment (Eighth Amendment)

Supreme Court's equal protection

When the Founding Fathers wrote in the Declaration of Independence that "all men are created equal," they meant "men," and, in fact, defined citizens as white men who owned land. However, as the country has developed and changed, the definition has expanded to more wholly include all people. "Equality" does not mean all people are inherently the same, but it does mean they all should be granted the same rights and should be treated the same by the government. Amendments to the Constitution have granted citizenship and voting rights to all Americans. The Supreme Court evaluates various laws and court decisions to determine if they properly represent the idea of equal protection. One sample case was Brown v. Board of Education, in 1954, which declared separate-but-equal to be unconstitutional.

Civil liberty challenges

The civil rights movements of the 1960s and ongoing struggle for women's rights and rights of other minorities have led to challenges to existing law. In addition, debate has raged over how much information the government should be required to divulge to the public. Major issues in today's political climate include:
- Continued debate over women's rights, especially as regards equal pay for equal work
- Debate over affirmative action to encourage hiring of minorities
- Debate over civil rights of homosexuals, including marriage and military service
- Decisions as to whether any minorities should be compensated for past discriminatory practices
- Balance between the public's right to know and the government's need to maintain national security
- Balance between the public's right to privacy and national security

Civil liberties vs. civil rights

While the terms civil liberties and civil rights are often used synonymously, in actuality their definitions are slightly different. The two concepts work together, however, to define the basics of a free state.
1. "Civil liberties" defines the role of the state in providing equal rights and opportunities to individuals within that state. An example is non-discrimination policies with regards to granting citizenship.
2. "Civil rights" defines the limitations of state rights, describing those rights that belong to individuals and which cannot be infringed upon by the government. Examples of these rights include freedom of religion, political freedom, and overall freedom to live how we choose.

- 95 -

Suffrage and franchise

Suffrage and franchise are both terms referring to the right to vote. Which individuals actually have the right to vote has changed as the US has developed as a nation.

In the early years, only white male landowners were granted suffrage. By the nineteenth century, most states had franchised, or granted the right to vote to, all adult white males. The Fifteenth Amendment of 1870 granted suffrage to former slaves. The Nineteenth Amendment gave women the right to vote, and in 1971 the Twenty-sixth Amendment expanded voting rights to include any US citizen over the age of eighteen. However, those who have not been granted full citizenship and citizens who have committed certain crimes do not have voting rights.

Voting process changes over the years

The first elections in the US were held by public ballot. However, election abuses soon became common, since public ballot made it easy to intimidate, threaten, or otherwise influence the votes of individuals or groups of individuals. New practices were put into play, including registering voters before elections took place, and using a secret or Australian ballot. In 1892, the introduction of the voting machine further privatized the voting process, since it allowed voters to vote in complete privacy. Even today debate continues about the accuracy of various voting methods, including high-tech voting machines and even low tech punch cards.

Political parties' affect

Different types and numbers of political parties can have a significant effect on how a government is run. If there is a single party, or a one-party system, the government is defined by that one party, and all policy is based on that party's beliefs. In a two-party system, two parties with different viewpoints compete for power and influence. The US is basically a two-party system, with checks and balances to make it difficult for one party to gain complete power over the other. There are also multi-party systems, with three or more parties. In multiparty systems, various parties will often come to agreements in order to form a majority and shift the balance of power.

Development of political parties in the US

George Washington was adamantly against the establishment of political parties, based on the abuses perpetrated by such parties in Britain. However, political parties developed in US politics almost from the beginning. Major parties throughout US History have included:

- Federalists and Democratic-Republicans—formed in the late 1700s and disagreed on the balance of power between national and state government
- Democrats and Whigs—developed before the Civil War, based on disagreements about various issues such as slavery
- Democrats and Republicans—developed after the Civil War, with issues centering on the treatment of the post-war South.

While third parties sometimes enter the picture in US politics, the government is basically a two-party system, dominated by the Democrats and Republicans.

Functions of political parties

Political parties form organizations at all levels of government. Activities of individual parties include:

- Recruiting and backing candidates for offices

- Discussing various issues with the public, increasing public awareness
- Working toward compromise on difficult issues
- Staffing government offices and providing administrative support

At the administrative level, parties work to ensure that viable candidates are available for elections and that offices and staff are in place to support candidates as they run for office and afterwards, when they are elected.

Political candidates selection

Historically, in the quest for political office, a potential candidate has followed one of the following four processes:

1. Nominating conventions—an official meeting of the members of a party for the express purpose of nominating candidates for upcoming elections. The Democratic National Convention and the Republican National Convention, convened to announce candidates for presidency, are examples of this kind of gathering.
2. Caucuses—a meeting, usually attended by a party's leaders. Some states still use caucuses, but not all.
3. Primary elections—the most common method of choosing candidates today, the primary is a publicly held election to choose candidates.
4. Petitions—signatures are gathered to place a candidate on the ballot. Petitions can also be used to place legislation on a ballot.

The average citizen's participation

In addition to voting for elected officials, American citizens are able to participate in the political process through several other avenues. These include:
- Participating in local government
- Participating in caucuses for large elections
- Volunteering to help political parties
- Running for election to local, state, or national offices

Individuals can also donate money to political causes, or support political groups that focus on specific causes such as abortion, wildlife conservation or women's rights. These groups often make use of representatives who lobby legislators to act in support of their efforts.

Political campaign funding

Political campaigns are very expensive ventures. In addition to the basic necessities of a campaign office, including office supplies, office space, etc., a large quantity of the money that funds a political campaign goes toward advertising. Television advertising in particular is quite costly.
Money to fund a political campaign can come from several sources including:
- The candidate's personal funds
- Donations by individuals
- Special interest groups

The most significant source of campaign funding is special interest groups. Groups in favor of certain policies will donate money to candidates they believe will support those policies. Special interest groups also do their own advertising in support of candidates they endorse.

Importance of free press and the media

The right to free speech guaranteed in the first amendment to the Constitution allows the media to report on government and political activities without fear of retribution. Because the media has access to information about the government, its policies and actions, as well as debates and discussions that occur in Congress, it can ensure that the people are informed about the inner workings of the government. The media can also draw attention to injustices, imbalances of power, and other transgressions the government or government officials might commit.

However, media outlets may, like special interest groups, align themselves with certain political viewpoints and skew their reports to fit that viewpoint. The rise of the Internet has made media reporting even more complex, as news can be found from an infinite variety of sources, both reliable and unreliable.

Anarchism, communism and dictatorship

Anarchists believe that all government should be eliminated and that individuals should rule themselves. Historically, anarchists have used violence and assassination to further their beliefs.

Communism is based on class conflict, revolution and a one-party state. Ideally, a communist government would involve a single government for the entire world. Communist government controls the production and flow of goods and services rather than leaving this to companies or individuals.

Dictatorship involves rule by a single individual. If rule is enforced by a small group, this is referred to as an oligarchy. Few malevolent dictatorships have existed. Dictators tend to rule with a violent hand, using a highly repressive police force to ensure control over the populace.

Fascism and monarchy

Fascism centers on a single leader and is, ideologically, an oppositional belief to Communism. Fascism includes a single party state and centralized control. The power of the fascist leader lies in the "cult of personality," and the fascist state often focuses on expansion and conquering of other nations.

Monarchy was the major form of government for Europe through most of its history. A monarchy is led by a king or a queen. This position is hereditary, and the rulers are not elected. In modern times, constitutional monarchy has developed, where the king and queen still exist but most of the governmental decisions are made by democratic institutions such as a parliament.

Presidential System and Socialism

A Presidential System, like a parliamentary system, has a legislature and political parties, but there is no difference between the head of state and the head of government. Instead of separating these functions, an elected president performs both. Election of the president can be direct or indirect, and the president may not necessarily belong to the largest political party.In Socialism, the state controls production of goods, though it does not necessarily own all means of production. The state also provides a variety of social services to citizens and helps guide the economy. A democratic form of government often exists in socialist countries.

Totalitarian and authoritarian systems

A totalitarian system believes everything should be under the control of the government, from resource production to the press to religion and other social institutions. All aspects of life under a totalitarian system must conform to the ideals of the government.

Authoritarian governments practices widespread state authority, but do not necessarily dismantle all public institutions. If a church, for example, exists as an organization but poses no threat to the authority of the state, an authoritarian government might leave it as it is. While all totalitarian governments are by definition authoritarian, a government can be authoritarian without becoming totalitarian.

Parliamentary and democratic systems

In a parliamentary system, government involves a legislature and a variety of political parties. The head of government, usually a Prime Minister, is typically the head of the dominant party. A head of state can be elected, or this position can be taken by a monarch, such as in Great Britain's constitutional monarchy system.

In a democratic system of government, the people elect their government representatives. The term democracy is a Greek term that means "for the rule of the people." There are two forms of democracy— direct and indirect. In a direct democracy, each issue or election is decided by a vote where each individual is counted separately. An indirect democracy employs a legislature that votes on issues that affect large number of people whom the legislative members represent. Democracy can exist as a Parliamentary system or a Presidential system. The US is a presidential, indirect democracy

Realism, liberalism, institutionalism and constructivism

The theory of realism states that nations are by nature aggressive, and work in their own self-interest. Relations between nations are determined by military and economic strength. The nation is seen as the highest authority.

Liberalism believes states can cooperate, and that they act based on capabilities rather than power. This term was originally coined to describe Woodrow Wilson's theories on international cooperation.

In institutionalism, institutions provide structure and incentive for cooperation among nations. Institutions are defined as a set of rules used to make international decisions. These institutions also help distribute power and determine how nations will interact.

Constructivism, like liberalism, is based on international cooperation, but recognizes that perceptions countries have of each other can affect their relations.

Foreign policy

Foreign policy is a set of goals, policies and strategies that determine how an individual nation will interact with other countries. These strategies shift, sometimes quickly and drastically, according to actions or changes occurring in the other countries. However, a nation's foreign policy is often based on a certain set of ideals and national needs.

Examples of US foreign policy include isolationism versus internationalism. In the 1800s, the US leaned more toward isolationism, exhibiting a reluctance to become involved in foreign affairs. The World Wars led to a period of internationalism, as the US entered these wars in support of other countries and joined the United Nations. Today's foreign policy tends more toward interdependence, or globalism, recognizing the widespread affects of issues like economic health.

<u>Figures involved in foreign policy</u>
US foreign policy is largely determined by Congress and the president, influenced by the secretary of state, secretary of defense, and the national security adviser. Executive officials actually carry out policies. The main departments in charge of these day-to-day issues are the US Department of State, also referred to as the State Department. The Department of State carries out policy, negotiates treaties, maintains diplomatic relations, assists citizens traveling in foreign countries, and ensures that the president is properly informed of any international issues. The Department of Defense, the largest executive department in the US, supervises the armed forces and provides assistance to the president in his role as commander in chief.

Types of international organizations

Intergovernmental organizations (IGOs). These organizations are made up of members from various national governments. The UN is an example of an intergovernmental organization. Treaties among the member nations determine the functions and powers of these groups.Nongovernmental organizations (NGOs). An NGO lies outside the scope of any government and are usually supported through private donations. An example of an NGO is the International Red Cross, which works with governments all over the world when their countries are in crisis, but is formally affiliated with no particular country or government.

Diplomats and international relations

Diplomats are individuals who reside in foreign countries in order to maintain communications between that country and their home country. They help negotiate trade agreements, environmental policies, and convey official information to foreign governments. They also help resolve conflicts between the countries, often working to sort out issues without making the conflicts official in any way. Diplomats, or ambassadors, are appointed in America by the president. Appointments must be approved by Congress.

UN

The United Nations (UN) helps form international policies by hosting representatives of various countries who then provide input into policy decisions. Countries who are members of the UN must agree to abide by all final UN resolutions, but this is not always the case in practice, as dissent is not uncommon. If countries do not follow UN resolutions, the UN can decide on sanctions against those countries, often economic sanctions, such as trade restriction. The UN can also send military forces to problem areas, with "peace keeping" troops brought in from member nations. An example of this function is the Korean War, the first war in which an international organization played a major role.

Principles of Economics

Economics

Economics is the study of the ways specific societies allocate resources to individuals and groups within that society. Also important are the choices society makes regarding what efforts or initiatives are funded and which are not. Since resources in any society are finite, allocation becomes a vivid reflection of that society's values.

In general, the economic system that drives an individual society is based on:
- What goods are produced
- How those goods are produced
- Who acquires the goods or benefits from them

Economics consists of two main categories, macroeconomics, which studies larger systems, and microeconomics, which studies smaller systems.

Market economy

A market economy is based on supply and demand. Demand has to do with what customers want and need, as well as how quantity those consumers are able to purchase based on other economic factors. Supply refers to how much can be produced to meet demand, or how much suppliers are willing and able to sell. Where the needs of consumers meet the needs of suppliers is referred to as a market equilibrium price. This price varies depending on many factors, including the overall health of a society's economy, overall beliefs and considerations of individuals in society, and other factors.

The following is a list of terms defined in the context of a market economy:
- Elasticity—based on how the quantity of a particular product responds to the price demanded for that product. If quantity responds quickly to changes in price, the supply/demand for that product is said to be elastic. If they do not respond quickly, then it is inelastic.
- Market efficiency—when a market is capable of producing output high enough to meet consumer demand, that market is efficient.
- Comparative advantage—in the field of international trade, this refers to a country focusing on a specific product that it can produce more efficiently and more cheaply, or at a lower opportunity cost, than another country, thus giving it a comparative advantage in production of that product.

Comparison to planned economy

In a market economy, supply and demand are determined by consumers. In a planned economy, a public entity or planning authority makes the decisions about what resources will be produced, how they will be produced, and who will be able to benefit from them. The means of production, such as factories, are also owned by a public entity rather than by private interests. In market socialism, the economic structure falls somewhere between the market economy and the planned economy. Planning authorities determine allocation of resources at higher economic levels, while consumer goods are driven by a market economy.

> ➤ **Review Video: Basics of Market Economy**
> *Visit **mometrix.com/academy** and enter **Code: 791556**

Microeconomics

While economics generally studies how resources are allocated, microeconomics focuses on economic factors such as the way consumers behave, how income is distributed, and output and input markets. Studies are limited to the industry or firm level, rather than an entire country or society. Among the elements studied in microeconomics are factors of production, costs of production, and factor income. These factors determine production decisions of individual firms, based on resources and costs.

> ➢ **Review Video: Microeconomics**
> *Visit mometrix.com/academy and enter* **Code: 779207**

Classification of markets

The conditions prevailing in a given market are used to classify markets. Conditions considered include:
- Existence of competition
- Number and size of suppliers
- Influence of suppliers over price
- Variety of available products
- Ease of entering the market

Once these questions are answered, an economist can classify a certain market according to its structure and the nature of competition within the market.

> ➢ **Review Video: Classification of Markets**
> *Visit mometrix.com/academy and enter* **Code: 904798**

Market failure

When any of the elements for a successfully competitive market are missing, this can lead to a market failure. Certain elements are necessary to create what economists call "perfect competition." If one of these factors is weak or lacking, the market is classified as having "imperfect competition." Worse than imperfect competition, though, is a market failure.

There are five major types of market failure:
- Competition is inadequate
- Information is inadequate
- Resources are not mobile
- Negative externalities, or side effects
- Failure to provide public goods

Externalities are side effects of a market that affect third parties. These effects can be either negative or positive.

> ➢ **Review Video: Market Failure**
> *Visit mometrix.com/academy and enter* **Code: 889023**

Factors of production and costs of production

Every good and service requires certain resources, or inputs. These inputs are referred to as factors of production. Every good and service requires four factors of production:
- Labor
- Land
- Capital
- Entrepreneurship

These factors can be fixed or variable, and can produce fixed or variable costs. Examples of fixed costs include land and equipment. Variable costs include labor. The total of fixed and variable costs makes up the costs of production.

Factor income

Factors of production all have an associated factor income. Factors that earn income include:
- Labor—earns wages
- Capital—earns interest
- Land—earns rent
- Entrepreneurs—earn profit

Each factor's income is determined by its contribution. In a market economy, this income is not guaranteed to be equal. How scarce the factor is and the weight of its contribution to the overall production process determines the final factor income.

Output market

The four kinds of market structures in an output market are:
- Perfect competition—all existing firms sell an identical product. The firms are not able to control the final price. In addition, there is nothing that makes it difficult to become involved in or leave the industry. Anything that would prevent entering or leaving an industry is called a barrier to entry. An example of this market structure is agriculture.
- Monopoly—a single seller controls the product and its price. Barriers to entry, such as prohibitively high fixed cost structures, prevent other sellers from entering the market.
- Monopolistic competition—a number of firms sell similar products, but they are not identical, such as different brands of clothes or food. Barriers to entry are low.
- Oligopoly—only a few firms control the production and distribution of products, such as automobiles. Barriers to entry are high, preventing large numbers of firms from entering the market.

Monopolies

Four types of monopolies are:
- Natural monopoly—occurs when a single supplier has a distinct advantage over the others
- Geographic monopoly—only one business offers the product in a certain area
- Technological monopoly—a single company controls the technology necessary to supply the product
- Government monopoly—a government agency is the only provider of a specific good or service

<u>Control by the US government</u>
The US government has passed several acts to regulate businesses, including:
- Sherman Antitrust Act (1890) — prohibited trusts, monopolies, and any other situations that eliminated competition.
- Clayton Antitrust Act (1914) — prohibited price discrimination.
- Robinson-Patman Act (1936) — strengthened provisions of the Clayton Antitrust Act.

The government has also taken other actions to ensure competition, including requirements for public disclosure. The Securities and Exchange Commission (SEC) requires companies that provide public stock to provide financial reports on a regular basis. Because of the nature of their business, banks are further regulated and required to provide various types of information to the government.

Marketing and utility

Marketing consists of all of the activity necessary to convince consumers to acquire goods. One major way to move products into the hands of consumers is to convince them that any single product will satisfy a need. The ability of a product or service to satisfy the need of a consumer is called utility.

There are four types of utility:
- Form utility—a product's desirability lies in its physical characteristics.
- Place utility—a product's desirability is connected to its location and convenience.
- Time utility—a product's desirability is determined by its availability at a certain time.
- Ownership utility—a product's desirability is increased because ownership of the product passes to the consumer.

Marketing behavior will stress any or all of the types of utility to the consumer to which the product is being marketed.

Determining a product's market

Successful marketing depends not only on convincing customers they need the product, but also on focusing the marketing towards those who have a need or desire for the product. Before releasing a product into the general marketplace, many producers will test markets to determine which will be the most receptive to the product.

There are three steps usually taken to evaluate a product's market:
- Market research—researching a market to determine if the market will be receptive to the product.
- Market surveys—a part of market research, market surveys ask specific questions of consumers to help determine the marketability of a product to a specific group.
- Test marketing—releasing the product into a small geographical area to see how it sells. Often test marketing is followed by wider marketing if the product does well.

Marketing plan

The four major elements of a marketing plan are:
- Product—any elements pertaining directly to the product, including packaging, presentation, or services to include along with it.
- Price—calculates cost of production, distribution, advertising, etc. as well as the desired profit to determine the final price.

- Place—what outlets will be used to sell the product, whether traditional outlets such as brick and mortar stores or through direct mail or Internet marketing.
- Promotion—ways to let consumers know the product is available, through advertising and other means.

Once these elements have all been determined, the producer can proceed with production and distribution of his product.

> **Review Video: Marketing Plan**
> *Visit mometrix.com/academy and enter Code: 379598*

Distribution channels

Distribution channels determine the route a product takes on its journey from producer to consumer, and can also influenced the final price and availability of the product. There are two major forms of distributions: wholesale and retail. A wholesale distributor buys in large quantities and then resells smaller amounts to other businesses. Retailers sell directly to the consumers rather than to businesses. In the modern marketplace, additional distribution channels have grown up with the rise of markets such as club warehouse stores as well as purchasing through catalogs or over the Internet. Most of these newer distribution channels bring products more directly to the consumer, eliminating the need for middlemen.

Distribution of income and poverty

Distribution of income in any society lies in a range from poorest to richest. In most societies, income is not distributed evenly. To determine income distribution, family incomes are ranked, lowest to highest. These rankings are divided into sections called quintiles, which are compared to each other. The uneven distribution of income is often linked to higher levels of education and ability in the upper classes, but can also be due to other factors such as discrimination and existing monopolies. The income gap in America continues to grow, largely due to growth in the service industry, changes in the American family unit and reduced influence of labor unions. Poverty is defined by comparing incomes to poverty guidelines. Poverty guidelines determine the level of income necessary for a family to function. Those below the poverty line are often eligible for assistance from government agencies.

Consumer behavior

The two major types of consumer behavior as defined in macroeconomics are:
- Marginal propensity to consume defines the tendency of consumers to increase spending in conjunction with increases in income. In general, individuals with greater income will buy more. As individuals increase their income through job changes or growth of experience, they will also increase spending.
- Utility is a term that describes the satisfaction experienced by a consumer in relation to acquiring and using a good or service. Providers of goods and services will stress utility to convince consumers they want the products being presented.

Macroeconomics

Macroeconomics examines economies on a much larger level than microeconomics. While microeconomics studies economics on a firm or industry level, macroeconomics looks at economic trends and structures on a national level. Variables studied in macroeconomics include:
- Output
- Consumption
- Investment
- Government spending
- Net exports

The overall economic condition of a nation is defined as the Gross Domestic Product, or GDP. GDP measures a nation's economic output over a limited time period, such as a year.

GDP

The two major ways to measure the Gross Domestic Product of a country are:
- The expenditures approach calculates the GDP based on how much money is spent in each individual sector.
- The income approach calculates based on how much money is earned in each sector.

Both methods yield the same results and both of these calculation methods are based on four economic sectors that make up a country's macro economy:
- Consumers
- Business
- Government
- Foreign sector

Several factors must be considered in order to accurately calculate the GDP using the incomes approach. Income factors are:
- Wages paid to laborers, or Compensation of Employees
- Rental income derived from land
- Interest income derived from invested capital
- Entrepreneurial income

Entrepreneurial income consists of two forms. Proprietor's Income is income that comes back to the entrepreneur himself. Corporate Profit is income that goes back into the corporation as a whole. Corporate profit is divided by the corporation into corporate profits taxes, dividends, and retained earnings. Two other figures must be subtracted in the incomes approach. These are indirect business taxes, including property and sales taxes, and depreciation.

Effects of the population
Changes in population can affect the calculation of a nation's GDP, particularly since GDP and GNP are generally measure per capita. If a country's economic production is low, but the population is high, the income per individual will be lower than if the income is high and the population is lower. Also, if the population grows quickly and the income grows slowly, individual income will remain low or even drop drastically.

Population growth can also affect overall economic growth. Economic growth requires both consumers to purchase goods and workers to produce them. A population that does not grow quickly enough will not supply enough workers to support rapid economic growth.

Ideal balance in an economy and phases in national economies

Ideally, an economy functions efficiently, with the aggregate supply, or the amount of national output, equal to the aggregate demand, or the amount of the output that is purchased. In these cases, the economy is stable and prosperous.

However, economies more typically go through phases. These phases are:
- Boom—GDP is high and the economy prospers
- Recession—GDP falls, unemployment rises
- Trough—the recession reaches its lowest point
- Recovery—Unemployment lessens, prices rise, and the economy begins to stabilize again

These phases happen often, in cycles that are not necessarily predictable or regular.

Unemployment and inflation

When demand outstrips supply, prices are driven artificially high, or inflated. This occurs when too much spending causes an imbalance in the economy. In general, inflation occurs because an economy is growing too quickly. When there is too little spending and supply has moved far beyond demand, a surplus of product results. Companies cut back on production, reduce the number of workers they employ, and unemployment rises as people lose their jobs. This imbalance occurs when an economy becomes sluggish. In general, both these economic instability situations are caused by an imbalance between supply and demand. Government intervention is often necessary to stabilize an economy when either inflation or unemployment becomes too serious.

Five different forms of unemployment are:
- Frictional—when workers change jobs and are unemployed while waiting for a new job.
- Structural—when economical shifts reduce the need for workers.
- Cyclical—when natural business cycles bring about loss of jobs.
- Seasonal—when seasonal cycles reduce the need for certain jobs.
- Technological—when advances in technology result in elimination of certain jobs.

Any of these factors can increase unemployment in certain sectors.

Inflation is classified by the overall rate at which it occurs:
- Creeping inflation—an inflation rate of about one to three percent annually.
- Galloping inflation—a high inflation rate of 100 to 300 percent annually.
- Hyperinflation—an inflation rate over 500 percent annually. Hyperinflation usually leads to complete monetary collapse in a society, as individuals become unable to generate sufficient income to purchase necessary goods.

Government intervention policies

When an economy becomes too imbalanced, either due to excessive spending or not enough spending, government intervention often becomes necessary to put the economy back on track. Government Fiscal Policy can take several forms, including:
- Monetary policy
- Contractionary policies
- Expansionary policies

Contractionary policies help counteract inflation. These include increasing taxes and decreasing government spending to slow spending in the overall economy. Expansionary policies increase government spending and lower taxes in order to reduce unemployment and increase the level of spending in the economy overall. Monetary policy can take several forms, and affects the amount of funds available to banks for making loans.

Populations and population growth

Populations are studied by size, rates of growth due to immigration, the overall fertility rate, and life expectancy. For example, though the population of the United States is considerably larger than it was two hundred years ago, the rate of population growth has decreased greatly, from about three percent per year to less than one percent per year.

In the US, the fertility rate is fairly low, with most women choosing not to have large families, and life expectancy is high, creating a projected imbalance between older and younger people in the near future. In addition, immigration and the mixing of racially diverse cultures are projected to increase the percentages of Asian, Hispanic and African Americans.

Money

Money is used in three major ways:
- As an accounting unit
- As a store of value
- As an exchange medium

In general, money must be acceptable throughout a society in exchange for debts or to purchase goods and services. Money should be relatively scarce, its value should remain stable, and it should be easily carried, durable, and easy to divide up. There are three basic types of money: commodity, representative and fiat. Commodity money includes gems or precious metals. Representative money can be exchanged for items such as gold or silver which have inherent value. Fiat money, or legal tender, has no inherent value but has been declared to function as money by the government. It is often backed by gold or silver, but not necessarily on a one-to-one ratio.

US money

Money in the US is not just currency. When economists calculate the amount of money available, they must take into account other factors such as deposits that have been placed in checking accounts, debit cards and "near moneys" such as savings accounts, that can be quickly converted into cash. Currency, checkable deposits and traveler's checks, referred to as M1, are added up, and then M2 is calculated by adding savings deposits, CDs and various other monetary deposits. The final result is the total quantity of available money.

Monetary policy and the Federal Reserve System

The Federal Reserve System, also known as the Fed, implements all monetary policy in the US. Monetary policy regulates the amount of money available in the American banking system. The Fed can decrease or increase the amount of available money for loans, thus helping regulate the national economy. Monetary policies implemented by the Fed are part of expansionary or contractionary monetary policies that help counteract inflation or unemployment. The Discount Rate is an interest rate charged by the Fed when banks borrow money from them. A lower discount rate leads banks to borrow more money, leading to increased spending. A higher discount rate has the opposite effect.

Banks

Banks earn their income by loaning out money and charging interest on those loans. If less money is available, fewer loans can be made, which affects the amount of spending in the overall economy. While banks function by making loans, they are not allowed to loan out all the money they hold in deposit. The amount of money they must maintain in reserve is known as the reserve ratio. If the reserve ratio is raised, less money is available for loans and spending decreases. A lower reserve ratio increases available funds and increases spending. This ratio is determined by the Federal Reserve System.

Open Market Operations

The Federal Reserve System can also expand or contract the overall money supply through Open Market Operations. In this case, the Fed can buy or sell bonds it has purchased from banks, or from individuals. When they buy bonds, more money is put into circulation, creating an expansionary situation to stimulate the economy. When the Fed sells bonds, money is withdrawn from the system, creating a contractionary situation to slow an economy suffering from inflation. Because of international financial markets, however, American banks often borrow and lend money in markets outside the US. By shifting their attention to international markets, domestic banks and other businesses can circumvent whatever contractionary policies the Fed may have put into place in order to help a struggling economy.

International trade

International trade can take advantage of broader markets, bringing a wider variety of products within easy reach. By contrast, it can also allow individual countries to specialize in particular products that they can produce easily, such as those for which they have easy access to raw materials. Other products, more difficult to make domestically, can be acquired through trade with other nations. International trade requires efficient use of native resources as well as sufficient disposable income to purchase native products and imported products. Many countries in the world engage extensively in international trade, but others still face major economic challenges.

Developing nations

The five major characteristics of a developing nation are:
- Low GDP
- Rapid growth of population
- Economy that depends on subsistence agriculture
- Poor conditions, including high infant mortality rates, high disease rates, poor sanitation, and insufficient housing
- Low literacy rate

Developing nations often function under oppressive governments that do not provide private property rights and withhold education and other rights from women. They also often feature an extreme disparity between upper and lower classes, with little opportunity for lower classes to improve their position.

Stages of economic development
Economic development occurs in three stages that are defined by the activities that drive the economy:
- Agricultural stage
- Manufacturing stage
- Service sector stage

In developing countries, it is often difficult to acquire the necessary funding to provide equipment and training to move into the advanced stages of economic development. Some can receive help from developed countries via foreign aid and investment or international organizations such as the International Monetary Fund or the World Bank. Having developed countries provide monetary, technical, or military assistance can help developing countries move forward to the next stage in their development.

Obstacles to economic growth
Developing nations typically struggle to overcome obstacles that prevent or slow economic development. Major obstacles can include:
- Rapid, uncontrolled population growth
- Trade restrictions
- Misused resources, often perpetrated by the nation's government
- Traditional beliefs that can slow or reject change.

Corrupt, oppressive governments often hamper the economic growth of developing nations, creating huge economic disparities and making it impossible for individuals to advance, in turn preventing overall growth. Governments sometimes export currency, called capital flight, which is detrimental to a country's economic development. In general, countries are more likely to experience economic growth if their governments encourage entrepreneurship and provide private property rights.

Problems with rapid industrialization

Rapid growth throughout the world leaves some nations behind, and sometimes spurs their governments to move forward too quickly into industrialization and artificially rapid economic growth. While slow or nonexistent economic growth causes problems in a country, overly rapid industrialization carries its own issues. Four major problems encountered due to rapid industrialization are:
- Use of technology not suited to the products or services being supplied
- Poor investment of capital
- Lack of time for the population to adapt to new paradigms
- Lack of time to experience all stages of development and adjust to each stage

Economic failures in Indonesia were largely due to rapid growth that was poorly handled.

E-commerce

The growth of the Internet has brought many changes to our society, not the least of which is the ways we do business. Where supply channels used to have to move in certain ways, many of these channels are now bypassed as e-commerce makes it possible for nearly any individual to set up a direct market to consumers, as well as direct interaction with suppliers. Competition is fierce. In many instances e-commerce can provide nearly instantaneous gratification, with a wide variety of products. Whoever provides the best product most quickly often rises to the top of a marketplace. How this added element to the marketplace will affect the economy in the near and not-so-near future remains to be seen. Many industries are still struggling with the best ways to adapt to the rapid, continuous changes.

Knowledge economy

The knowledge economy is a growing sector in the economy of developed countries, and includes the trade and development of:
- Data
- Intellectual property
- Technology, especially in the area of communications

Knowledge as a resource is steadily becoming more and more important. What is now being called the Information Age may prove to bring about changes in life and culture as significant as those brought on by the Agricultural and Industrial Revolutions.

Cybernomics

Related to the knowledge economy is what has been dubbed "cybernomics," or economics driven by e-commerce and other computer-based markets and products. Marketing has changed drastically with the growth of cyber communication, allowing suppliers to connect one-on-one with their customers. Other issues coming to the fore regarding cybernomics include:
- Secure online trade
- Intellectual property rights
- Rights to privacy
- Bringing developing nations into the fold

As these issues are debated and new laws and policies developed, the face of many industries continues to undergo drastic change. Many of the old ways of doing business no longer work, leaving industries scrambling to function profitably within the new system.

Principles of Geography

Geography

Geography literally means the study of the earth. Geographers study physical characteristics of the earth as well as man-made borders and boundaries. They also study the distribution of life on the planet, such as where certain species of animals can be found, as well as how different forms of life interact. Major elements of the study of geography include:
- Locations
- Regional characteristics
- Spatial relations
- Natural and manmade forces that change elements of the earth

These elements are studied from regional, topical, physical and human perspectives. Geography also focuses on the origins of the earth as well as the history and backgrounds of different human populations.

<u>Physical and cultural geography</u>
Physical geography is the study of the physical characteristics of the earth, how they relate to each other, how they were formed, and how they develop. These characteristics include climate, land, and water, and also how they affect human populations in various areas. Different landforms in combination with various climates and other conditions determine characteristics of various cultures.

Cultural geography is the study of how the various aspects of physical geography affect individual cultures. Cultural geography also compares various cultures, how their lifestyles and customs are affected by their geographical location, climate, and other factors, and how they interact with their environment.

> ➤ **Review Video:** <u>Physical vs. Cultural Geography</u>
> *Visit **mometrix.com/academy** and enter **Code: 912136***

Divisions of geographical study

The four divisions of geographical study and tools used are:
- Topical—the study of a single feature of the earth or one specific human activity that occurs world-wide.
- Physical—the various physical features of the earth, how they are created, the forces that change them, and how they are related to each other and to various human activities.
- Regional—specific characteristics of individual places and regions.
- Human—how human activity affects the environment. This includes study of political, historical, social, and cultural activities.

Tools used in geographical study include special research methods like mapping, field studies, statistics, interviews, mathematics, and use of various scientific instruments.

Ancient geographers

The following are three important ancient geographers and their contributions to the study of geography:
- Eratosthenes lived in ancient Greek times, and mathematically calculated the circumference of the earth.
- Strabo wrote a description of the ancient world called Geographica. The work consisted of seventeen volumes.
- Ptolemy, primarily an astronomer, was also an experienced mapmaker. His skills also contributed to overall knowledge of the earth's geography.

Analysis of areas of human population

In cities, towns, or other areas where many people have settled, geographers focus on distribution of populations, neighborhoods, industrial areas, transportation, and other elements important to the society in question. For example, they would map out the locations of hospitals, airports, factories, police stations, schools, and housing groups. They would also make note of how these facilities are distributed in relation to the areas of habitation, such as the number of schools a certain neighborhood, or how many grocery stores are located in a specific suburban area. Another area of study and discussion is the distribution of towns themselves, from widely spaced rural towns to large cities that merge into each other to form a megalopolis.

Cartographers and maps

A cartographer is a mapmaker. Mapmakers produce detailed illustrations of geographic areas to record where various features are located within that area. These illustrations can be compiled into maps, charts, graphs, and even globes. When constructing maps, cartographers must take into account the phenomenon of distortion. Because the earth is round, a flat map does not accurately represent the correct proportions, especially if a very large geographical area is being depicted. Maps must be designed in such a way as to minimize this distortion and maximize accuracy. Accurately representing the earth's features on a flat surface is achieved through projection.

> ➢ **Review Video: Cartography and Technology**
> *Visit **mometrix.com/academy** and enter **Code: 642071***

Map projections

The three major types of projection used in creating world maps are:
- Cylindrical projection—created by wrapping the globe of the Earth in a cylindrical piece of paper, then using a light to project the globe onto the paper. The largest distortion occurs at the outermost edges.
- Conical projection—the paper is shaped like a cone and contacts the globe only at the cone's base. This type of projection is most useful for middle latitudes.
- Flat-Plane projections—also known as a Gnomonic projection, this type of map is projected onto a flat piece of paper that only touches the globe at a single point. Flat-plane projections make it possible to map out Great-Circle Routes, or the shortest route between one point and another on the globe, as a straight line.

Four specific types of map projections that are commonly used today are:
- Winkel tripel projection—the most common projection used for world maps, since it was accepted in 1998 by the National Geographic Society as a standard. The Winkel tripel projection balances size and shape, greatly reducing distortion.
- Robinson projection—east and west sections of the map are less distorted, but continental shapes are somewhat inaccurate.
- Goode's interrupted equal-area projection—Sizes and shapes are accurate, but distances are not. This projection basically represents a globe that has been cut in a way that allows it to lie flat.
- Mercator projection—though distortion is high, particularly in areas farther from the equator, this cylindrical projection is commonly used by seafarers.

Map elements

The five major elements of any map are:
- Title—tells basic information about the map, such as the area represented.
- Legend—also known as the key, the legend explains what symbols used on a particular map represent, such as symbols for major landmarks.
- Grid—most commonly represents the Geographic Grid System, or latitude and longitude marks used to precisely locate specific locations.
- Directions—a compass rose or other symbol used to indicate the cardinal directions.
- Scale—shows the relation between a certain distance on the map and the actual distance. For example, one inch might represent one mile, or ten miles, or even more depending on the size of the map.

> **Review Video:** <u>5 Elements of Any Map</u>
> *Visit **mometrix.com/academy** and enter **Code:** 313443*

Equal area map and conformal map

An equal area map is designed such that the proportional sizes of various areas are accurate. For example, if one land mass is one-fifth the size of another, the lines on the map will be shifted to accommodate for distortion so that the proportional size is accurate. In many maps, areas farther from the equator are greatly distorted; this type of map compensates for this phenomenon.

A conformal map focuses on representing the correct shape of geographical areas, with less concern for comparative size.

Consistent scale map and thematic map

With a consistent scale map, the same scale, such as one inch=ten miles, is used throughout the entire map. This is most often used for maps of smaller areas, as maps that cover larger areas, such as the full globe, must make allowances for distortion. Maps of very large areas often make use of more than one scale, with scales closer to the center representing a larger area than those at the edges.

A thematic map is constructed to show very specific information about a chosen theme. For example, a thematic map might represent political information, such as how votes were distributed in an election, or show population distribution or climactic features.

Relief map

A relief map is constructed to show details of various elevations across the area of the map. Higher elevations are represented by different colors than lower elevations. Relief maps often also show additional details, such as the overall ruggedness or smoothness of an area. Mountains would be represented as ridged and rugged, while deserts would be shown as smooth. Elevation in relief maps can also be represented by contour lines, or lines that connect points of the same elevation. Some relief maps even feature textures, reconstructing details in a sort of miniature model.

Mountains, hills, plains and valleys

The following are geographical features of mountains, hills, plains, and valleys:
- Mountains are elevated areas that measure 2,000 feet or more above sea level. Often steep and rugged, they usually occur in groups called chains or ranges. Six of the seven continents on Earth contain at least one range.
- Hills are of lower elevation than mountains, at about 500-2,000 feet. Hills are usually more rounded, and are found everywhere on Earth.
- Plains are large, flat areas and are usually very fertile. The majority of Earth's population is supported by crops grown on the Earth's vast plains.
- Valleys lie between hills and mountains. Depending on where they are located, their specific features can vary greatly, from fertile and habitable to rugged and inhospitable.

Plateaus, deserts, deltas, mesas, basins, foothills, marshes and swamps

Plateaus, deserts, deltas, mesas, basins, foothills, marshes and swamps are described below:
- Plateaus are elevated, but flat on top. Some plateaus are extremely dry, such as the Kenya Plateau, because surrounding mountains prevent them from receiving moisture.
- Deserts receive less than ten inches of rain per year. They are usually large areas, such as the Sahara Desert in Africa or the Australian Outback.
- Deltas occur at river mouths. Because the rivers carry sediment to the deltas, these areas are often very fertile.
- Mesas are flat, steep-sided mountains or hills. The term is sometimes used to refer to plateaus.
- Basins are areas of low elevation where rivers drain.
- Foothills are the transition area between the plains and the mountains, usually consisting of hills that gradually increase in size as they approach the mountain range.
- Marshes and swamps are also lowlands, but they are very wet and largely covered in vegetation such as reeds and rushes.

Bodies of water

Oceans, seas, lakes, rivers and canals are described below:
- Oceans are the largest bodies of water on Earth. They are salt water, and cover about two-thirds of the earth's surface. The four major oceans are the Atlantic, Pacific, Indian and Arctic.
- Seas are generally also salt water, but are smaller than oceans and surrounded by land. Examples include the Mediterranean Sea, the Caribbean Sea, and the Caspian Sea.
- Lakes are bodies of freshwater found inland. Sixty percent of all lakes are located in Canada.

- Rivers are moving bodies of water that flow from higher elevations to lower. They usually start as rivulets or streams, and grow until they finally empty into a sea or an ocean.
- Canals, such as the Panama Canal and the Suez Canal, are manmade waterways connecting two large bodies of water.

> ➢ **Review Video:** Geographical Features
> *Visit mometrix.com/academy and enter Code:* **773539**

Communities

Communities, or groups of people who settle together in a specific area, typically gather where certain conditions exists. These conditions include:
- Easy access to resources such as food, water, and raw materials
- Ability to easily transport raw materials and goods, such as access to a waterway
- Room to house a sufficient work force

People also tend to form groups with others who are similar to them. In a typical community, people can be found who share values, a common language, and common or similar cultural characteristics and religious beliefs. These factors will determine the overall composition of a community as it develops.

Cities

Cities develop and grow as an area develops. Modern statistics show over half of the world's people living in cities. That percentage is even higher in developed areas of the globe. Cities are currently growing more quickly in developing regions, and even established cities continue to experience growth throughout the world. In developing or developed areas, cities often are surrounded by a metropolitan area made up of both urban and suburban sections. In some places, cities have merged into each other and become a megalopolis, or a single, huge city.

Cities develop differently in different areas of the world. The area available for cities to grow, as well as cultural and economic forces, drives how cities develop. For example, North American cities tend to cover wider areas. European cities tend to have better developed transportation systems. In Latin America, the richest inhabitants can be found in the city centers, while in North America wealthier inhabitants tend to live in suburban areas.

In other parts of the world, transportation and communication between cities is less developed. Recent technological innovations such as the cell phone have increased communication even in these areas. Urban areas must also maintain communication with rural areas in order to procure food, resources and raw materials that cannot be produced within the city limits.

Weather and climate

Weather and climate are physical systems that affect geography. Though they deal with similar information, the way this information is measured and compiled is different. Weather involves daily conditions in the atmosphere that affect temperature, precipitation (rain, snow, hail or sleet), wind speed, air pressure, and other factors. Weather focuses on the short-term—for example what the conditions will be today, tomorrow, or over the next few days. By contrast, climate aggregates information about daily and seasonal weather conditions in a region over a long period of time. The climate takes into account average monthly and yearly temperatures, average precipitation over long periods of time, and the growing season of an area.

Climates are classified according to latitude, or how close they lie to the Earth's equator. The three major divisions are:
- Low Latitudes, lying from 0 to 23.5 degrees latitude
- Middle Latitudes, found from 23.5 to 66.5 degrees
- High Latitudes, found from 66.5 degrees to the poles

Desert, savanna and rainforest climates occur in low latitudes:
- Rainforest climates, near the equator, experience high average temperatures and humidity, as well as relatively high rainfall.
- Savannas are found to either side of the rainforest region. Mostly grasslands, they typically experience dry winters and wet summers.
- Beyond the savannas lie the desert regions, with hot, dry climates, sparse rainfall (less than ten inches per year on average) and temperature fluctuations of up to fifty degrees from day into night.

The climate regions found in the middle latitudes are:
- Mediterranean - The Mediterranean climate occurs between 30 and 40 degrees latitude, both north and south, and on the western coasts. Characteristics include a year-long growing season, hot, dry summers followed by mild winters, and sparse rainfall that occurs mostly during the winter months.
- Humid-subtropical - Humid-subtropical regions are located on southeastern coastal areas. Winds that blow in over warm ocean currents produce long summers, mild winters, and a long growing season. These areas are highly productive, and support a larger part of the Earth's population than any other climate.
- Humid-continental - The humid continental climate produces the familiar four seasons typical of a good portion of the US. Some of the most productive farmlands in the world lie in these climates. Winters are cold, summers are hot and humid.
- Marine - Marine climates are found near water or on islands. Ocean winds help make these areas mild and rainy. Summers are cooler than humid-subtropical summers, but winters also bring milder temperatures due to the warmth of the ocean winds.
- Steppe - Steppe climates, or prairie climates, are found far inland in large continents. Summers are hot and winters are cold, but rainfall is sparser than in continental climates.
- Desert - Desert climates occur where steppe climates receive even less rainfall. Examples include the Gobi desert in Asia as well as desert areas of Australia and the southwestern US.

The high latitudes consist of two major climate areas, the tundra and taiga.
- Tundra means marshy plain. Ground is frozen throughout long, cold winters, but there is little snowfall. During the short summers, it becomes wet and marshy. Tundras are not amenable to crops, but many plants and animals have adapted to the conditions.
- Taigas lie south of tundra regions, and include the largest forest areas in the world, as well as swamps and marshes. Large mineral deposits exist here, as well as many animals valued for their fur. In the winter, taiga regions are colder than the tundra, and summers are hotter. The growing season is short.

A vertical climate exists in high mountain ranges. Increasing elevation leads to varying temperatures, growing conditions, types of vegetation and animals, and occurrence of human habitation, often encompassing elements of various other climate regions.

Factors that affect climate

Because the earth is tilted, its rotation brings about the changes in seasons. Regions closer to the equator, and those nearest the poles, experience very little change in seasonal temperatures. Mid-range latitudes are most likely to experience distinct seasons. Large bodies of water also affect climate. Ocean currents and wind patterns can change the climate for an area that lies in typically cold latitude, such as England, to a much more temperate climate. Mountains can affect both short-term weather and long-term climates. Some deserts occur because precipitation is stopped by the wall of a mountain range.

Over time, established climate patterns can shift and change. While the issue is hotly debated, it has been theorized that human activity has also led to climate change.

Human systems

Human systems affect geography in the way in which they settle, form groups that grow into large-scale habitations, and even create permanent changes in the landscape. Geographers study movements of people, how they distribute goods among each other and to other settlements or cultures, and how ideas grow and spread. Migrations, wars, forced relocations, and trade all can spread cultural ideas, language, goods and other practices to wide-spread areas. Some major migrations or the conquering of one people by another have significantly changed cultures throughout history. In addition, human systems can lead to various conflicts or alliances to control access to and the use of natural resources.

North America
North America consists of the countries of the United States and Canada. These two countries support similarly diverse cultures, as both were formed from groups of native races as well as large numbers of immigrants. Both functioned for a period under British rule. The United States broke from British rule via violent revolution, while Canada became independent in 1931 through diplomatic means. Agriculture is important to both countries, while service industries and technology also play a large part in the North American economy. North America in general supports a high standard of living and a high level of development, and supports trade with countries throughout the world

Latin America
Including Mexico, Central America and South America, Latin America is largely defined by its prevailing languages. The majority of countries in Latin America speak Spanish or Portuguese. Most of Latin America has experienced a similar history, having been originally dominated by Native cultures, conquered by European nations. The countries of Latin America have since gained independence, but there is a wide disparity between various countries' economic and political factors. Most Latin American countries rely on only one or two exports, usually agricultural, with suitable lands often controlled by rich families. Most societies in Latin America feature major separations between classes, both economically and socially. Challenges faced by developing Latin American countries include geographical limitations, economic issues, and sustainable development, including the need to preserve the existing rainforests.

Europe
Europe contains a wide variety of cultures, ethnic groups, physical geographical features, climates, and resources, all of which have influenced the distribution of its varied population. Europe in general is industrialized and developed, with cultural differences giving each individual country its own unique characteristics. Greek and Roman influences played a major role in European culture, as did Christian

- 118 -

beliefs. European countries spread their beliefs and cultural elements throughout the world by means of migration and colonization. They have had a significant influence on nearly every other continent in the world. While Western Europe has been largely democratic, Eastern Europe functioned under Communist rule for many years. The recent formation of the European Union (EU) has increased stability and positive diplomatic relations among European nations. Like other industrialized regions, Europe is now focusing on various environmental issues.

Russia

After numerous conflicts, Russia became a Communist state, known as the USSR. With the collapse of the USSR in 1991, the country has struggled in its transition to a market driven economy. Attempts to build a workable system have led to the destruction of natural resources as well as problems with nuclear power, including accidents such as Chernobyl. To complete the transition to a market economy, Russia needs to improve its transportation and communication systems, and find a way to more efficiently use its natural resources.

The population of Russia is not distributed evenly, with three quarters of the population living west of the Ural Mountains. The people of Russia encompass over a hundred different ethnic groups. Over eighty percent of the population is ethnically Russian, and Russian is the official language of the country.

North Africa and Southwest and Central Asia

The largely desert climate of these areas has led most population centers to arise around sources of water, such as the Nile River. This area is the home of the earliest known civilizations and the place of origin for Christianity, Judaism and Islam. After serving as the site of huge, independent civilizations in ancient times, North Africa and Southwest and Central Asia were largely parceled out as European Colonies during the eighteenth and nineteenth centuries. The beginning of the twentieth century saw many of these countries gain their independence. Islam has served as a unifying force for large portions of these areas, and many of the inhabitants speak Arabic. In spite of the arid climate, agriculture is a large business, but the most valuable resource is oil. Centuries of conflict throughout this area has led to ongoing political problems. These political problems have also contributed to environmental issues.

Southern Africa

South of the Sahara Desert, Africa is divided into a number of culturally diverse nations. The inhabitants are unevenly distributed due to geographical limitations that prevent settlement in vast areas. AIDS has become a major plague throughout this part of Africa, killing millions, largely due to restrictive beliefs that prevent education about the disease, as well as abject poverty and unsettled political situations that make it impossible to manage the pandemic. The population of this area of Africa is widely diverse due to extensive migration. Many of the people still rely on subsistence farming for their welfare. Starvation and poverty are rampant due to drought and political instability. Some areas are far more stable than others due to greater availability of resources. These have been able to begin the process of industrialization.

South Asia

South Asia is home to one of the first human civilizations, which grew up in the Indus River Valley. With a great deal of disparity between rural and urban life, South Asia has much to do to improve the quality of life for its lower classes. Two major religions, Hinduism and Buddhism, have their origins in this region. Parts of South Asia, most notably India, were subject to British rule for several decades, and are still working to improve independent governments and social systems. Overall, South Asia is very culturally diverse, with a wide mix of religions and languages throughout. Many individuals are farmers, but a growing number have found prosperity in the spread of high-tech industries. Industrialization is growing in South Asia, but continues to face environmental, social, religious and economic challenges.

East Asia

Governments in East Asia are varied, ranging from communist to democratic governments, with some governments that mix both approaches. Isolationism throughout the area limited the countries' contact with other nations until the early twentieth century. The unevenly distributed population of East Asia consists of over one and a half billion people with widely diverse ethnic backgrounds, religions and languages. More residents live in urban areas than in rural areas, creating shortages of farm workers for some. Japan, Taiwan and South Korea are overall more urban, while China and Mongolia are more rural. Japan stands as the most industrial country of East Asia. Some areas of East Asia are suffering from major environmental issues. Japan has dealt with many of these problems and now has some of the strictest environmental laws in the world.

Southeast Asia

Much of Southeast Asia was colonized by European countries during the eighteenth and nineteenth centuries, with the exception of Siam, now known as Thailand. All the countries of the area are now independent, but the twentieth century saw numerous conflicts between communist and democratic forces.

Southeast Asia has been heavily influenced by both Buddhist and Muslim religions. Industrialization is growing, with the population moving in large numbers from rural to urban areas. Some have moved to avoid conflict, oppression, and poverty.

Natural disasters, including volcanoes, typhoons and flash flooding, are fairly common in Southeast Asia, creating extensive economic damage and societal disruption.

Australia, Oceana and Antarctica

South Pacific cultures originally migrated from Southeast Asia, creating hunter-gatherer or sometimes settled agricultural communities. European countries moved in during later centuries, seeking the plentiful natural resources of the area. Today, some South Pacific islands remain under the control of foreign governments, and culture in these areas mix modern, industrialized society and indigenous culture. Population is unevenly distributed, largely due to the inhabitability of many parts of the South Pacific, such as the extremely hot desert areas of Australia. Agriculture still drives much of the economy, with tourism growing. Antarctica remains the only continent not claimed by a single country. There are no permanent human habitations in Antarctica, but scientists and explorers visit the area on a temporary basis.

Human-environment interaction

Geography also studies the way people interact with, use and change their environment. The effects, reasons and consequences of these changes are studied, as are the ways the environment limits or influences human behavior. This kind of study can help determine the best course of action when a nation or group of people are considering making changes to the environment, such as building a dam or removing natural landscape to build or expand roads. Study of the consequences can help determine if these actions are manageable and how long-term detrimental results can be mitigated.

Physical geography and climate

US and Canada

The US and Canada have a similar distribution of geographical features, with shared mountain ranges in both east and west, similar stretches of fertile plains through the center, and some shared lakes and waterways. Both areas were shaped by glaciers, which also deposited highly fertile soil. Because they are so large, Canada and the US experience several varieties of climate, including continental climates with four seasons in median areas, tropical climates in the southern part of the US, and arctic climes in the far north. Human intervention has greatly influenced the productivity of agricultural regions, and many areas have been reshaped to accommodate easier, more economical transportation.

Latin America

Latin America contains a wide variety of geographical features including high mountains such as the Andes, wide plains, and high altitude plateaus. The region contains numerous natural resources, but many of them have remained unused due to various obstacles, including political issues, geographic barriers, and lack of sufficient economic power.

Climate zones in Latin America are largely tropical, with rainforests and savannahs, but vertical climate zones and grasslands are also included.

Europe

Europe spans a wide area with a variety of climate zones. In the east and south are mountain ranges, while the north is dominated by a plains region. The long coastline and the island nature of some countries, such as Britain, mean the climate is often warmer than other lands at similar latitudes, as the area is warmed by ocean currents. Many areas of western Europe have a moderate climate, while areas of the south are dominated by the classic Mediterranean climate. Europe carries a high level of natural resources. Numerous waterways help connect the inner regions with the coastal areas. Much of Europe is industrialized, and agriculture has existed in the area for thousands of years.

Russia

Russia's area encompasses part of Asia and Europe. From the standpoint of square footage alone, Russia is the largest country in the world. Due to its size Russia encompasses a wide variety of climatic regions, including plains, plateaus, mountains and tundra.

Russia's climate can be quite harsh, with rivers that are frozen through most of the year making transportation of the country's rich natural resources more difficult. Siberia, in the north of Russia, is dominated by permafrost. Native peoples in this area still live hunting and gathering existence, live in portable yurts and subsisting largely on herds of reindeer or caribou. Other areas include taiga with extensive, dense woods in north central Russia and more temperate steppes and grasslands in the southwest.

North Africa and Southwest and Central Asia

This area of the world is complex in its geographical structure and climate, incorporating seas, peninsulas, rivers, mountains, and numerous other features. Earthquakes remain common, with tectonic plates in the area remaining active. Much of the world's oil lies in this area. The tendency of the large rivers of North Africa, especially the Nile, to follow a set pattern of drought and extreme fertility, led people to settle there from prehistoric times. As technology has advanced, people have tamed this river, making its activity more predictable and the land around it more productive. The extremely arid nature of many other parts of this area has also led to human intervention such as irrigation to increase agricultural production.

Southern Africa

South of the Sahara Desert, the high elevations and other geographical characteristics have made it very difficult for human travel or settlement to occur. The geography of the area is dominated by a series of plateaus. There are also mountain ranges and a large rift valley in the eastern part of the country. Contrasting the wide desert areas, Southern Africa contains numerous lakes, rivers, and world-famous waterfalls. The area contains tropical climates, including rain forests, as well as savannahs, steppes, and desert areas. The main natural resources are minerals, including gems, and water.

South Asia
The longest alluvial plain, a plain caused by shifting floodplains of major rivers and river systems over time, exists in South Asia. South Asia boasts three major river systems in the Ganges, Indus and Brahmaputra. It also has large deposits of minerals, including iron ore that are in great demand internationally. South Asia holds mountains, plains, plateaus, and numerous islands. The climates range from tropical to highlands and desert areas. South Asia also experiences monsoon winds that cause a long rainy season. Variations in climate, elevation and human activity influence agricultural production.

East Asia
East Asia includes North and South Korea, Mongolia, China, Japan and Taiwan. Mineral resources are plentiful but not evenly distributed throughout. The coastlines are long, and while the population is large, farmlands are sparse. As a result, the surrounding oceans have become a major source of sustenance. East Asia is large enough to also encompass several climate regions. Ocean currents provide milder climates to coastal areas, while monsoons provide the majority of the rainfall for the region. Typhoons are somewhat common, as are earthquakes, volcanoes and tsunamis. The latter occur because of the tectonic plates that meet beneath the continent, and remain somewhat active.

Southeast Asia
Southeast Asia lies largely on the equator, and roughly half of the countries of the region are island nations. These countries include Borneo, Thailand, Vietnam, Laos, Myanmar, New Guinea and Malaysia. Malaysia is partially on the mainland and partially an island country. The island nations of Southeast Asia feature mountains that are considered part of the Ring of Fire, an area where tectonic plates remain quite active, leading to extensive volcanic activity as well as earthquakes and tsunamis. Southeast Asia boasts many rivers as well as abundant natural resources, including gems, fossil fuels and minerals. There are basically two seasons—wet and dry. The wet season arrives with the monsoons. In general, Southeast Asia consists of tropical rainforest climates, but there are some mountain areas and tropical savannas.

Australia, Oceania and Antarctica
In the far southern hemisphere of the globe, Australia and Oceania present their own climatic combinations. Australia, the only island on earth that is also a continent, has extensive deserts as well as mountains and lowlands. The economy is driven by agriculture, including ranches and farms, and minerals. While the steppes bordering extremely arid inland areas are suitable for livestock, only the coastal areas receive sufficient rainfall for crops without using irrigation. Oceania refers to literally thousands of Pacific islands, created by volcanic activity. Most of these have tropical climates with wet and dry seasons. New Zealand, Australia's nearest neighbor, boasts rich forests as well as mountain ranges and relatively moderate temperatures, including rainfall throughout the year. Antarctica is covered with ice. Its major resource consists of scientific information. It supports some wildlife, such as penguins, and little vegetation, mostly mosses or lichens.

Plate tectonics

According to the geological theory of plate tectonics, the earth's crust is made up of ten major and several minor tectonic plates. These plates are the solid areas of the crust. They float on top of the earth's mantle, which is made up of molten rock. Because the plates float on this liquid component of the earth's crust, they move, creating major changes in the earth's surface. These changes can happen very slowly, over time, such as in continental drift, or can happen rapidly, such as when earthquakes occur. Interaction between the different continental plates can create mountain ranges, volcanic activity, major earthquakes, and deep rifts.

> ➤ **Review Video: Plate Tectonic Theory**
> *Visit* **mometrix.com/academy** *and enter* **Code: 535013**

Plate boundaries

Plate tectonics defines three types of plate boundaries, determined by the way in which the edges of the plates interact. These plate boundaries are:

- Convergent boundaries—the bordering plates move toward one another. When they collide directly, this is known as continental collision, which can create very large, high mountain ranges such as the Himalayas and the Andes. If one plate slides under the other, this is called subduction. Subduction can lead to intense volcanic activity. One example is the Ring of Fire that lies along the northern Pacific coastlines.
- Divergent boundaries—plates move away from each other. This movement leads to rifts such as the Mid-Atlantic Ridge and east Africa's Great Rift Valley.
- Transform boundaries—plate boundaries slide in opposite directions against each other. Intense pressure builds up along transform boundaries as the plates grind along each other's edges, leading to earthquakes. Many major fault lines, including the San Andreas Fault, lie along transform boundaries.

Erosion, weathering, transportation and deposition

Erosion involves movement of any loose material on the earth's surface. This can include soil, sand, or rock fragments. These loose fragments can be displaced by natural forces such as wind, water, ice, plant cover, and human factors. Mechanical erosion occurs due to natural forces. Chemical erosion occurs as a result of human intervention and activities. Weathering occurs when atmospheric elements affect the earth's surface. Water, heat, ice, and pressure all lead to weathering. Transportation refers to loose material being moved by wind, water or ice. Glacial movement, for example, carries everything from pebbles to boulders, sometimes over long distances. Deposition is the result of transportation. When material is transported, it is eventually deposited, and builds up to form formations like moraines and sand dunes.

Effects of human interaction and conflict on geographical boundaries

Human societies and their interaction have led to divisions of territories into countries and various other subdivisions. While these divisions are at their root artificial, they are important to geographers in the discussion of interactions of various populations.

Geographical divisions often occur through conflict between different human populations. The reasons behind these divisions include:

- Control of resources
- Control of important trade routes
- Control of populations

Conflict often occurs due to religious or political differences, language differences, or race differences. Natural resources are finite and so often lead to conflict over how they are distributed among populations.

State sovereignty

State sovereignty recognizes the division of geographical areas into areas controlled by various governments or groups of people. These groups control not only the territory, but also all its natural resources and the inhabitants of the area. The entire planet Earth is divided into political or administratively sovereign areas recognized to be controlled by a particular government with the exception of the continent of Antarctica.

Alliances

Alliances form between different countries based on similar interests, political goals, cultural values, or military issues. Six existing international alliances include:
- North Atlantic Treaty Organization (NATO)
- Common Market
- European Union (EU)
- United Nations (UN)
- Caribbean Community
- Council of Arab Economic Unity

In addition, very large companies and multi-national corporations can create alliances and various kinds of competition based on the need to control resources, production, and the overall marketplace.

Agricultural revolution

The agricultural revolution began six thousand years ago when the plow was invented in Mesopotamia. Using a plow drawn by animals, people were able to cultivate crops in large quantities rather than gathering available seeds and grains and planting them by hand.
Because large-scale agriculture was labor intensive, this led to the development of stable communities where people gathered to make farming possible. As stable farming communities replaced groups of nomadic hunter-gatherers, human society underwent profound changes. Societies became dependent on limited numbers of crops as well as subject to the vagaries of weather. Trading livestock and surplus agricultural output led to the growth of large-scale commerce and trade routes.

Modification of surrounding environments by human populations

The agricultural revolution led human societies to begin changing their surroundings in order to accommodate their needs for shelter and room to cultivate food and to provide for domestic animals. Clearing ground for crops, redirecting waterways for irrigation purposes, and building permanent settlements all create major changes in the environment. Large-scale agriculture can lead to loose topsoil and damaging erosion. Building large cities leads to degraded air quality, water pollution from energy consumption, and many other side effects that can severely damage the environment. Recently, many countries have taken action by passing laws to reduce human impact on the environment and reduce the potentially damaging side effects. This is called environmental policy.

Ecology

Ecology is the study of the way living creatures interact with their environment. Biogeography explores the way physical features of the earth affect living creatures.

Ecology bases its studies on three different levels of the environment. These are:

- Ecosystem—a specific physical environment and all the organisms that live there.
- Biomes—a group of ecosystems, usually consisting of a large area with similar flora and fauna as well as similar climate and soil. Examples of biomes include deserts, tropical rain forests, taigas, and tundra.
- Habitat—an area in which a specific species usually lives. The habitat includes the necessary soil, water, and resources for that particular species, as well as predators and other species that compete for the same resources.

Interactions between species

Different interactions occur among species and members of single species within a habitat. These interactions fall into three categories:

- Competition — Competition occurs when different animals, either of the same species or of different species, compete for the same resources. Robins can compete with other robins for available food, but other insectivores also compete for these same resources.
- Predation— Predation occurs when one species depends on the other species for food, such as a fox who subsists on small mammals.
- Symbiosis — Symbiosis occurs when two different species exist in the same environment without affecting the other. Some symbiotic relationships are beneficial to one or both organisms without harm occurring to either.

Ability to adapt

If a species is relocated from one habitat to another, it must adapt in order to survive. Some species are more capable of adapting than others. Those that cannot adapt will not survive. There are different ways a creature can adapt, including behavior modification as well as structure or physiological changes. Adaptation is also vital if an organism's environment changes around it. Although the creature has not been relocated, it finds itself in a new environment that requires changes in order to survive. The more readily an organism can adapt, the more likely it is to survive. The almost infinite ability of humans to adapt is a major reason why they are able to survive in almost any habitat in any area of the world.

Biodiversity

Biodiversity refers to the variety of habitats that exist on the planet, as well as the variety of organisms that can exist within these habitats. A greater level of biodiversity makes it more likely that an individual habitat will flourish along with the species that depend upon it. Changes in habitat, including climate change, human intervention, or other factors, can reduce biodiversity by causing the extinction of certain species.

Practice Test

Multiple Choice Questions

1. Some countries in the Americas still have large populations of indigenous or partly indigenous peoples. Of the following, which pair of countries does not have comparatively as large of an indigenous population as the other countries?
    a. Guatemala and Peru
    b. Ecuador and Bolivia
    c. Paraguay and Mexico
    d. Argentina and Uruguay

2. Which of the following statements is *not* true regarding English expansionism in the 16th century?
    a. England's defeat of the Spanish Armada in 1588 brought a decisive end to their war with Spain.
    b. King Henry VIII's desire to divorce Catherine of Aragon strengthened English expansionism.
    c. Queen Elizabeth's support for the Protestant Reformation strengthened English expansionism.
    d. Sir Francis Drake and other English sea captains plundered the Spaniards' plunders of Indians.

3. Which of the following is *not* true regarding the Virginia Companies?
    a. One of these companies, the Virginia Company of Plymouth, made its base in North America.
    b. One of these companies, the Virginia Company of London, made its base in Massachusetts.
    c. One company had a charter to colonize America between the Hudson and Cape Fear rivers.
    d. One company had a charter to colonize America from the Potomac River to north Maine.

4. Which of the following statements is *not* true regarding the colony of Jamestown?
    a. The colony of Jamestown was established by the Virginia Company of London in 1607.
    b. The colony of Jamestown became the first permanent English colony in North America.
    c. The majority of settlers in early Jamestown died of starvation, disease, or Indian attacks.
    d. John Smith's governance helped Jamestown more than John Rolfe's tobacco discovery.

5. Which of the following conquistadores unwittingly gave smallpox to the Indians and destroyed the Aztec empire in Mexico?
    a. Balboa
    b. Ponce de Leon
    c. Cortes
    d. De Vaca

6. Which of these factors was *not* a direct contributor to the beginning of the American Revolution?
    a. The attitudes of American colonists toward Great Britain following the French and Indian War
    b. The attitudes of leaders in Great Britain toward the American colonies and imperialism
    c. James Otis's court argument against Great Britain's Writs of Assistance as breaking natural law
    d. Lord Grenville's Proclamation of 1763, Sugar Act, Currency Act, and especially Stamp Act

7. Which of the following statements is *not* true regarding the Tea Act of 1773?
    a. The British East India Company was suffering financially because Americans were buying tea smuggled from Holland.
    b. Parliament granted concessions to the British East India Company to ship tea straight to America, bypassing England.
    c. Colonists found that even with added taxes, tea directly shipped by the British East India Company cost less, and they bought it.
    d. American colonists refused to buy less expensive tea from the British East India Company on the principle of taxation.

8. Which of the following were dispatch riders notifying Americans of British troop movements reported by American surveillance in 1775?
    a. Paul Revere
    b. William Dawes
    c. John Parker
    d. (a) and (b)

9. Which of the following is true concerning the formation of new state governments in the new United States of America following freedom from British rule?
    a. By the end of 1777, new constitutions had been created for twelve of the American states.
    b. The states of Connecticut and Massachusetts retained their colonial charters, minus the British parts.
    c. The state of Massachusetts required a special convention for its constitution, setting a good example.
    d. The state of Massachusetts did not formally begin to use its new constitution until 1778.

10. Which of the following is *not* a true statement regarding the Louisiana Purchase?
    a. Jefferson sent a delegation to Paris to endeavor to purchase only the city of New Orleans from Napoleon.
    b. Napoleon, anticipating U.S. intrusions into Louisiana, offered to sell the U.S. the entire Louisiana territory.
    c. The American delegation accepted Napoleon's offer, though they were only authorized to buy New Orleans.
    d. The Louisiana Purchase, once it was completed, increased the territory of the U.S. by 50% overnight.

11. Which of the following is *not* correct about the growth of America in the first half of the 19th century?
    a. By 1840, two thirds of all Americans resided west of the Allegheny Mountains.
    b. The population of America doubled every 25 years during this time period.
    c. The trend of westward expansion increased as more people migrated west.
    d. Immigration to America from other countries was not substantial prior to 1820.

12. Which of the following did *not* occur during the War of 1812?
   a. Early in the war, the U.S. executed a three-pronged invasion of Canada and succeeded on two of three fronts.
   b. Early in the war, Americans won naval battles against the British, but were soon beaten back by the British.
   c. Admiral Oliver Hazard Perry's fleet defeated the British navy on Lake Erie in September, 1813.
   d. William Henry Harrison invaded Canada and defeated the British and the Indians in the Battle of the Thames.

13. Which of the following is *not* correct concerning the growth of American labor unions?
   a. The new factory system separated workers from owners, which tended to depersonalize workplaces.
   b. The goal of attaining an 8-hour work day stimulated growth in labor organizing in the early 1800s.
   c. The first organized workers' strike was in Paterson, New Jersey in 1828, and was by child laborers.
   d. Recurring downturns in the economy tended to limit workers' demands for rights until the 1850s.

14. Which of the following is *not* true regarding public schools in the early 19th century?
   a. Virtually no public schools existed in America prior to around 1815.
   b. Schools were mainly financed by private corporate or religious groups.
   c. Thomas Jefferson's plan of a free school in Virginia was realized.
   d. American schools were elitist, catering to the rich and to males in academics.

15. Which of the following was *not* an immediate effect of rapid urban growth in the 1800s?
   a. Poor sanitation conditions in the cities
   b. Epidemics of diseases in the cities
   c. Inadequate police and fire protection
   d. Widespread urban political corruption

16. Which of the following laws was instrumental in spurring westward migration to the Great Plains between 1860 and 1880?
   a. The Homestead Act
   b. The Timber Culture Act
   c. The Desert Land Act
   d. All of these laws were instrumental in spurring westward migration to the Great Plains during that period.

17. Which of the following did *not* contribute to ending America's neutrality in World War I?
   a. Germany's declaration of a war zone surrounding the British Isles in February, 1913
   b. Germany's declaration of a war on Russia after Archduke Ferdinand's assassination
   c. Germany's sinking the British ship *Lusitania,* which killed 128 American passengers
   d. Germany's declaration of unrestricted submarine warfare on all ships in the war zone

18. Of the following international diplomatic conferences, which one made US-Soviet differences apparent?
   a. The Potsdam conference
   b. The conference at Yalta
   c. Dumbarton Oaks conference
   d. The Tehran conference

19. Which statement about relations between the Middle East and the US and Europe in the 1950s is incorrect?
    a. President Nasser of Egypt refused to align with the US in the Cold War.
    b. President Eisenhower removed US funding from the Aswan Dam in 1956.
    c. President Nasser nationalized the Suez Canal, which was owned by England.
    d. In 1956, Egypt attacked Israel, and England and France joined in the war.

20. Which of the following statements regarding events in the Middle East that took place during the Reagan administration is *not* correct?
    a. Israel invaded Lebanon to get rid of the Palestine Liberation Organization's camps there.
    b. When a terrorist bombing killed 240 US Marines, Reagan escalated military action.
    c. Lebanon was already in the midst of a civil war when Israeli troops invaded the country.
    d. President Reagan deployed US Marines to Lebanon in 1982 on a peacekeeping mission.

21. Of the following, which person or group was *not* instrumental in advancement of civil rights and desegregation during the 1940s and 1950s?
    a. The President
    b. The Supreme Court
    c. The Congress
    d. The NAACP

22. Of the programs enacted by President Lyndon B. Johnson's administration, which was most closely related to John F. Kennedy's legacy?
    a. The Economic Opportunity Act
    b. The Civil Rights Act
    c. The Great Society program
    d. All of these were equally related to JFK's legacy.

23. Which statement regarding US international trade policy in the 1990s is incorrect?
    a. In 1994, the General Agreement on Tariffs and Trade (GATT) was approved by Congress.
    b. The GATT included 57 countries who agreed they would remove or reduce many of their tariffs.
    c. The GATT created the World Trade Organization (WTO) to settle international trade differences.
    d. The NAFTA (North American Free Trade Agreement), ratified in 1994, had originally been set up by George H.W. Bush's administration.

24. Which of the following statements regarding the Branch Davidians in 1993 is *not* true?
    a. The Branch Davidians were a Seventh Day Adventist sect living on a compound located near Waco, Texas.
    b. The Bureau of Alcohol, Tobacco, and Firearms got a search warrant for the Branch Davidian compound.
    c. When attempts to look for weapon stockpiles led to gunfire and deaths, the FBI attacked the compound.
    d. The incident at the Branch Davidian compound in Waco developed into a siege that lasted for six months.

25. Which statement about factors related to the growth of the US economy between 1945 and 1970 is incorrect?
    a. The Baby Boom's greatly increased birth rates contributed to economic growth during this time.
    b. The reduction in military spending after World War II contributed to the stronger US economy.
    c. Government programs and growing affluence nearly quadrupled college enrollments in 20 years.
    d. Increased mobility and bigger families caused fast suburban expansion, especially in the Sunbelt.

26. Which of the following statements regarding immigration to America during the 1980s is *not* true?
    a. Twice as many immigrants came to America during the 1980s than during the 1970s.
    b. Latin Americans comprised the largest proportion of immigrants to America in the 1980s.
    c. Most immigrants to the US in the 1980s were Latin American, Asian, and Caribbean.
    d. The 1986 Immigration Reform and Control Act impeded illegal Mexican immigration.

27. Which is *not* correct regarding black activism during the 1960s?
    a. There was a riot in the Los Angeles ghetto of Watts in 1965.
    b. There was a riot involving black activists in Newark, New Jersey, after the Watts riot.
    c. The Mississippi Freedom Democrats unseated that state's delegation at the convention.
    d. There was a riot involving black activists in Detroit, Michigan, after the riot in Watts.

28. What was the earliest written language in Mesopotamia?
    a. Sumerian
    b. Elamite
    c. Akkadian
    d. Aramaic

29. During which of these periods were pyramids *not* built in Egypt?
    a. The Old Kingdom
    b. The Middle Kingdom
    c. The New Kingdom
    d. The Third Dynasty

30. The Indus Valley or Harappan civilization existed in what is now:
    a. Iran
    b. India
    c. Pakistan
    d. All of these

31. The Yellow River Valley began to emerge as a cultural center during the:
    a. Shang Dynasty
    b. Neolithic Era
    c. Xia Dynasty
    d. Paleolithic Era

32. Which statement is *not* true regarding ancient Greek democracy?
    a. Democracy began to develop approximately 500 B.C.E.
    b. One of the first, best-known democracies was in Athens
    c. It was a direct democracy, not using any representatives
    d. It was a democracy completely open to all of the public

33. Which of the following statements is incorrect regarding these religions under the Roman Empire?
    a. The Romans generally protected the Jews until the rebellion in Judea (66 C.E.)
    b. Julius Caesar circumvented Roman law to help Jews have freedom of worship
    c. The Druids were a religious group that the Romans ignored but also tolerated
    d. Romans viewed Christianity as a Jewish sect for its first two centuries

34. Which of the following came chronologically the earliest in what is now the Republic of Ghana?
    a. The Kingdom of Ghana
    b. The Akan state of Bono
    c. The Ashanti federation
    d. The states of the Fante

35. Which of the following is *not* true about the Crusades?
    a. Their purpose was for European rulers to retake the Middle East from Muslims
    b. The Crusades succeeded at European kings' goal of reclaiming the "holy land"
    c. The Crusades accelerated the already incipient decline of the Byzantine Empire
    d. Egypt saw a return as a major Middle Eastern power as a result of the Crusades

36. Which of the following events did *not* contribute to the growth of the Italian Renaissance?
    a. The Black Death killed 1/3 of the population of Europe
    b. The lower classes benefited from the need for laborers
    c. The middle classes developed from a need for services
    d. All these events contributed to the Italian Renaissance

37. Which of the following was *not* a characteristic of the Renaissance in 14th-16th century Europe?
    a. The development of linear perspective in the art of painting
    b. The rejection of classical antiquity as a source of education
    c. The educational reform that grew slowly but spread widely
    d. The innovation of using the Scientific Method for learning

38. Which of the following is *not* correct regarding assumptions of mercantilism?
    a. The money and the wealth of a nation are identical properties
    b. In order to prosper, a nation should try to increase its imports
    c. In order to prosper, a nation should try to increase its exports
    d. Economic protectionism by national governments is advisable

39. Which of the following choices is/are *not* considered among causes of the French Revolution?
    a. Famines causing malnutrition and starvation
    b. War debt, Court spending, bad monetary system
    c. Resentment against the Catholic Church's rule
    d. Resentment against the Protestant Reformation

40. Of the following statements, which is true about the March on Versailles during the French Revolution?
    a. The March on Versailles was an action undertaken by equal numbers of both men and women
    b. The March on Versailles was an action undertaken primarily by women
    c. The March on Versailles happened prior to the storming of the Bastille
    d. The March on Versailles was not effective in accomplishing its purpose

41. Which of the following statements is accurate regarding the end of the First World War?
    a. The Treaty of Versailles brought peace among all countries involved in the war
    b. The Treaty of Versailles contained a clause for establishing the United Nations
    c. President Woodrow Wilson had proposed forming a coalition of world nations
    d. President Wilson succeeded in getting the USA to ratify the League of Nations

42. Which of the following empire(s) no longer existed following the armistice ending World War I?
    a. The Austro-Hungarian Empire
    b. The Ottoman Empire
    c. The German Empire
    d. All of these empires

43. Which of the following events of Communism occurred the earliest?
    a. Chairman Mao's Communist Party of China formed the People's Republic
    b. Joseph Stalin became party leader in Russia and made his first 5-year plan
    c. Lenin created the New Economic Policy allowing capitalism within limits
    d. Bolsheviks instituted a policy of "war communism" nationalizing property

44. During the decolonization of the Cold War years, which of the following events occurred chronologically latest?
    a. The Eastern Bloc and Satellite states became independent from the Soviet Union
    b. Canada became totally independent from British Parliament via the Canada Act
    c. The Bahamas, in the Caribbean, became independent from the United Kingdom
    d. The Algerian War ended, and Algeria became independent from France

45. Why was U.S. industrialization confined to the Northeast until after the Civil War?
    a. Because the Civil War delayed the development of water-powered manufacturing
    b. Because the Northeast had faster-running rivers than the rivers found in the South
    c. Because Slater's first cotton mill with horse-drawn production lost so much money
    d. Because the technical innovations for milling textiles had not as yet been invented

46. Which of the following statements is *not* an accurate statement about the Puritans in England?
    a. The Puritans unconditionally gave all their support to the English Reformation
    b. The Puritans saw the Church of England as too much like the Catholic Church
    c. The Puritans became a chief political power because of the English Civil War
    d. The Puritans' clergy mainly departed from the Church of England after 1662

47. Which of the following statements is true regarding the Puritans?
    a. In terms of their theology, the Puritans were considered Calvinists
    b. Many Puritans agreed with the radical criticisms of the Swiss Calvinists
    c. Many of those identified as Calvinists opposed the Puritans
    d. All these statements are true regarding the Puritan movement

48. A monotheistic religious practice was central to which of the following cultures?
    a. Egyptians.
    b. Hebrews.
    c. Sumerians.
    d. Babylonians.

49. Which of the following statements is *not* true about the Gilded Age in America?
    a. The Gilded Age was the era of the "robber barons" in the business world
    b. The Gilded Age got its name from the excesses of the wealthy upper class
    c. The Gilded Age had philanthropy Carnegie called the "Gospel of Wealth"
    d. The Gilded Age is a term whose origins have not been identified clearly

50. Which of the following is *not* true about Democracy and the formation of the United States?
    a. The founding fathers stated in the Constitution that the USA would be a democracy
    b. The Declaration of Independence did not dictate democracy but stated its principles
    c. The United States Constitution stipulated that government be elected by the people
    d. The United States Constitution had terms to protect some, but not all, of the people

51. Who wrote about the concept of the Social Contract, which was incorporated into the Declaration of Independence?
    a. Thomas Hobbes
    b. John Locke
    c. Neither of these
    d. Both of these

52. Which of the following statements does *not* describe the average European diet before the expansion of trade routes?
    a. Europeans ate for survival, not enjoyment.
    b. They had an abundance of preservatives such as salt that could make food last longer.
    c. Grain-based foods such as porridge and bread were staple meals.
    d. Spices were unavailable.

53. Which of the following statements is *not* true of daily life for the average European in the 1500s?
    a. Life was not significantly different from the medieval era.
    b. The majority of people worked in agriculture.
    c. Life expectancy was short.
    d. Most people were literate, due to well-financed public education programs.

54. Which of these is true concerning the French Revolution, America, and Europe?
    a. When France's revolution spread and they went to war with other European countries, George Washington allied with the French.
    b. During the time period around 1792, American merchants were trading with countries on both sides of the war.
    c. American traders conducted business with various countries, profiting the most from the British West Indies.
    d. The Spanish navy retaliated against America for trading with the French by capturing American trading ships.

55. Which group overtook Rome in the mid-600s B.C. and established much of its infrastructure, including sewers, roads, and fortifications, only to be driven out of the city in 509 B.C.?
    a. Latins.
    b. Etruscans.
    c. Greeks.
    d. Persians.

56. The writers of The Federalist Papers published under the pen name "Publius." Who were the authors?
    a. James Madison, John Jay, and Alexander Hamilton
    b. George Washington, Thomas Jefferson, and James Madison
    c. Alexander Hamilton, Benjamin Franklin, and Thomas Jefferson
    d. Benjamin Franklin, John Jay, and Thomas Jefferson

57. What demographics have recently shown support for Democratic candidates?
    a. Men and young voters
    b. Women and young voters
    c. Women and gun owners
    d. Men and gun owners

58. One reason the Articles of Confederation created a weak government was because it limited Congress's ability to do what?
    a. Declare war
    b. Conduct a census
    c. Vote
    d. Tax

59. The philosophy of the late 17th-18th centuries that influenced the Constitution was from the Age of:
    a. Enlightenment
    b. Empire
    c. Discovery
    d. Industry

60. The votes of how many states were needed to ratify the Constitution?
    a. Five
    b. Ten
    c. Nine
    d. Seven

61. Power divided between local and central branches of government is a definition of what term?
    a. Bicameralism
    b. Checks and balances
    c. Legislative oversight
    d. Federalism

62. The Senate and the House of Representatives are an example of:
    a. Bicameralism
    b. Checks and balances
    c. Legislative oversight
    d. Federalism

63. When the Senate held an impeachment hearing against Andrew Johnson for overstepping his authority, what did they invoke?
    a. Checks and balances
    b. Bicameralism
    c. Legislative oversight
    d. Supremacy

64. Which statement describes the authority of most local officials?
   a. Members of local government are generally elected by the people, but their authority is granted by the state
   b. Members of local government are given their authority directly from the people
   c. Members of local government have constitutionally-granted authority
   d. Members of local government are elected by the people, but the state Supreme Court determines their authority

65. The Animal and Plant Health Inspection Service, the Food and Nutrition Service, and the Forest Service are members of which department?
   a. The Department of Health and Human Services
   b. The Department of Agriculture
   c. The Department of the Interior
   d. The Department of Transportation

66. A filibuster is used to delay a bill. Where can a filibuster take place?
   I.   The House
   II.   The Senate
   III. Committees
   a. I only
   b. II only
   c. I and II
   d. I, II, and III

67. Which organization is maintained by Congress to oversee the effectiveness of government spending?
   a. The House Committee on Oversight and Government Reform
   b. The Office of Management and Budget
   c. Government Accountability Office
   d. The Department of the Interior

68. The civil rights act that outlawed segregation in schools and public places also:
   a. Gave minorities the right to vote
   b. Established women's right to vote
   c. Outlawed unequal voter registration
   d. Provided protection for children

69. How many Southern states originally ratified the 14th Amendment?
   a. Three
   b. Five
   c. One
   d. Ten

70. Senators were originally chosen by state legislatures. In what year was the constitution amended to allow for them to be elected by popular vote?
   a. 1826
   b. 1891
   c. 1913
   d. 1935

71. How many judges are on a panel that decides federal appeals?
    a. Five
    b. Three
    c. Nine
    d. Six

72. What petition needs to be filed to request that the Supreme Court hear a case?
    a. Writ of certiorari
    b. Writ of habeas corpus
    c. Writ of mandamus
    d. Writ of attachment

73. Every citizen 18 years of age and older has the constitutional right to vote. What do states govern in the voting process?
    a. The registration for elections
    b. The administration of elections
    c. Both A and B
    d. State governments are not involved in federal elections

74. The Supreme Court has nine members. How is this number determined?
    a. It is outlined in the Constitution
    b. Congress determines the number
    c. The President determines the number
    d. The Court decides on the number

75. What are campaign funds given directly to a candidate called?
    a. Soft money
    b. Hard money
    c. Bundling
    d. Independent expenditure

76. Presidential candidates are eligible for public funding if they raise $5,000 per state in how many states?
    a. Twenty
    b. Ten
    c. Twenty-five
    d. Seventeen

77. What judicial system did America borrow from England?
    a. Due process
    b. Federal law
    c. Commerce law
    d. Common law

78. Most state governments have a bicameral legislature. Which one of the following states does not?
    a. Utah
    b. Nebraska
    c. Washington
    d. Louisiana

79. What is the main difference between a primary election and a caucus?
   a. A primary election is privately run by political parties, and a caucus is held by local governments
   b. Caucuses are always held on the same day, but the dates of state primaries vary
   c. A caucus is privately run by political parties, and a primary is an indirect election run by state and local governments
   d. Primary elections are all held on the same date, but the dates of caucuses vary

80. Who negotiates treaties?
   a. The President
   b. The House of Representatives
   c. Ambassadors
   d. The Senate

81. Delegates awarded to Puerto Rico, Guam, and American Samoa in the Democratic National Convention are:
   a. PLEO delegates
   b. Base delegates
   c. District delegates
   d. Bonus delegates

82. The shortest distance between New York and Paris goes
   a. over Florida and Spain.
   b. along the 42nd parallel.
   c. over Labrador and Greenland.
   d. over Philadelphia and London.

83. On which type of map are different countries represented in different colors, with no two adjacent countries sharing a color?
   a. Physical map
   b. Political map
   c. Climate map
   d. Contour map

84. On a map of Africa, there is a small box around Nairobi. This city is depicted in greater detail in a box at the bottom of the map. What is the name for this box at the bottom of the map?
   a. Inset
   b. Legend
   c. Compass Rose
   d. Key

85. Which of the following gives the clearest relative location of Milwaukee?
   a. in Wisconsin
   b. on Lake Michigan
   c. 44° N, 88° W
   d. 100 miles north of Chicago

86. On which type of map would Nigeria be bigger than Australia?
    a. Contour map of elevation
    b. Flow-line map of the spice trade
    c. Mercator projection
    d. Cartogram of population

87. Which of the following are not included in a geographical definition of Southeast Asia?
    a. Myanmar, Laos, Cambodia, and Thailand
    b. Vietnam, the Malay Peninsula, and Brunei
    c. East Malaysia, Indonesia, and the Philippines
    d. These are all geographical parts of Southeast Asia

88. How many intermediate directions are there?
    a. 2
    b. 4
    c. 8
    d. 16

89. What is the name for a line that connects points with equal total rainfall?
    a. Isotherm
    b. Isoline
    c. Isobar
    d. Isohyet

90. Which part of a hurricane features the strongest winds and greatest rainfall?
    a. Eye wall
    b. Front
    c. Eye
    d. Outward spiral

91. What is the most common type of volcano on earth?
    a. Lava dome
    b. Composite volcano
    c. Shield volcano
    d. Cinder cone

92. Which map describes the movement of people, trends, or materials across a physical area?
    a. Political Map
    b. Cartogram
    c. Qualitative Map
    d. Flow-line Map

93. Which of the following exemplifies the multiplier effect of large cities?
    a. The presence of specialized equipment for an industry attracts even more business.
    b. The large population lowers the price of goods.
    c. Public transportation means more people can commute to work.
    d. A local newspaper can afford to give away the Sunday edition.

94. Where is the area of greatest corn production?
    a. South Africa
    b. Kazakhstan
    c. United States
    d. Mexico

95. Thai food has become increasingly popular in the United States, though it is prepared in slightly different ways here. This is an example of
    a. Cultural divergence.
    b. Assimilation.
    c. Cultural convergence.
    d. Acculturation.

96. Which type of chart is best at representing the cycle of demographic transition?
    a. Pie chart
    b. Political map
    c. Line graph
    d. Flow-line map

97. Last year, 4 residents of Henrytown died. The population of Henrytown is 500. What is the death rate of Henrytown?
    a. 1
    b. 4
    c. 8
    d. 12

98. In which stage of demographic transition does fertility remain high while mortality declines?
    a. High stationary stage
    b. Early expanding stage
    c. Late expanding stage
    d. Low stationary stage

99. Which of the following countries are separated by a geometric border?
    a. Turkish Cyprus and Greek Cyprus
    b. North Korea and South Korea
    c. France and Spain
    d. England and Ireland

100. On a political map of India, the northernmost part of the border with Pakistan is represented as a dotted line. Why is this so?
    a. Pakistan does not have control of this border.
    b. This area has never been comprehensively mapped.
    c. Indian Sikhs are threatening to secede.
    d. The borders of the Kashmir region remain in dispute.

101. The price of oil drops dramatically, saving soda pop manufacturers great amounts of money spent on making soda pop and delivering their product to market. Prices for soda pop, however, stay the same. This is an example of what?
    a. Sticky prices
    b. Sticky wages
    c. The multiplier effect
    d. Aggregate expenditure

102. John Maynard Keynes advocated what?
    a. Supply-side economics
    b. Demand-side economics
    c. Laissez faire economics
    d. The Laffer Curve

103. Assume a society has a given production possibilities frontier (PPF) representing the production of guns and butter. Which of the following would cause the PPF to move outward?
    a. The invention of a new machine that makes guns more efficiently
    b. An increase in the production of butter
    c. An increase in the production of guns
    d. A decrease in the production of guns and butter

104. Which of the following is a supply shock likely to produce?
        I.   An increase in input prices
        II.   An increase in price levels
        III.   A decrease in employment
        IV.   A decrease in GDP
    a. I and III only
    b. II and IV only
    c. I, II, and III only
    d. I, II, III, and IV

105. Which of the following would *not* cause aggregate supply (AS) to change?
    a. An increase or decrease in land availability
    b. The labor force suddenly increases dramatically
    c. A new oil discovery causes dramatic decreases in power production
    d. Worker productivity remains the same

106. Assume that aggregate demand (AD) decreases. How will this decrease affect real GDP if there is a lot of unemployment as opposed to full employment?
    a. If there is a lot of unemployment, prices will rise dramatically
    b. If there is a lot of unemployment, GDP will stay the same
    c. If there is full employment, GDP will increase dramatically
    d. None of the above

107. Assume that aggregate demand is at AD1 and the government borrows money and then spends that money in order to attempt to move aggregate demand to AD3. According to the theory of "crowding out," where is AD likely to wind up?

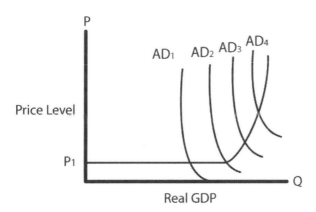

a. AD1
b. AD2
c. AD3
d. AD4

108. Which of the following will bring about greater income equity in a society?
    a. imposing a progressive income tax.
    b. imposing high estate taxes.
    c. imposing a gift tax.
    d. All of the above

Consider the following table to answer Question 109:

Inputs	1	2	3	4
Output	20	50	80	100

109. What does the data in this table most directly describe?
    a. The Law of Diminishing Marginal Returns
    b. Law of Increasing Opportunity Cost
    c. Law of Demand
    d. Consumer surplus

110. Ivy loses her job because her skills as a seamstress are no longer required due to a new piece of machinery that does the work of a seamstress more quickly and for less money. Which type of unemployment is this?
    a. Frictional
    b. Structural
    c. Cyclical
    d. Careless

111. Which is considered part of the natural rate of unemployment?
    I.   Structural unemployment
    II.   Frictional unemployment
    III. Cyclical unemployment
    a. I only
    b. II only
    c. III only
    d. I and II only

112. Inflation has what effects?
    a. Harms all members of an economy
    b. Helps all members of an economy
    c. Harms no members of an economy
    d. Harms some members of an economy, helps others

113. Hyperinflation is most likely to be associated with:
    I.   Demand-pull inflation
    II.   Cost-push inflation
    a. I
    b. II
    c. I and II
    d. I or II

114. Which of the following is not a part of the business cycle?
    a. Expansion
    b. Contraction
    c. Recovery
    d. Stagflation

115. Assume a nation's economy is in recession. The nation has an MPC of 0.9 and the government wants to enact fiscal policy to shift the AD curve by $10 billion dollars. What must the government do to its current spending rate?
    a. Decrease spending by $10 billion
    b. Increase spending by $10 billion
    c. Decrease spending by $1 billion
    d. Increase spending by $1 billion

116. How do banks create money?
    a. By printing it
    b. By taking it out of the Federal Reserve
    c. By loaning it out
    d. By putting it into the Federal Reserve

117. Which of the following might happen if the FOMC uses Treasury Bills to pursue a contractionary monetary policy?
    a. The money supply decreases
    b. The international value of the American dollar increases
    c. The price of US goods to foreigners increases
    d. All of the above

118. Which of the following correctly states the equation of exchange?
    a. MV = PQ
    b. MP x VQ
    c. P / VQ
    d. VP = MQ

119. Which of the following best defines American GDP?
    a. The value, in American dollars, of all goods and services produced within American borders during one calendar year
    b. The value, in American dollars, of all goods and services produced by American companies during one calendar year
    c. The total value, in American dollars, of all American household incomes during one calendar year
    d. The value, in American dollars, of a "market basket" of goods and services in one year divided by the value of the same market basket in a previous year multiplied by 100

120. "Self-actualization" is a term associated with the _____ approach to understanding human behavior
    a. Behaviorist
    b. Humanistic
    c. Psychodynamic
    d. All of the above

121. Which of the following is *not* one of the Big Five personality traits?
    a. Aggression
    b. Conscientiousness
    c. Extroversion
    d. Neuroticism

122. Sigmund Freud is associated with which of the following approaches?
    a. Behaviorist
    b. Humanistic
    c. Psychodynamic
    d. None of the above

123. The train tracks seemed to be moving as I drove by the stationary train. Which of the following terms would explain this?
    a. Difference threshold
    b. Interposition
    c. Linear perspective
    d. Motion parallax

124. According to George Murdock, which of the following is *not* a general characteristic of all cultural practices?
    a. Religion
    b. Folklore
    c. Property disputes
    d. Laws

125. A father from a patriarchal society who passes on his property to his youngest son is practicing:
   a. Ultimogeniture
   b. Primogeniture
   c. Neolocality
   d. Patrilocality

126. Of the factors listed below, which one is *not* among Max Weber's independent factors associated with his theory of social stratification?
   a. Social class
   b. Personal power
   c. Social status
   d. Race

127. The sociologist who is credited with developing the action theory of society is:
   a. Talcott Parsons
   b. Robert Merton
   c. C. Wright Mills
   d. Dennis Wong.

128. Which of the following questions would most likely be asked by a historian concerned with the philosophy of history?
   a. What issues shaped the writing of Plato's Republic?
   b. Should history be measured by changes in individual lives or by larger political trends?
   c. Why were the religions of Shinto and Buddhism able to merge in Japan?
   d. Should historians study modern primitive cultures as a means of learning about past civilizations?

129. Which of the following is *not* necessarily an example of an educator introducing his own bias into the educational process?
   a. A teacher only using materials and sources that he knows are reputable and declining to use unverified material in his lessons.
   b. A textbook author choosing to only use sources that place his favorite U.S. president in a good light and his least favorite U.S. president in a bad light.
   c. A teacher only using primary sources that he agrees with and ridiculing a student who provides a verifiable primary source that offers a conflicting opinion.
   d. All of the above are examples of bias

Use the following statistical table to answer Question 130

Median U.S. income by amount of schooling, in dollars
Source: U.S. Census Bureau, Current Population Survey, Annual Social and Economic Supplements.

Year	9-12th grade, no diploma	High School graduate	Some College, no degree	Associates Degree	Bachelors Degree or higher
2007	24,492	40,456	50,419	60,132	84,508
2002	23,267	35,646	45,333	51,058	73,600
1997	19,851	33,779	40,015	45,258	63,292

130. Which of the following could you infer from the data presented above?
    a. Persons without a high school diploma receive smaller monetary increases in their income than persons with a high school diploma.
    b. Increased education increases a person's earning potential
    c. Income generally increases over time.
    d. All of the above

Constructed Response

It is our duty now to begin to lay the plans and determine the strategy for the winning of a lasting peace and the establishment of an American standard of living higher than ever before known. We cannot be content, no matter how high that general standard of living may be, if some fraction of our people—whether it be one-third or one-fifth or one-tenth—is ill-fed, ill-clothed, ill-housed, and insecure...We have come to a clear realization of the fact that true individual freedom cannot exist without economic security and independence...People who are hungry and out of a job are the stuff of which dictatorships are made.
President Franklin Delano Roosevelt, State of the Union Address, January 11, 1944

1. Describe how the passage above justifies President Franklin Roosevelt's domestic policy during his presidency.

If evils will result from the commingling of the two races upon public highways established for the benefit of all, they will be infinitely less than those that will surely come from state legislation regulating the enjoyment of civil rights upon the basis of race. We boast of the freedom enjoyed by our people above all other peoples. But it is difficult to reconcile that boast with a state of the law which, practically, puts the brand of servitude and degradation upon a large class of our fellow-citizens, our equals before the law. The thin disguise of 'equal' accommodations for passengers in railroad coaches will not mislead any one, nor atone for the wrong this day done.
Supreme Court Justice John Marshall Harlan, *Plessy v. Ferguson* dissenting opinion

2. Briefly describe how the events in the decades that followed the *Plessy v. Ferguson* decision either confirmed or refuted the quote above taken Justice Harlan's dissent in *Plessy v. Ferguson*.

3. Discuss how the concept of "liberty" was used by proponents of either side in their arguments in the *Plessy v. Ferguson* case.

Answers and Explanations

1. D: Of those countries listed here, the two countries whose respective indigenous populations are not as large as the populations of the other countries are Argentina and Uruguay. Argentina's population is approximately 86.4% of European descent, roughly 8% of mestizo (of mixed European and Amerindian heritage), and an estimated 4% of Arab or East Asian ancestry. Uruguay's population is estimated to be 88% of European descent, 4% of African, and 2% of Asian, with 6% of mestizo ancestry in its rural northwest region. Guatemala and Peru (a) have larger indigenous populations. Guatemala, in Central America, has approximately over 40% of its population as Indigenous peoples. Peru, in South America, is estimated to have 45% indigenous peoples and 37% partly indigenous peoples for a total of 82%. Ecuador and Bolivia (b) in South America still have indigenous peoples. The population of Ecuador has an estimated 25% indigenous and 65% partly indigenous peoples, for a total of 90%. Paraguay in South America and Mexico in North America (c) both have sizeable indigenous populations. Paraguay's population is estimated to include 95% partly indigenous peoples. Mexico is estimated to have 30% indigenous and 60% partly indigenous peoples in its population for a total of 90%. El Salvador and Honduras in Central America also still have numbers of indigenous peoples. The population of El Salvador is estimated to include 90% partly indigenous peoples and 8% purely indigenous peoples for a total of 98%. Honduras is estimated to have 90% partly indigenous and 7% purely indigenous peoples for a total of 97% of its population.

2. A: It is not true that England's defeat of the Spanish Armada in 1588 ended their war with Spain. It did establish England's naval dominance and strengthened England's future colonization of the New World, but the actual war between England and Spain did not end until 1604. It is true that Henry VIII's desire to divorce Catherine of Aragon strengthened English expansionism (b). Catherine was Spanish, and Henry split from the Catholic Church because it prohibited divorce. Henry's rejection of his Spanish wife and his subsequent support of the Protestant movement angered King Philip II of Spain and destroyed the formerly close ties between the two countries. When Elizabeth became Queen of England, she supported the Reformation as a Protestant, which also contributed to English colonization (c). Sir Francis Drake, one of the best known English sea captains during this time period, would attack and plunder Spanish ships that had plundered American Indians (d), adding to the enmity between Spain and England. Queen Elizabeth invested in Drake's voyages and gave him her support in claiming territories for England.

3. B: The Virginia Company of London was based in London, not Massachusetts. It had a charter to colonize American land between the Hudson and Cape Fear rivers (c). The other Virginia Company was the Virginia Company of Plymouth, which was based in the American colony of Plymouth, Massachusetts (a). It had a charter to colonize North America between the Potomac River and the northern boundary of Maine (d). Both Virginia Companies were joint-stock companies, which had often been used by England for trading with other countries.

4. D: It is not true that John Smith's governance helped Jamestown more than John Rolfe's discovery that a certain type of East Indian tobacco could be grown in Virginia. Smith's strong leadership from 1608-1609 gave great support to the struggling colony. However, when Smith's return to England left Jamestown without this support, the future of the colony was again in question. In 1612, however, when John Rolfe found that an East Indian tobacco strain popular in Europe could be farmed in Virginia, the discovery gave Jamestown and Virginia a lucrative crop. Therefore, both Smith's time in office and Rolfe's discovery were beneficial to Jamestown. Jamestown was established by the Virginia Company of London in 1607 (a), and

it became the first permanent settlement by the English in North America (b). It is also true that Jamestown survived in spite of the fact that most of its early settlers died from starvation, disease, and Indian attacks (c). It is also true that many of Jamestown's settlers came from the English upper class and were unwilling to farm the land, while others came hoping to find gold or other treasures, and persisted in their search for these instead of working to make the land sustainable.

5. C: Hernando Cortes conquered the Mexican Aztecs in 1519. He had several advantages over the Indians, including horses, armor for his soldiers, and guns. In addition, Cortes' troops unknowingly transmitted smallpox to the Aztecs, which devastated their population as they had no immunity to this foreign illness. Vasco Nunez de Balboa (a) was the first European explorer to view the Pacific Ocean when he crossed the Isthmus of Panama in 1513. Juan Ponce de Leon (b) also visited and claimed Florida in Spain's name in 1513. Cabeza de Vaca (d) was one of only four men out of 400 to return from an expedition led by Panfilio de Narvaez in 1528, and was responsible for spreading the story of the Seven Cities of Cibola (the "cities of gold"). Hernando de Soto led an expedition from 1539-1541 to the southeastern part of America.

6. A: The attitudes of American colonists after the 1763 Treaty of Paris ended the French and Indian War was not a direct contributor to the American Revolution. American colonists had a supportive attitude toward Great Britain then, and were proud of the part they played in winning the war. Their good will was not returned by British leaders (b), who looked down on American colonials and sought to increase their imperial power over them. Even in 1761, a sign of Americans' objections to having their liberty curtailed by the British was seen when Boston attorney James Otis argued in court against the Writs of Assistance (c), search warrants to enforce England's mercantilist trade restrictions, as violating the kinds of natural laws espoused during the Enlightenment. Lord George Grenville's aggressive program to defend the North American frontier in the wake of Chief Pontiac's attacks included stricter enforcement of the Navigation Acts, the Proclamation of 1763, the Sugar Act (or Revenue Act), the Currency Act, and most of all the Stamp Act (d). Colonists objected to these as taxation without representation. Other events followed in this taxation dispute, which further eroded Americans' relationship with British government, including the Townshend Acts, the Massachusetts Circular Letter, the Boston Massacre, the Tea Act, and the resulting Boston Tea Party. Finally, with Britain's passage of the Intolerable Acts and the Americans' First Continental Congress, which was followed by Britain's military aggression against American resistance, actual warfare began in 1775. While not all of the colonies wanted war or independence by then, things changed by 1776, and Jefferson's Declaration of Independence was formalized. James Otis, Samuel Adams, Patrick Henry, the Sons of Liberty, and the Stamp Act Congress also contributed to the beginning of the American Revolution.

7. C: Colonists did find that tea shipped directly by the British East India Company cost less than smuggled Dutch tea, even with tax. The colonists, however, did not buy it. They refused, despite its lower cost, on the principle that the British were taxing colonists without representation (d). It is true that the British East India Company lost money as a result of colonists buying tea smuggled from Holland (a). They sought to remedy this problem by getting concessions from Parliament to ship tea directly to the colonies instead of going through England (b) as the Navigation Acts normally required. Boston Governor Thomas Hutchinson, who sided with Britain, stopped tea ships from leaving the harbor, which after 20 days would cause the tea to be sold at auction. At that time, British taxes on the tea would be paid. On the 19th night after Hutchinson's action, American protestors held the Boston Tea Party, dressing as Indians and dumping all the tea into the harbor to destroy it so it could not be taxed and sold. Many American colonists disagreed with the Boston Tea Party because it involved destroying private property. When Lord North and the British Parliament responded by passing the Coercive Acts and the Quebec Act, known collectively in America as the Intolerable Acts, Americans changed their minds, siding with the Bostonians against the British.

8. D: Paul Revere (a) and William Dawes (b) were both dispatch riders who set out on horseback from Massachusetts to spread news of British troop movements across the American countryside around the beginning of the War of Independence. John Parker (c) was the captain of the Minutemen militia, who were waiting for the British at Lexington, Massachusetts.

9. C: Massachusetts did set a valuable example for other states by stipulating that its constitution should be created via a special convention rather than via the legislature. This way, the constitution would take precedence over the legislature, which would be subject to the rules of the constitution. It is not true that twelve states had new constitutions by the end of 1777 (a). By this time, ten of the states had new constitutions. It is not true that Connecticut and Massachusetts retained their colonial charters minus the British parts (b). Connecticut and Rhode Island were the states that preserved their colonial charters. They simply removed any parts referring to British rule. Massachusetts did not formalize its new constitution in 1778 (d). This state did not actually finish the process of adopting its new constitution until 1780. Finally, it is not true that Pennsylvania began with a viable constitution featuring checks and balances. It is true that Maryland and Virginia did initially provide such workable constitutions. Pennsylvania, however, began with such a hyper-democratic document with so little in the way of checks and balances that officials found it impossible to manage and quickly got rid of it, eventually coming up with a more reasonable constitution.

10. D: The Louisiana Purchase actually increased the U.S.'s territory by 100% overnight, not 50%. The Louisiana territory doubled the size of the nation. It is true that Jefferson initially sent a delegation to Paris to see if Napoleon would agree to sell only New Orleans to the United States (a). It is also true that Napoleon, who expected America to encroach on Louisiana, decided to avoid this by offering to sell the entire territory to the U.S. (b). It is likewise true that America only had authority to buy New Orleans. Nevertheless, the delegation accepted Napoleon's offer of all of Louisiana (c). Due to his belief in strict interpretation of the Constitution, Jefferson did require approval from Congress to make the purchase. When his advisors characterized the purchase as being within his purview based on the presidential power to make treaties, Congress agreed.

11. A: By 1840, more than one third of all Americans lived west of the Alleghenies, but not two thirds. It is correct that in the first half of the 19th century, the American population doubled every 25 years (b). It is also correct that westward expansion increased as more people moved west (c) during these years. It is correct that there was not a lot of immigration to the U.S. from other countries before 1820 (d). It is also true that foreign immigration to America increased quickly around that time, with most immigrants coming from the British Isles.

12. A: The U.S. did carry out a three-pronged invasion of Canada early in the war, but they did not succeed on two fronts. Instead, they lost on all three. Americans did win sea battles against the British early in the war, but were soon beaten back to their homeports and then blockaded by powerful British warships (b). Admiral Perry did defeat the British on Lake Erie on September 10, 1813 (c). Perry's victory allowed William Henry Harrison to invade Canada (d) in October of 1813, where he defeated British and Indians in the Battle of the Thames. *Old Ironsides* was one of the ships that won early naval battles during the war before Britain drove American ships to retreat.

13. B: Growth in labor organizing was stimulated by organizers wanting to achieve the goal of a shorter workday. However, what they were aiming for in the 1800s was a 10-hour day, not an 8-hour day, which was not realized until 1936. It is true that when the factory system supplanted the cottage industry, owners and workers became separate, and this depersonalized workplaces (a). Child laborers did conduct the first organized workers' strike in Paterson, N.J., in 1828 (c). Although the first strike did occur this early, there were not a lot of strikes or labor negotiations during this time period due to periodic

downturns in the economy (d), which had the effect of keeping workers dependent and less likely to take action against management. The campaign to attain a 10-hour work day did stimulate a period of growth in labor organizing, but this growth period ended with the depression of 1837.

14. C: Thomas Jefferson did describe a plan for Virginia to have a free school, but it was not realized. Jefferson's plan was never implemented. It is true that there were really no public schools worth mentioning in America before around 1815 (a). Once there were schools, they were mainly paid for by private organizations – corporate ones in the Northeastern states and religious ones in the Southern and Mid-Atlantic states (b). America's early schools did cater to rich people, and specialized in providing academic instruction to males (d). The few schools for females in existence taught homemaking and fine arts rather than academic subjects. The New York Free School was a very unusual instance of an early American school that provided education for the poor. This school tried out the Lancastrian system, wherein older students tutor younger students, which not only employed a sound educational principle, but also helped the school to operate within its limited budget.

15. D: Political corruption was not an immediate effect of the rapid urban growth during this time. The accelerated growth of cities in America did soon result in services being unable to keep up with that growth. The results of this included deficiencies in clean water delivery and garbage collection, causing poor sanitation (a). That poor sanitation led to outbreaks of cholera and typhus, as well as typhoid fever epidemics (b). Police and fire fighting services could not keep up with the population increases, and were often inadequate (c). With people moving to the cities at such a fast rate, there were also deficits in housing and public transportation.

16. D: All the laws named were instrumental in spurring westward migration to the Great Plains. The Homestead Act (a), passed in 1862, gave settlers 160 acres of land at no monetary cost in exchange for a commitment to cultivating the land for five years. The Timber Culture Act (b), passed in 1873, gave the settlers 160 acres more of land in exchange for planting trees on one quarter of the acreage. The Desert Land Act (c), passed in 1877, allowed buyers who would irrigate the land to buy 640 acres for only 25 cents an acre. Thus,, all of these laws were instrumental to spurring westward migration to the Great Plains during that period, is correct.

17. B: Germany's declaration of war on Russia in 1914, following the assassination of Archduke Ferdinand (b), did not contribute to ending American neutrality in World War I. Once Germany declared war, England, France, Italy, Russia, and Japan joined as the Allied Powers against the Central Powers of Germany and Austria-Hungary, and US President Woodrow Wilson declared America's neutrality. When Germany designated the area surrounding the British Isles as a war zone in February 1913 (a), and warned all ships from neutral countries to stay out of the zone, an end to American neutrality was prompted. President Wilson's responded to Germany's declaration by proclaiming that America would hold Germany responsible for any American losses of life or property. When Germany sank the British passenger vessel *Lusitania,* 128 American passengers were killed (c). This further eroded Wilson's resolve to remain neutral. In February 1917, Germany declared unrestricted submarine warfare on any ship in the war zone (d); this signified that ships from any country would face German attack. President Wilson's reaction to this declaration was to cease diplomatic relations with Germany. Meanwhile, England intercepted a telegram from Germany to Mexico asking Mexico to join forces with Germany.. This infuriated the American public. President Wilson then asked for a declaration of war on Germany on April 2, 1917, which Congress approved.

18. A: The postwar conference that brought US-Soviet differences to light was (a) the Potsdam conference in July of 1945. The conference at Yalta (b), in February of 1945, resulted in the division of Germany into Allied-controlled zones. The Dumbarton Oaks conference (c) (1944) established a Security Council, on

which with the US, England, Soviet Union, France, and China served as the five permanent members. Each of the permanent members had veto power, and a General Assembly, with limited power, was also established. The Tehran conference (d) included FDR's proposal for a new international organization to take the place of the League of Nations. This idea would later be realized in the form of the United Nations. Earlier in 1943, at the Casablanca Conference, President Roosevelt and Prime Minister Churchill agreed to a policy of unconditional surrender for all enemies of the Allied powers .

19. D: In 1956, Egypt did not attack Israel. On October 29, 1956, Israel attacked Egypt. England and France did join this war within two days. It is true that Egyptian President Gamal Abdul Nasser refused to take America's side in the Cold War (a). In reaction to his refusal, President Eisenhower's administration pulled its funding from the Aswan Dam project in Egypt (b). Nasser then nationalized the British-owned Suez Canal (c). Eisenhower further declared in 1957 that America would provide aid to any country in the Middle East facing Communist control. Pursuant to Eisenhower's declaration, the US invaded Lebanon in 1958 to resolve a conflict in government.

20. B: Reagan escalated military action in response to a terrorist bombing that killed 240 US Marines, is not true. Reagan sent the Marines to Lebanon in 1982 as part of a peacekeeping effort (d) after Israel invaded Lebanon on a mission to eradicate its PLO camps (a). At the time, Lebanon was already engaged in a civil war (c). When the terrorist attack killed 240 Marines, Reagan withdrew the rest of the troops rather than escalate the action. In 1988, an uprising of Palestinians known as the First Intifada started on the Jordan River's much-contested West Bank. In response to this uprising, Reagan initiated peace talks with the PLO's leader, Yasser Arafat. However, the goal of peace in the Middle East never materialized.

21. C: The person or group *not* instrumental in advancing civil rights and desegregation immediately after WWII was (c), Congress. As African American soldiers came home from the war, racial discord increased. President Harry Truman (a) appointed a Presidential Committee on Civil Rights in 1946. This committee published a report recommending that segregation and lynching be outlawed by the federal government. However, Congress ignored this report and took no action. Truman then used his presidential powers to enforce desegregation of the military and policies of "fair employment" in federal civil service jobs. The National Association for the Advancement of Colored People (NAACP) (d) brought lawsuits against racist and discriminatory practices, and in resolving these suits, the Supreme Court (b) further eroded segregation. For example, the Supreme Court ruled that primaries allowing only whites would be illegal, and it ended the segregation of interstate bus lines. The landmark civil rights laws were not passed by Congress until the 1960s

22. B: Of the programs enacted by Johnson, the one most closely related to JFK's legacy was (b), the Civil Rights Act, which Johnson pushed through Congress using allusions to Kennedy's and his goals. While Kennedy received congressional backing for a raise in minimum wage and public housing improvements, his efforts regarding civil rights were thwarted by conservative Republicans and Southern Democrats in Congress. However, as the Civil Rights movement progressed through the campaigns of the Freedom Riders, Kennedy developed a strong commitment to the cause.
The Economic Opportunity Act gave almost $1 billion to wage Johnson's War on Poverty. The Great Society (c) was Johnson's name for his comprehensive reform program which included a variety of legislation (see also question #102).

23. B: The GATT countries did agree to abolish or decrease many of their tariffs, but this agreement did not include only 57 countries. Then number of signatories was much larger, totaling 117 countries. The GATT was approved by Congress in 1994 (a). In addition to having 117 countries agree to increase free trade, the GATT also set up the World Trade Organization (WTO) for the purpose of settling any differences among nations related to trade (c). Another instance of free trade policy established in the

1990s was the Senate's ratification of NAFTA. The negotiation of this agreement was originally made by the first Bush administration, with President Bush and the leaders of Canada and Mexico signing it in 1992 (d), but it still needed to be ratified. When he was elected President following the senior Bush's second term, Bill Clinton also supported NAFTA, and the Senate ratified it in 1994.

24. D: It is not true that (d) the Waco siege at the Branch Davidian compound lasted for six months. In fact, once the FBI attacked the compound, the resulting siege lasted for 51 days. It is true that the Branch Davidians were a Protestant sect that had split off from the Seventh Day Adventists and lived on a compound near Waco, Texas (a). Following reports of gunfire and weapons caches there, the Bureau of Alcohol, Tobacco and Firearms (ATF) conducted surveillance and obtained a search warrant (b). When ATF attempted to execute the warrant, gunfire was exchanged between the compound and ATF agents, and four agents were killed, whereupon the FBI became involved and attacked the compound (c). Following the 51-day siege, the FBI gassed the main building as Davidians set several fires in the building. Various sources claim the deaths totaled 76-86. One of the fatalities was Branch Davidian leader David Koresh, whose original name was Vernon Wayne Howell. Note: Despite videotaped records, there is still much controversy surrounding this event.

25. B: There was not a reduction in military spending after the war. Although the manufacturing demand for war supplies and the size of the military decreased, the government had increased military spending from $10 billion in 1947 to more than $50 billion by 1953—a more than fivefold increase. This increase strengthened the American economy. Other factors contributing to the strengthened economy included the significantly higher birth rates during the Baby Boom (a) from 1946 to 1957, which stimulated the growth of the building and automotive industries by increased demand. Government programs, such as the GI Bill (the Servicemen's Readjustment Act of 1944), other veterans' benefits, and the National Defense Education Act all encouraged college enrollments, which increased by nearly four times (c). Additionally, larger families, increased mobility and low-interest loans offered to veterans led to suburban development and growth (d) as well as an increased home construction. Improvements in public health were also results of the new affluence; the rate of infant deaths decreased significantly, and as a result, from 1946-1957, the American life span rose from 67 to 71 years. Moreover, Dr. Jonas Salk developed the polio vaccine in 1955, which virtually wiped out poliomyelitis, preventing many deaths and disabilities in children.

26. D: The statement that the 1986 Immigration Reform and Control Act impeded illegal Mexican immigration is not true. This legislation punished employers with sanctions for hiring undocumented employees, but despite this the illegal immigration of Mexicans to America was largely unaffected by the law. It is true that twice as many people immigrated to America in the 1980s than in the 1970s (a): the number reached over nine million in the 80s. It is true that the majority of immigrants were Latin American (b). In addition to Latin Americans, other large groups of immigrants in the 1980s were Asians and Caribbean inhabitants (c).

27. C: T he Mississippi Freedom Democratic Party did attend the 1964 Democratic convention; however, they were unable garner Lyndon Johnson's support to unseat the regular delegation from Mississippi. A riot did break out in Watts in 1965 (a), and in the following three years, more riots occurred in Newark, N.J. (b) and in Detroit, Michigan (d). These riots were manifestations of the frustrations experienced by blacks regarding racial inequities in American society. Another demonstration of black unrest was the increasing activity of the Black Panthers and the Black Muslims in the 1960s. Both were militant organizations demanding civil rights reforms.

28. A: The earliest written language in Mesopotamia was Sumerian. Ancient Sumerians began writing this language around 3500 B.C.E. Elamite (b), from Iran, was the language spoken by the ancient Elamites and

was the official language of the Persian Empire from the 6th to 4th centuries B.C.E. Written Linear Elamite was used for a very short time in the late 3rd century B.C.E. The written Elamite cuneiform, used from about 2500 to 331 B.C.E., was an adaptation of the Akkadian (c) cuneiform. Akkadian is the earliest found Semitic language. Written Akkadian cuneiform first appeared in texts by circa 2800 B.C.E., and full Akkadian texts appeared by circa 2500 B.C.E. The Akkadian cuneiform writing system is ultimately a derivative of the ancient Sumerian cuneiform writing system, although these two spoken languages were not related linguistically. Aramaic (d) is another Semitic language, but unlike Akkadian, Aramaic is not now extinct. Old Aramaic, the written language of the Old Testament and the spoken language used by Jesus Christ, was current from c. 1100-200 C.E. Middle Aramaic, used from 200-1200 C.E., included literary Syriac (Christian groups developed the writing system of Syriac in order to be able to write spoken Aramaic) and was the written language of the Jewish books of Biblical commentary (Namely, the Talmud, the Targum, and the Midrash). Modern Aramaic has been used from 1200 to the present. Hurrian was the language spoken and written by the Hurrians or Khurrites, a people who migrated into Northern Mesopotamia, from circa 2300-1000 B.C.E. They are thought to have emigrated from Armenia, settled in Syria, and spread through Southeast Anatolia and Northern Mesopotamia, thereby establishing the Mitanni Kingdom in Northern Mesopotamia during that time period.

29. C: The New Kingdom was the period during which no more pyramids were built in Egypt. The Pyramids were built between the years of 2630 and 1814 B.C.E., and the New Kingdom spanned from circa 1550-1070 B.C. As a result, the last pyramid was built approximately 264 years before the New Kingdom began. 2630 B.C.E. marked the beginning of the reign of the first Pharaoh, Djoser, who had the first pyramid built at Saqqara. 1814 B.C.E. marked the end of the reign of the last Pharaoh, Amenemhat III, who had the last pyramid built at Hawara. In between these years, a succession of pharaohs built many pyramids. The Old Kingdom (a) encompasses both the Third (d) and Fourth Dynasties; therefore, all three of these choices encompass pyramid-building periods. Djoser's had his first pyramid built during the Third Dynasty (d). The Pharaohs Kufu, Khafre, and Menkaure, respectively, build the famous Pyramids of Giza during the Fourth Dynasty during their reigns at different times between circa 2575 and 2467 B.C.E., the period of the Fourth Dynasty. The Middle Kingdom (b) encompassed the 11th through 14th Dynasties, from circa. 2080 to 1640 B.C.E.—also within the time period (2630-1814 B.C.E.) when pyramids were built by the Pharaohs.

30. D: The ancient Indus Valley civilization, also known in its mature phase as the Harappan civilization, existed in what now encompasses all of the listed countries today. This culture flourished from circa 2600-1900 B.C.E., during the Bronze Age. This civilization included the most eastern portion of Balochistan in what is now Iran (a); the most western parts of what is now India (b); the majority of what is now Pakistan (c); and the southeastern part of Afghanistan.

31. B: Historians have determined that the Yellow River Valley in China began to develop into a cultural center during the Neolithic Era between c. 12,000-10,000 B.C.E. The Shang Dynasty (a) occurred between c. 1700-1046 B.C.E.—still part of the Ancient Era, but very long after the Neolithic era. The Xia Dynasty (c) ruled between circa 2100-1600 B.C.E., preceding the Shang Dynasty but still long after the Neolithic Era. The Paleolithic Era (d) came even before the Neolithic Era. Archaeological evidence exists of Homo erectus in China from more than a million years ago, during the Paleolithic Era, but the Yellow River Valley was not an emergent cultural center that long ago. The Zhou Dynasty ruled from circa 1066-221 B.C.E., later than the Neolithic Era, the Xia Dynasty, and overlapping with and then succeeding the Shang Dynasty.

32. D: Ancient Greek democracy was not completely open to all of the public. However, participating persons were not chosen or excluded based on their respective socioeconomic levels. The city-state of Athens had one of the first and most well-known democracies in ancient Greece (b). It began around 500

B.C.E. (a). The experiment of Athenian democracy was unique in that it was a direct democracy, meaning people voted directly for or against proposed legislation without any representation (c) such as the House of Representatives and the Senate, as we have in modern democracies.

33. C: The Druids were neither ignored nor tolerated by the Romans. Conversely, the Druids were viewed as "non-Roman" and therefore were suppressed. Augustus (63 B.C.E.-14 C.E.) forbade Romans to practice Druid rites. According to Pliny, the Senate under Tiberius (42 B.C.E.-37 C.E.) issued a decree suppressing Druids, and in 54 C.E., Claudius outlawed Druid rites entirely. It is correct that the Romans generally protected the Jews up until the rebellion in Judea in 66 C.E. (a). In fact, Julius Caesar circumvented the Roman laws against "secret societies" by designating Jewish synagogues as "colleges," which in essence permitted Jews to have freedom of worship (b). After the rebellion in Judea, according to Suetonius, the Emperor Claudius appeared to have expelled all Jews, probably including early Christians, from Rome. The Roman Empire viewed Christianity as a Jewish sect, which was how Christianity began, for 200 years following its emergence (d). It is also correct that according to Tacitus, when much of the public saw the Emperor Nero as responsible for the Great Fire of Rome in 64 C.E. (the origin of the old saying "Nero fiddled while Rome burned"), Nero blamed the Christians for the fire in order to deflect guilt from himself. Following their persecution of Jews, the Roman Empire would continue to persecute Christians for the next two centuries.

34. A: The earliest existing empire was the Kingdom of Ghana, also known as the Ghana Empire, from circa 790-1076, located north of modern-day Ghana. The Akan peoples formed the first of their states, Bono (b), after the Kingdom of Ghana fell around the turn of the 12th-13th centuries. The Akan peoples also established the Ashanti federation (c) and the states of the Fante people (d), but these existed later than Bono. The Fante repelled Portuguese colonizers in the 15th century. The Fante peoples still exist and never lost their state, despite the Ashanti Empire's expansion. (Kofi Annan, former Secretary General of the United Nations, is Fante, as is Ghanaian President John Atta Mills.) A number of conflicts have existed between the Fante and the Ashanti. The Empire of Ashanti formed first a loose confederation of city-states, then a centralized kingdom, in the 18th century, uniting much of sub-Saharan Africa until Europeans came to dominate the region.

35. B: It is not true that the Crusades succeeded at Christians' reclaiming the "holy land" (the Middle East) from Muslims. Despite their number (nine not counting the Northern Crusades) and longevity (1095-1291 not counting later similar campaigns), the Crusades never accomplished this purpose (a). While they did not take back the Middle East, the Crusades did succeed in exacerbating the decline of the Byzantine Empire (c), which lost more and more territory to the Ottoman Turks during this period. In addition, the Crusades resulted in Egypt's rise once again to become a major power (d) of the Middle East as it had been in the past. It is also true that during the Crusades, some Christians and Muslims became allies against common enemies. For example, during the Fifth Crusade, in Anatolia, Christian Crusaders with German, Dutch, Flemish, and Frisian soldiers allied themselves with the Sultanate of Rûm, a Seljuk Turk Sultanate that attacked the Ayyubids in Syria, in order to further their aim of attacking and capturing the port of Damietta in Egypt.

36. D: All these events contributed to the Italian Renaissance. After the Black Death killed a third of Europe's population (a), the survivors were mainly upper classes with more money to spend on art, architecture, and other luxuries. The plague deaths also resulted in a labor shortage, thereby creating more work opportunities for the surviving people in lower classes (b). As a result, these survivors' positions in society appreciated. Once plague deaths subsided and population growth in Europe began to reassert itself, a greater demand existed for products and services. At the same time, the number of people available to provide these products and services was still smaller than in the past. Consequently, more merchants, artisans, and bankers emerged in order to provide the services and products people

Copyright © Mometrix Media. You have been licensed one copy of this document for personal use only. Any other reproduction or redistribution is strictly prohibited. All rights reserved.

wanted, thereby creating a class of citizens between the lower class laborers and the upper class elite (c). After the two major Italian banks collapsed, wealthy investors who would normally have reinvested their disposable income did not do this, since the economy did not favor it. Instead, they invested their money in artistic and cultural products.

37. B: The rejection of classical antiquity as a source of education was not a characteristic of the European Renaissance. In fact, the opposite was true. The knowledge of the ancient classical civilizations temporarily was lost to Europeans during the middle ages. As a result, this time period often was called the "Dark Ages." After the fall of the Roman Empire, the loss of the unifying Roman rule eliminated the cultural exchange formerly facilitated by trading and other travel. Outside of the Catholic Church, illiteracy became widespread. The European Renaissance saw a revival of interest in classical sources of knowledge. During this period, Renaissance painters developed the use of linear perspective in art (a); reforms in education progressed gradually but spread widely over Europe (c); and scientists first began to use the Scientific Method for discovery (d), which required empirical evidence in order to support scientists' ideas.

38. B: In order to prosper, a nation should not try to increase its imports. Mercantilism is an economic theory including the idea that prosperity comes from a positive balance of international trade. For any one nation to prosper, that nation should increase its exports (c) but decrease its imports. Exporting more to other countries while importing less from them will give a country a positive trade balance. This theory assumes that money and wealth are identical (a) assets of a nation. In addition, this theory also assumes that the volume of global trade is an unchangeable quantity. Mercantilism dictates that a nation's government should apply a policy of economic protectionism (d) by stimulating more exports and suppressing imports. Some ways to do accomplish this task have included granting subsidies for exports and imposing tariffs on imports. Mercantilism can be regarded as essentially the opposite of the free trade policies that have been encouraged in more recent years.

39. D: Resentment against the Protestant Reformation was not a cause given for the French Revolution. Choices (a), (b), and (c) are just a few among many causes cited for the war. Famines caused malnutrition and even starvation among the poorest people (a). Escalating bread prices contributed greatly to the hunger. Louis XV had amassed a great amount of debt from spending money on many wars in addition to the American Revolution. Military failures as well as a lack of social services for veterans exacerbated these debts. In addition, the Court of Louis XVI and Marie Antoinette spent excessively and obviously on luxuries even while people in the country were starving, and France's monetary system was outdated, inefficient, and thus unable to manage the national debt (b). Much of the populace greatly resented the Catholic Church's control of the country (c). However, there was not great resentment against the Protestant Reformation (d); there were large minorities of Protestants in France, who not only exerted their influence on government institutions, but undoubtedly also contributed to the resentment of the Catholic Church. Because (d) is not a cause of the French Revolution as the other choices are, answer, all of these, is incorrect.

40. B: The only true statement is the March on Versailles was made primarily by women. Therefore, an equal number of both men and women did not undertake the March on Versailles (a). The women took action because of the dire economic conditions from which they suffered, especially the high prices on bread and food shortages. The storming of the Bastille occurred on July 14, 1789; the March on Versailles occurred on October 5, 1789, almost three months later, not prior to it (c). (The date of July 14th is so famous as Bastille Day in France that generally it is familiar in other countries as well.) It is not true that the March on Versailles was not effective in accomplishing its purpose (d). In fact, the marchers did achieve their goal: They stormed the palace and killed several guards. La Fayette, in charge of the National Guard to control the mob, convinced the royals to move from Versailles to Paris and to stop blocking the

National Assembly, and the royal family complied with these demands. The women did not march right to Versailles with no preliminaries. First, they assembled in markets around Paris and marched to the Hôtel de Ville. There they made their demands of the Paris city officials. When those officials did not give acceptable responses, the women then joined a march to the palace at Versailles. While the march to Versailles included men and weapons, some 7,000 women made up the majority of the marchers.

41. C: The only accurate statement about the end of WWI is that President Wilson had proposed that the nations of the world form a coalition to prevent future world wars. While he did not give the coalition a name, he clearly expressed his proposal that such a group form in the fourteenth of his Fourteen Points. The Treaty of Versailles (1919) did not bring peace among all countries involved in the war (a); Germany and the United States arrived at a separate peace in 1921. Furthermore, the Treaty of Versailles did not contain a clause for establishing the United Nations (b); it contained a clause for establishing the League of Nations. The League of Nations was created as dictated by the treaty, but when the Second World War proved that this group had failed to prevent future world wars, it was replaced by the United Nations after World War II. President Wilson did not succeed in getting the USA to ratify the League of Nations (d). Although he advocated vigorously for the League of Nations, the U.S. Senate never ratified the proposal. While the USA signed the League of Nations charter, the Senate never ratified it, and the USA never joined the League of Nations.

42. D: All of these empires no longer existed following the armistice ending WWI. The Austro-Hungarian Empire (a), the Ottoman Empire (b), and the German Empire (c) were all among the Central powers that lost the war. As empires capitulated, armistices and peace treaties were signed and the map of Europe was redrawn as territories formerly occupied by Central powers were partitioned. For example, the former Austro-Hungarian Empire was partitioned into Austria, Hungary, Czechoslovakia, Yugoslavia, Transylvania, and Romania. The Treaty of Lausanne (1923) gave Turkey both independence and recognition as successor to the former Ottoman Empire after Turkey refused the earlier Treaty of Sèvres (1920), and Mustafa Kemal Ataturk led the Turkish Independence War. Greece, Bulgaria, and other former Ottoman possessions became independent. The Lausanne Treaty defined the boundaries of these countries as well as the boundaries of Iraq, Syria, Cyprus, Sudan, and Egypt. The Russian Empire was among the Allied powers. Russia not only sustained losses in WWI, but Russia also lost additional numbers in the Russian Revolution of 1917, which destroyed the Empire. Bolsheviks took power in Russia under Lenin and signed the Treaty of Brest-Litovsk with Germany in 1918, thereby formally ending Russia's part in WWI and ending the Eastern Front theatre of the war. The former Russian Empire territories of Latvia, Lithuania, Estonia, Finland, and Poland became independent. Therefore, by the end of the Second World War, these four multinational empires no longer existed.

43. D: The earliest occurring chronological event was during the Russian Revolution, the Bolsheviks in 1918 instituted a policy of "war communism," nationalizing all productive property, putting railroads and factories under government control, and collecting and rationing food. Lenin created the New Economic Policy (NEP) in 1921 after the Russian Revolution had been going on for three years and the Kronstadt Rebellion had occurred. Lenin stated that the NEP would give "a limited place for a limited time to capitalism" (c). This policy continued until 1928, when Joseph Stalin became party leader and created his first Five-Year Plan (b). Meanwhile, the Russian Revolution had ended in 1922, and once the war was over the Bolsheviks formed the Union of Soviet Socialist Republics (USSR), often called the Soviet Union, in 1922. Chairman Mao's Communist Party of China formed the People's Republic (a) of China in 1949, eleven years later than the latest of the Russian events named here.

44. A: The latest occurring decolonization event was the Eastern Bloc and Soviet Satellite states of Armenia, Azerbaijan, Estonia, Georgia, Kazakhstan, Kyrgyzstan, Latvia, Lithuania, Moldova, Russia, Tajikistan, Turkmenistan, Ukraine, and Uzbekistan all became independent from the Soviet Union in

1991. (Note: This was the last decolonization of the Cold War years, as the end of the Soviet Union marked the end of the Cold War.) Canada completed its independence from British Parliament via the Canada Act (b) in 1982. In the Caribbean, the Bahamas gained independence from the United Kingdom (c) in 1973. Algeria won its independence from France when the Algerian War of Independence, begun in 1954, ended in 1962 (d). In Africa, Libya gained independence from Italy and became an independent kingdom in 1951.

45. B: U.S. industrialization was confined to the Northeast until after the Civil War because the Northeast had faster-running rivers than the South. The earliest American factories used horse-drawn machines. When waterpower was developed and proved superior, the Northeast's faster rivers were more suited to water-powered mills than the South's slower rivers. The war did not delay the development of water power (a). Waterpower was developed before the Civil War in the late 1790s. Steam power, a more efficient alternative to water power, was developed after the Civil War and eventually replaced waterpower. With steam-powered engines, industry could spread to the South, since steam engines did not depend on rapidly running water like water-powered engines. While British emigré Samuel Slater's first cotton mill using horse-drawn production did lose a lot of money (c), this was not a reason for industrial delay. In fact, Slater's Beverly Cotton Manufactory in Massachusetts, the first American cotton mill, in spite of its financial problems, was successful in both its volume of cotton production and in developing the water-powered technology that ultimately would succeed the horse-drawn method. Slater's second cotton mill in Pawtucket, Rhode Island, was water-powered. Industrial delay was not because milling technology had not yet been invented (d). Slater learned of new textile manufacturing techniques as a youth in England, and he brought this knowledge to America in 1789. Resistance of Southern owners of plantations and slaves did not slow the spread of industrialism. Rather, as seen in (b) above, the South did not have the geographic capability to sustain waterpower. Once steam power was developed, the South joined in industrialization.

46. A: The inaccurate statement is the Puritans unconditionally supported the English Reformation. While they agreed with the Reformation in principle, they felt that it had not pursued those principles far enough and should make greater reforms. Similarly, they felt that the Church of England (or Anglican Church), though it had separated from the Catholic Church in the Protestant Reformation, still allowed many practices they found too much like Catholicism (b). The Puritans did become a chief political power in England because of the first English Civil War (c) between Royalists and Parliamentarians. The Royalists had a profound suspicion of the radical Puritans. Among the Parliament's elements of resistance, the strongest was that of the Puritans. They joined in the battle initially for ostensibly political reasons as others had, but soon they brought more attention to religious issues. Following the Restoration in 1660 and the Uniformity Act of 1662, thereby restoring the Church of England to its pre-English Civil War status, the great majority of Puritan clergy defected from the Church of England (d). It is also accurate that the Puritans in England disagreed about separating from the Church of England. Some Puritans desired complete separation; they were known first as Separatists and after the Restoration as Dissenters. Others did not want complete separation but instead desired further reform in the Church of England. While they remained part of the Church of England, they were called Non-Separating Puritans, and after the Restoration, they were called Nonconformists.

47. D: These are all true. Because the Puritans took on a Reformed theology, they were in this sense Calvinists (a). However, many Puritans endorsed radical views that criticized such Calvinists as founder John (Jean) Calvin and Huldrych (Ulrich) Zwingli in Switzerland. Not only were Puritans critical of Calvinists despite their mutual Reformed approaches, reciprocally many Calvinists were opposed to the Puritans as well (c). The Puritan movement changed less in American colonies than in England during the 1660s. Following the Restoration (1660) and the Uniformity Act (1662) in England, nearly all of the Puritan clergy objected and left the Church of England, thereby creating a dramatic change in the

movement in that country. Nevertheless, in America, the Puritans who had emigrated from England continued their original Puritan traditions for a longer time, as they had neither the same Anglican Church as in England nor the legislation restoring earlier church status against which the English Puritans had reacted.

48. B: is the best answer. Of the cultures listed, only the Hebrews worshipped one God. Egyptians, Sumerians, Babylonians, and Hittites all practiced polytheistic religions that worshipped a host of deities.

49. D: It is not true that the Gilded Age is a term whose origins have not been identified clearly. In 1873, Mark Twain and Charles Dudley Warner co-authored a book entitled The Gilded Age: A Tale of Today. Twain and Warner first coined this term to describe the extravagance and excesses of America's wealthy upper class (b), who became richer than ever due to industrialization. Furthermore, the Gilded Age was the era of the "robber barons" (a) such as John D. Rockefeller, Cornelius Vanderbilt, J.P. Morgan, and others. Because they accumulated enormous wealth through extremely aggressive and occasionally unethical monetary manipulations, critics dubbed them "robber barons" because they seemed to be elite lords of robbery. While these business tycoons grasped huge fortunes, some of them—such as Andrew Carnegie and Andrew Mellon—were also philanthropists, using their wealth to support and further worthy causes such as literacy, education, health care, charities, and the arts. They donated millions of dollars to fund social improvements. Carnegie himself dubbed this large philanthropic movement the "Gospel of Wealth" (c). Another characteristic of the Gilded Age was the Beaux Arts architectural style, a neo-Renaissance style modeled after the great architectural designs of the European Renaissance. The Panic of 1893 ended the Gilded and began a severe four-year economic depression. The Progressive Era followed these events. (see #69).

50. A: It is not true that the founding fathers specifically stated in the Constitution that the USA would be a democracy. The founding fathers wanted the new United States to be founded on principles of liberty and equality, but they did not specifically describe these principles with the term "Democracy." Thus, the Declaration of Independence, like the Constitution after it, did not stipulate a democracy, although both did state the principles of equality and freedom (b). The Constitution also provided for the election of the new government (c), and for protection of the rights of some, but not all, of the people (d). Notable exceptions at the time were black people and women. Only later were laws passed to protect their rights over the years. Because (b), (c), and (d) are all true, answer, these statements are all untrue, is incorrect.

51. D: Both of these men wrote about the idea of a Social Contract between government and the people that was used in the Declaration of Independence as a democratic principle. Thomas Hobbes (c) wrote about it in his Leviathan (1651), describing it in the context of an authoritarian monarchy. John Locke (d) wrote about it in his Second Treatise of Government (1689), describing it in the context of a liberal monarchy. Jean-Jacques Rousseau wrote about it in his Du Contrat Social, or The Social Contract (1762), in the context of a liberal republic similar to what the new USA would become. These works supplied a theoretical basis for constitutional monarchies, liberal democracies, and republicanism. Since answer (b), all of these, is correct, answer (a), none of these, is incorrect.

52. B: is the answer. Preservatives such as salt were only introduced to the European diet after trade routes opened and these goods could be brought to Europe.

53. D: is the answer. Despite the growing amount of literacy in the 1500s, due principally to the invention of the printing press and the availability of texts, the majority of Europeans remained illiterate.

54. B: In 1792, when the French Revolution turned into European war, American traders conducted business with both sides. It is not true that Washington allied with the French (a) at this time. Washington

issued a Proclamation of Neutrality in 1792 when the French went to war with European countries. While they did trade with both sides, American merchants profited the most from the French West Indies, not the British West Indies (c). The Spanish navy did not retaliate against America for trading with the French (d). Though Spain was an ally of Britain, it was the British who most often seized American ships and forced their crews to serve the British navy. Edmond-Charles Genêt, or Citizen Genêt, a French ambassador to the United States during the French Revolution, defied Washington's policy of neutrality by encouraging the American people to support the French. Washington was embarrassed by this violation. He did not agree with it.

55. B: is the best choice. The Etruscans were from a kingdom to the north that seized control of Rome from the Latins in the mid 600s B.C. They began urbanizing the settlement, improving roads, adding drainage systems, etc. They were driven out of the region in 509 B.C. during an uprising of the Latins

56. A: James Madison, John Jay, and Alexander Hamilton published The Federalist in the Independent Journal in New York. It was a response to the Anti-Federalists in New York, who were slow to ratify the Constitution because they feared it gave the central government too much authority.

57. B: Female support for Democratic candidates has increased since the 1980s, and younger, college-age voters are more likely to vote Democrat. The 2008 election saw particularly strong support for Obama from women and young voters.

58. D: Congress did not have the authority to levy taxes under the Articles of Confederation. Without the ability to levy taxes, there was no way to finance programs, which weakened the government.

59. A: The Age of Enlightenment was a time of scientific and philosophical achievement. Also called the Age of Reason, it was a time when human thought and reason were prized.

60. C: The Constitution was not ratified immediately. Only five states accepted it in early 1788; Massachusetts, New York, Rhode Island, and Virginia were originally opposed to the Constitution. Rhode Island reluctantly accepted it in 1790.

61. D: Federalists who helped frame the Constitution believed the central government needed to be stronger than what was established under the Articles of Confederation. Anti-federalists were against this and feared a strong federal government. A system of checks and balances was established to prevent the central government from taking too much power.

62. A: The Senate and House of Representatives make up a bicameral legislature. The Great Compromise awarded seats in the Senate equally to each state, while the seats in the House of Representatives were based on population.

63. A: Checks and balances were established to keep one branch of government from taking too much authority. When Johnson violated the Tenure of Office Act by replacing Secretary of War Edwin Stanton, Johnson was impeached, but the final vote in the Senate trial came up one vote short of the number needed to convict him.

64. A: The citizens usually elect members of the local government such as mayors and city council. However, the state grants local governments their authority. State and local governments work independently and do not share authority the way the federal and state governments share power.

65. B: The Animal and Plant Health Inspection Service, the Food and Nutrition Service, and the Forest Service are agencies in the Department of Agriculture. The Department of Agriculture ensures food safety, works with farmers, promotes trade, and protects natural resources.

66. B: The House has strict rules that limit debate. A filibuster can only occur in the Senate where Senators can speak on topics other than the bill at hand and introduce amendments. A filibuster can be ended by a supermajority vote of 60 Senators.

67. C: The Government Accountability Office was originally called the General Accounting Office and was established in 1921 to audit the budget, Congress, and the Director of the Treasury. The Government Accountability Office now oversees the effectiveness of government spending in every branch.

68. C: The Civil Rights Act of 1964 affected the Jim Crowe laws in the Southern states. Many minorities suffered under unfair voting laws and segregation. President Lyndon Johnson signed the Civil Rights Act of 1964 into law after the 1963 assassination of President Kennedy, who championed the reform.

69. C: Tennessee was the only Southern state to ratify the 14th Amendment. Although Southern states that ratified this amendment could be readmitted to the Union with more reform, President Andrew Johnson, who was at odds with Congress, advised them against it.

70. C: The 17th Amendment was ratified in 1913. This amendment allowed the citizens to choose their Senators by holding elections and participating in a popular vote.

71. B: The appellant presents arguments in a brief that explains to the three judges on the panel why the trial court was wrong. The respondent explains why the trial court made the right decision. The appeals court usually makes the final decision, unless they send it back to trial.

72. A: A writ of certiorari is filed if a case is lost in appeals or the highest state court. The writ of certiorari is a request for the Supreme Court to hear the case, but it does not guarantee the case will be heard.

73. C: Nebraska does not require voter registration, but all other states do and have their own process. State and local officials administer federal elections, and though each state has its own method for holding elections, federal elections are always held at the same time.

74. B: Congress has the authority to shape the judicial branch. The Supreme Court once operated with only six members. Nine has been the standard number since 1869.

75. B: Money given directly to a party candidate is hard money. The Federal Election Commission monitors hard money because of limitations on the amount and the money's source.

76. A: Presidential candidates are eligible for a match from the federal government (with a $250 per contribution limit) if they can privately raise $5,000 per state in twenty states. Candidates who accept public money agree to limit spending. Candidates who do not accept matching funds are free to use the money they raise privately.

77. D: America is a common law country because English common law was adopted in all states except Louisiana. Common law is based on precedent, and changes over time. Each state develops its own common laws.

78. B: All states have bicameral legislatures, except Nebraska. The bicameral legislatures in states resemble the federal legislature, with an upper house and a lower house.

79. C: A caucus is a private event run by political parties, and a primary is an indirect election run by state and local governments. Voters may award delegates to candidates for the national conventions, depending on state laws.

80. A: The President has the authority to negotiate and sign treaties. A two-thirds vote of the Senate, however, is needed to ratify a treaty for it to be upheld.

81. A: Presidential candidates are nominated at each party's national convention. The Republican and Democratic Conventions have their own processes for selecting delegates. Puerto Rico, Guam, and American Samoa are also awarded PLEO (Party Leaders and Elected Officials) delegates in the Democratic National Convention.

82. C: The shortest distance between New York and Paris goes over Labrador and Greenland. This is not apparent on a projection map, in which a straight line drawn between the two cities would extend straight out across the Atlantic Ocean, roughly along the 42nd parallel. The illusion that this straight line is the shortest path is a result of the distortions inherent in projection maps. On a globe, it would be easier to see that a plane flying from New York to Paris would cover the least ground by carving an arc, first up through eastern Canada and Greenland and then back down through the British Isles and northern France. This sort of path is known as a great circle route because it looks like an arc when it is drawn on a projection map.

83. B: On a political map, countries are represented in different colors, and countries that share a border are not given the same color. This is so that the borders between countries will be distinct. Political maps are used to illustrate those aspects of a country that have been determined by people: the capital, the provincial and national borders, and the large cities. Political maps sometimes include major physical features like rivers and mountains, but they are not intended to display all such information. On a physical, climate, or contour map, however, the borders between nations are more incidental. Colors are used on these maps to represent physical features, areas with similar climate, etc. It is possible that colors will overrun the borders and be shared by adjacent countries.

84. A: A smaller box in which some part of the larger map is depicted in greater detail is known as an inset. Insets provide a closer look at parts of the map that the cartographer deems to be more important (for instance, cities, national parks, or historical sites). Often, traffic maps will include several insets depicting the roads in the most congested area of the city. Legends, also known as keys, are the boxes in which the symbols used in the map are explained. A legend, or key, might indicate how railroads and boundaries are depicted, for example. A compass rose indicates how the map is oriented along the north-south axis. It is common for cartographers to tilt a map for ease of display, such that up may not be due north.

85. D: A relative location for Milwaukee is 100 miles north of Chicago. Relative location is a description of placement in terms of some other location. The latitude and longitude of Milwaukee are its absolute location because they describe its placement relative to an arbitrary but inalterable system of positioning. To say that Milwaukee is in Wisconsin or on Lake Michigan does not provide as much detail as answer choice D because Wisconsin is a big state and because Lake Michigan is a large body of water.

86. D: On a cartogram of population, Nigeria would be bigger than Australia. Even though the area of Australia is several times greater than that of Nigeria, Nigeria has a much larger population. A cartogram

is a map on which countries or regions are sized according to a certain variable. So, in a cartogram of population, the country with the most people will be the biggest. The countries would be depicted at their usual size in a contour map of elevation or in a flow-line map. On a Mercator projection, Nigeria would actually be smaller relative to Australia because it is closer to the equator.

87. D: These are all geographically parts of Southeast Asia. The countries of Myanmar (Burma), Laos, Cambodia, and Thailand (a) are considered Mainland Southeast Asia, as are Vietnam and the Malay Peninsula (b). Brunei (b), East Malaysia, Indonesia, and the Philippines (c) are considered Maritime Southeast Asia, as are Singapore and Timor-Leste. The Seven Sister States of India are also considered to be part of Southeast Asia, geographically and culturally. (The Seven Sister States of India are Arunachal Pradesh, Assam, Nagaland, Meghalaya, Manipur, Tripura, and Mizoram, which all have contiguous borders in northeastern India.)

88. B: There are four intermediate directions. They are northwest, northeast, southwest, and southeast. The intermediate directions are midway between each set of adjacent cardinal directions. The cardinal directions are north, south, east, and west. On a compass rose, the cardinal directions are typically indicated by large points, while the intermediate directions are represented by smaller points.

89. D: An isohyet is a line that connects points with equal total rainfall. On an isohyetal map then, a series of lines will indicate areas of greater or lesser rainfall. This is a form of contour map, the most common of which uses a series of lines to indicate changes in elevation. The other answer choices represent lines used in other forms of contour maps. An isotherm connects points with the same temperature. An isoline connects points with an equal value, as, for instance, on a contour map illustrating iron production. An isobar connects points with identical atmospheric pressure.

90. A: The eye wall of a hurricane has the strongest winds and the greatest rainfall. The eye wall is the tower-like rim of the eye. It is from this wall that clouds extend out, which are seen from above as the classic outward spiral pattern. A hurricane front is the outermost edge of its influence; although there will be heavy winds and rain in this area, the intensity will be relatively small. The eye of a hurricane is actually a place of surprising peace. In this area, dry and cool air rushes down to the ground or sea. Once there, the air is caught up in the winds of the eye wall and is driven outward at a furious pace.

91. B: The composite volcano, sometimes called the stratovolcano, is the most common type of volcano on earth. A composite volcano has steep sides, so the explosions of ash, pumice, and silica are often accompanied by treacherous mudslides. Indeed, it is these mudslides that cause most of the damage associated with composite volcano eruptions. Krakatoa and Mount Saint Helens are examples of composite volcanoes. A lava dome is a round volcano that emits thick lava very slowly. A shield volcano, one example of which is Mt. Kilauea in Hawaii, emits a small amount of lava over an extended period of time. Shield volcanoes are not known for violent eruptions. A cinder cone has steep sides made of fallen cinders, which themselves are made of the lava that intermittently shoots into the air.

92. D: A flow-line map describes the movement of people, trends, or materials across a physical area. The movements depicted on a flow-line map are typically represented by arrows. In more advanced flow-line maps, the width of the arrow corresponds to the quantity of the motion. Flow-line maps usually declare the span of time that is being represented. A political map depicts the man-made aspects of geography, such as borders and cities. A cartogram adjusts the size of the areas represented according to some variable. For instance, a cartogram of wheat production would depict Iowa as being much larger than Alaska. A qualitative map uses lines, dots, and other symbols to illustrate a particular point. For example, a qualitative map might be used to demonstrate the greatest expansion of the Persian Empire.

93. A: One example of the multiplier effect of large cities would be if the presence of specialized equipment for an industry attracted even more business. Large cities tend to grow even larger for a number of reasons: they have more skilled workers, they have greater concentrations of specialized equipment, and they have already-functioning markets. These factors all make it easier for a business to begin operations in a large city than elsewhere. Thus, the populations and economic productivity of large cities tend to grow quickly. Some governments have sought to mitigate this trend by clustering groups of similar industries in smaller cities.

94. C: The greatest area of corn production is in the United States, specifically in the so-called Corn Belt that runs from northern Florida and eastern Texas all the way up to Iowa and Pennsylvania. Corn has traditionally been the specialty grain of the Americas, although it is now grown as a subsistence crop all over the world. Indeed, all the incorrect answer choices are areas that produce significant amounts of corn, though not as much as the Corn Belt. Corn is useful because it can grow in various climates and can be converted into a number of different products.

95. C: The increasing popularity of Thai food in the United States is an example of cultural convergence, or the intersection of traits or customs from two distinct cultures. Thailand's cuisine has been introduced to the United States, but it has undergone subtle changes as a result of the desires and practices of the American consumer. The phenomenon of cultural convergence is credited with much of the innovation in any society. Cultural divergence, on the other hand, is the practice of shielding one culture from the influence of another. France, for instance, seeks to limit the influence of American culture on its citizens. Assimilation is the process by which a minority group gradually adopts the culture of the majority group. For example, many Native Americans assimilated into the European-style culture of the early American settlers. Acculturation is the process of obtaining the practices and ideas of a culture. A child undergoes acculturation, wherein he or she learns to think and act appropriately for his or her setting.

96. C: The cycle of demographic transition is best illustrated by a line graph. Demographic transition is a phenomenon in which a region's growth rate increases rapidly, peaks, and then decreases slowly over a long time. In the early phase of a region's development, both the birth and death rates are high, which can cause the population to fluctuate. As the people of the region become settled, the growth rate calms down, and the region enters a period of rapid increase. Political maps are better at depicting borders and the locations of cities, while pie charts are better at representing proportions. Flow-line maps are good for illustrating the movement of people, goods, or trends across a physical area.

97. C: The death rate of Henrytown is 8. Death rate is calculated as the number of deaths every year for every thousand people. Of course, the population of Henrytown is only 500, so it requires a quick calculation to obtain the death rate. This can be accomplished with the following equation: $4 / x = 500 / 1000$. This equation basically means "4 is to 500 as x is to 1000." The equation is solved by first cross multiplying, which yields $4{,}000 = 500x$. Then, both sides are divided by 500 to isolate the variable. This indicates that x is equal to 8.

98. B: In the early expanding stage of demographic transition, the fertility rate remains high, while the mortality rate declines sharply. Demographic transition is a model for how the population growth rate of a region changes over time. It consists of four stages. In the first, the high stationary stage, fertility and mortality rates are high, so the population rate varies, and there is little growth. In the second stage, some of the problems causing mortality have been solved, but fertility continues at the same rate. This means that the population begins to expand at a greater rate. In the third stage, the late expanding stage, the fertility rate begins to decline, but because the mortality rate remains low, there is continuing growth. In the low stationary stage, there are low rates of fertility and mortality, and consequently there is a low rate of growth.

99. B: North Korea and South Korea are separated by a geometric border, meaning that the boundary between the two nations is a straight line drawn on a map, without respect to landforms. Specifically, the boundary between the Koreas is the 38th parallel. Another example of a geometric border lies between the continental United States and Canada. The Turkish Cyprus–Greek Cyprus border is anthropogeographic, or drawn according to cultural reasons. The border between France and Spain is physiographic-political, a combination of the Pyrenees Mountains and European history. The Irish Sea separates England from Ireland.

100. D: The northernmost border between India and Pakistan is represented on political maps as a broken line because the borders of the Kashmir region remain in dispute. Both nations lay claim to this mountainous region, which has great water resources. This has been just one of the issues to complicate relations between these neighbors in South Asia. Although India controls most of Kashmir at present, the boundaries have not yet been fully resolved, and, on a political map, such undefined borders are usually represented with dotted lines.

101. A: The phenomenon of "sticky prices" refers to prices that stay the same even though it seems they should change (either increasing or decreasing).

102. B: John Maynard Keynes argued that government could help revitalize a recessionary economy by increasing government spending and therefore increasing aggregate demand. This is known as demand-side economics.

103. A: The production possibilities frontier shows the different possible combinations of goods (and/or services) a society can produce. If all other factors are even, producing more of Good A leads to a decreased production of Good B. If the PPF moves outward, that means a change in the factors of production that allows the economy to produce more goods—economic growth—has occurred. Only Answer A is an example of economic growth.

104. D: A supply shock is caused when there is a dramatic increase in input prices. This causes an increase in price levels and decreases in employment and GDP. A supply shock causes the AS curve to move to the left (in).

105. D: A change in productivity, such as workers becoming more or less productive, would affect how many goods can be supplied. No change in worker productivity would cause no change in AS. Items A, B, and C would all affect input prices and therefore would all affect AS.

106. D: When there is a lot of unemployment, the AS curve is horizontal. If AD decreases at this time, prices will tend to remain the same while GDP decreases. When there is full employment, the AS curve is vertical. If AD decreases at this time, prices will drop but GDP will tend to remain the same.

107. B: According to the theory of crowding out, when the government borrows money to increase spending, this will increase the price of money, leading to a drop in investment. That drop in investment will have a negative effect on AD, and so the government injection of funds will not have its full, desired effect (AD3), instead winding up at AD2.

108. D: If a society wants greater income equity, it can impose a progressive income tax, which taxes the wealthy at a higher rate; an inheritance tax, which prevents the wealthy from passing all

their wealth on to the next generation; and a gift tax, which prevents the wealthy from simply giving their wealth away.

109. A: The input and output data illustrates the Law of Diminishing Marginal Returns, which states that as inputs are added during production, there eventually comes a time when increased inputs coincide with a decrease in marginal return.

110. B: Structural unemployment is unemployment that results from a mismatch of job skills or location. In this case, Ivy's job skill—her ability to work as a seamstress—is no longer desired by employers. Frictional and cyclical are other forms of unemployment; economists do not use the term careless unemployment.

111. D: It is believed that some level of frictional and structural unemployment will always exist, and that the best economists (and politicians) can hope for is to reduce cyclical unemployment to zero. Therefore, frictional and structural unemployment are sometimes referred to as natural unemployment, meaning unemployment that naturally exists within an economy.

112. D: While rising prices may hurt many members of an economy, those same rising prices may benefit other members of the same economy. For example, rising prices may help those who sell goods and services and are able to keep their costs of production low, increasing their profit margin. Meanwhile, rising prices can hurt consumers because their income is now able to purchase fewer goods and services than before.

113. A: Demand-pull inflation is caused when total spending is in excess of total production. This causes price levels to rise, and can lead to hyperinflation.

114. D: The business cycle includes five stages: expansion, peak, contraction, trough, and recovery. Stagflation is the name for periods when inflation and unemployment are both increasing.

115. D: Because the MPC is 0.9, the multiplier is 10 (1/0.1). Therefore, to attain an increase of $10 billion in AD, the government must increase spending by $1 billion ($1 billion x 10 = $10 billion).

116. C: Banks create money by giving out loans. For example, assume a person puts $100 into a bank. The bank will keep a percentage of that money in reserves because of the reserve requirement. If the reserve requirement is 10% then the bank will put $10 in reserves and then loan out $90 of it to a second person. The money total, which started at $100, now includes the original $100 plus the $90, or a total of $190. The bank creates $90 by loaning it.

117. D: When the FOMC sells bonds, they raise interest rates. This draws money out of the American economy, and attracts foreign investors. This causes the value of the American dollar to rise overseas, which makes American goods more expensive to overseas buyers and causes American exports to drop.

118. A: The equation of exchange is MV = PQ. This means that M1 (a measure of the supply of money) multiplied by the velocity of money (the average number of times a typical dollar is spent on final goods and services a year) = the average price level of final goods and services in GDP x real output, or the quantity of goods and services in GDP.

119. A: Answer B is a definition of gross national product, and answers C and D define other economic measures.

120. B: Humanistic. The humanistic approach to understanding human behavior is driven by the idea that a person has a need to reach self-actualization, which includes the proclivity to seek after the highest possible growth and development that is attainable. In this approach, each individual has his or her own distinctive needs, desires, talents, skills, etc. According to the humanistic approach, a person who is well adjusted must be free to express his or her own uniqueness.

121. A: Aggression. The Big Five personality traits are agreeableness, conscientiousness, extroversion, neuroticism, and openness. This classification system is an attempt to collapse the many different traits pertaining to personality into a few foundational traits that describe consistent behavior.

122. C: Psychodynamic. The psychodynamic approach deals with the idea that a person's behavior, thoughts, and emotions come from society's restrictions on the manifestation of a person's innate drives. Freud believed that sexual and aggressive drives are the most significant in human beings. Since society limits both drives, Freud believed that people struggle with meeting their personal needs versus displeasing others. According to Freud, a person's personality is reliant on how these issues are solved during the first two years or so of childhood.

123. D: Motion parallax. Motion parallax is also known as relative motion. It is a monocular cue that causes stable objects to appear to be in motion when a person is in motion. Objects closer to the fixation point (the thing the person is looking at) appear to be moving backward. The closer the object is to the fixation point, the faster the object would seem to be moving. Things that are farther from the fixation point will appear to be moving with the person at a slower pace as the object gets farther away.

124. C: According to George Murdock, it is the preponderance of property rights, rather than property disputes, which is a characteristic of all cultural practices. It may be that property disputes arise from the characteristic of property rights, but property disputes are not, in and of themselves, one of Murdock's cultural universals.

125. A: If a father from a patriarchal society passes on his property to his youngest son, he is practicing ultimogeniture. (B) Primogeniture is incorrect because it refers to the practice of a father's passing his property to his eldest son, not his youngest. (C) Neolocality and (D) patrilocality are incorrect because they represent concepts unrelated to ultimogeniture. (E) Parsimony is incorrect because is it not a societal practice; it is merely another word for stinginess.

126. D: Race is the correct answer because it is not one of Max Weber's independent factors which form the basis for his theory of stratification. (A), (B), and (C) are all incorrect because they are among Weber's independent factors forming his theory of stratification. (E) is incorrect because there is a correct answer, (D).

127. A: Talcott Parsons is the sociologist credited with developing the action theory of society

128. B: The philosophy of history is concerned with the ultimate significance of history as a field of study and asks questions concerning how history should be studied, including what social unit is correct to use when studying history—whether it is more important to look at the individual lives of ordinary people or to concentrate on the so-called big picture, looking at the overall trends in a society or culture; only giving personal treatment to people, such as George Washington, who had particular significance to the events surrounding them. The philosophy of history also looks for broad historical trends and progress.

129. A: Bias is a form of prejudice, and a historical work is considered biased when it is unreasonably shaped by the author's personal or institutional prejudices. It is wise for a teacher to choose material that comes from reputable sources and to verify that all material used in classroom presentations is reliable and appropriate. As long as the teacher is willing to do these things and show a variety of historical opinions, this is not an example of bias.

130. D: The information in this table shows the median incomes of persons who have achieved various educational levels. Looking at the table, one can see that from 1997 to 2007, persons without a high school degree had their median income increase by less than $5,000 while persons with a high school degree had their median income increase by more than $6,000. One can also see that as a general matter, the more education a person has, the higher their income will be and that income typically increases over time.

Secret Key #1 - Time is Your Greatest Enemy

Pace Yourself

Wear a watch. At the beginning of the test, check the time (or start a chronometer on your watch to count the minutes), and check the time after every few questions to make sure you are "on schedule."

If you are forced to speed up, do it efficiently. Usually one or more answer choices can be eliminated without too much difficulty. Above all, don't panic. Don't speed up and just begin guessing at random choices. By pacing yourself, and continually monitoring your progress against your watch, you will always know exactly how far ahead or behind you are with your available time. If you find that you are one minute behind on the test, don't skip one question without spending any time on it, just to catch back up. Take 15 fewer seconds on the next four questions, and after four questions you'll have caught back up. Once you catch back up, you can continue working each problem at your normal pace.

Furthermore, don't dwell on the problems that you were rushed on. If a problem was taking up too much time and you made a hurried guess, it must be difficult. The difficult questions are the ones you are most likely to miss anyway, so it isn't a big loss. It is better to end with more time than you need than to run out of time.

Lastly, sometimes it is beneficial to slow down if you are constantly getting ahead of time. You are always more likely to catch a careless mistake by working more slowly than quickly, and among very high-scoring test takers (those who are likely to have lots of time left over), careless errors affect the score more than mastery of material.

Secret Key #2 - Guessing is not Guesswork

You probably know that guessing is a good idea. Unlike other standardized tests, there is no penalty for getting a wrong answer. Even if you have no idea about a question, you still have a 20-25% chance of getting it right.

Most test takers do not understand the impact that proper guessing can have on their score. Unless you score extremely high, guessing will significantly contribute to your final score.

Monkeys Take the Test

What most test takers don't realize is that to insure that 20-25% chance, you have to guess randomly. If you put 20 monkeys in a room to take this test, assuming they answered once per question and behaved themselves, on average they would get 20-25% of the questions correct. Put 20 test takers in the room, and the average will be much lower among guessed questions. Why?

1. The test writers intentionally write deceptive answer choices that "look" right. A test taker has no idea about a question, so he picks the "best looking" answer, which is often wrong. The monkey has no idea what looks good and what doesn't, so it will consistently be right about 20-25% of the time.

2. Test takers will eliminate answer choices from the guessing pool based on a hunch or intuition. Simple but correct answers often get excluded, leaving a 0% chance of being correct. The monkey has no clue, and often gets lucky with the best choice.

This is why the process of elimination endorsed by most test courses is flawed and detrimental to your performance. Test takers don't guess; they make an ignorant stab in the dark that is usually worse than random.

$5 Challenge

Let me introduce one of the most valuable ideas of this course—the $5 challenge.
- *You only mark your "best guess" if you are willing to bet $5 on it.*
- *You only eliminate choices from guessing if you are willing to bet $5 on it.*

Why $5? Five dollars is an amount of money that is small yet not insignificant, and can really add up fast (20 questions could cost you $100). Likewise, each answer choice on one question of the test will have a small impact on your overall score, but it can really add up to a lot of points in the end.

The process of elimination IS valuable. The following shows your chance of guessing it right:

If you eliminate wrong answer choices until only this many remain:	Chance of getting it correct:
1	100%
2	50%
3	33%

However, if you accidentally eliminate the right answer or go on a hunch for an incorrect answer, your chances drop dramatically—to 0%. By guessing among all the answer choices, you are GUARANTEED to have a shot at the right answer.

That's why the $5 test is so valuable. If you give up the advantage and safety of a pure guess, it had better be worth the risk.

What we still haven't covered is how to be sure that whatever guess you make is truly random. Here's the easiest way:
- *Always pick the first answer choice among those remaining.*

Such a technique means that you have decided, **before you see a single test question**, exactly how you are going to guess, and since the order of choices tells you nothing about which one is correct, this guessing technique is perfectly random.

This section is not meant to scare you away from making educated guesses or eliminating choices; you just need to define when a choice is worth eliminating. The $5 test, along with a pre-defined random guessing strategy, is the best way to make sure you reap all of the benefits of guessing.

Secret Key #3 - Practice Smarter, Not Harder

Many test takers delay the test preparation process because they dread the awful amounts of practice time they think necessary to succeed on the test. We have refined an effective method that will take you only a fraction of the time.

There are a number of "obstacles" in the path to success. Among these are answering questions, finishing in time, and mastering test-taking strategies. All must be executed on the day of the test at peak performance, or your score will suffer. The test is a mental marathon that has a large impact on your future.

Just like a marathon runner, it is important to work your way up to the full challenge. So first you just worry about questions, and then time, and finally strategy:

Success Strategy

1. Find a good source for practice tests.
2. If you are willing to make a larger time investment, consider using more than one study guide. Often the different approaches of multiple authors will help you "get" difficult concepts.
3. Take a practice test with no time constraints, with all study helps, "open book." Take your time with questions and focus on applying strategies.
4. Take a practice test with time constraints, with all guides, "open book."
5. Take a final practice test without open material and with time limits.

If you have time to take more practice tests, just repeat step 5. By gradually exposing yourself to the full rigors of the test environment, you will condition your mind to the stress of test day and maximize your success.

Secret Key #4 - Prepare, Don't Procrastinate

Let me state an obvious fact: if you take the test three times, you will probably get three different scores. This is due to the way you feel on test day, the level of preparedness you have, and the version of the test you see. Despite the test writers' claims to the contrary, some versions of the test WILL be easier for you than others.

Since your future depends so much on your score, you should maximize your chances of success. In order to maximize the likelihood of success, you've got to prepare in advance. This means taking practice tests and spending time learning the information and test taking strategies you will need to succeed.

Never go take the actual test as a "practice" test, expecting that you can just take it again if you need to. Take all the practice tests you can on your own, but when you go to take the official test, be prepared, be focused, and do your best the first time!

Secret Key #5 - Test Yourself

Everyone knows that time is money. There is no need to spend too much of your time or too little of your time preparing for the test. You should only spend as much of your precious time preparing as is necessary for you to get the score you need.

Once you have taken a practice test under real conditions of time constraints, then you will know if you are ready for the test or not.

If you have scored extremely high the first time that you take the practice test, then there is not much point in spending countless hours studying. You are already there.

Benchmark your abilities by retaking practice tests and seeing how much you have improved. Once you consistently score high enough to guarantee success, then you are ready.

If you have scored well below where you need, then knuckle down and begin studying in earnest. Check your improvement regularly through the use of practice tests under real conditions. Above all, don't worry, panic, or give up. The key is perseverance!

Then, when you go to take the test, remain confident and remember how well you did on the practice tests. If you can score high enough on a practice test, then you can do the same on the real thing.

General Strategies

The most important thing you can do is to ignore your fears and jump into the test immediately. Do not be overwhelmed by any strange-sounding terms. You have to jump into the test like jumping into a pool—all at once is the easiest way.

Make Predictions

As you read and understand the question, try to guess what the answer will be. Remember that several of the answer choices are wrong, and once you begin reading them, your mind will immediately become cluttered with answer choices designed to throw you off. Your mind is typically the most focused immediately after you have read the question and digested its contents. If you can, try to predict what the correct answer will be. You may be surprised at what you can predict.

Quickly scan the choices and see if your prediction is in the listed answer choices. If it is, then you can be quite confident that you have the right answer. It still won't hurt to check the other answer choices, but most of the time, you've got it!

Answer the Question

It may seem obvious to only pick answer choices that answer the question, but the test writers can create some excellent answer choices that are wrong. Don't pick an answer just because it sounds right, or you believe it to be true. It MUST answer the question. Once you've made your selection, always go back and check it against the question and make sure that you didn't misread the question and that the answer choice does answer the question posed.

Benchmark

After you read the first answer choice, decide if you think it sounds correct or not. If it doesn't, move on to the next answer choice. If it does, mentally mark that answer choice. This doesn't mean that you've definitely selected it as your answer choice, it just means that it's the best you've seen thus far. Go ahead and read the next choice. If the next choice is worse than the one you've already selected, keep going to the next answer choice. If the next choice is better than the choice you've already selected, mentally mark the new answer choice as your best guess.

The first answer choice that you select becomes your standard. Every other answer choice must be benchmarked against that standard. That choice is correct until proven otherwise by another answer choice beating it out. Once you've decided that no other answer choice seems as good, do one final check to ensure that your answer choice answers the question posed.

Valid Information

Don't discount any of the information provided in the question. Every piece of information may be necessary to determine the correct answer. None of the information in the question is there to throw you off (while the answer choices will certainly have information to throw you off). If two seemingly unrelated topics are discussed, don't ignore either. You can be confident there is a relationship, or it wouldn't be included in the question, and you are probably going to have to determine what is that relationship to find the answer.

Avoid "Fact Traps"

Don't get distracted by a choice that is factually true. Your search is for the answer that answers the question. Stay focused and don't fall for an answer that is true but irrelevant. Always go back to the question and make sure you're choosing an answer that actually answers the question and is not just a true statement. An answer can be factually correct, but it MUST answer the question asked. Additionally, two answers can both be seemingly correct, so be sure to read all of the answer choices, and make sure that you get the one that BEST answers the question.

Milk the Question

Some of the questions may throw you completely off. They might deal with a subject you have not been exposed to, or one that you haven't reviewed in years. While your lack of knowledge about the subject will be a hindrance, the question itself can give you many clues that will help you find the correct answer. Read the question carefully and look for clues. Watch particularly for adjectives and nouns describing difficult terms or words that you don't recognize. Regardless of whether you completely understand a word or not, replacing it with a synonym, either provided or one you more familiar with, may help you to understand what the questions are asking. Rather than wracking your mind about specific detailed information concerning a difficult term or word, try to use mental substitutes that are easier to understand.

The Trap of Familiarity

Don't just choose a word because you recognize it. On difficult questions, you may not recognize a number of words in the answer choices. The test writers don't put "make-believe" words on the test, so don't think that just because you only recognize all the words in one answer choice that that answer choice must be correct. If you only recognize words in one answer choice, then focus on that one. Is it correct? Try your best to determine if it is correct. If it is, that's great. If not, eliminate it. Each word and answer choice you eliminate increases your chances of getting the question correct, even if you then have to guess among the unfamiliar choices.

Eliminate Answers

Eliminate choices as soon as you realize they are wrong. But be careful! Make sure you consider all of the possible answer choices. Just because one appears right, doesn't mean that the next one won't be even better! The test writers will usually put more than one good answer choice for every question, so read all of them. Don't worry if you are stuck between two that seem right. By getting down to just two remaining possible choices, your odds are now 50/50. Rather than wasting too much time, play the odds. You are guessing, but guessing wisely because you've been able to knock out some of the answer choices that you know are wrong. If you are eliminating choices and realize that the last answer choice you are left with is also obviously wrong, don't panic. Start over and consider each choice again. There may easily be something that you missed the first time and will realize on the second pass.

Tough Questions

If you are stumped on a problem or it appears too hard or too difficult, don't waste time. Move on! Remember though, if you can quickly check for obviously incorrect answer choices, your chances of guessing correctly are greatly improved. Before you completely give up, at least try to knock out a couple of possible answers. Eliminate what you can and then guess at the remaining answer choices before moving on.

Brainstorm

If you get stuck on a difficult question, spend a few seconds quickly brainstorming. Run through the complete list of possible answer choices. Look at each choice and ask yourself, "Could this answer the question satisfactorily?" Go through each answer choice and consider it independently of the others. By systematically going through all possibilities, you may find something that you would otherwise overlook. Remember though that when you get stuck, it's important to try to keep moving.

Read Carefully

Understand the problem. Read the question and answer choices carefully. Don't miss the question because you misread the terms. You have plenty of time to read each question thoroughly and make sure you understand what is being asked. Yet a happy medium must be attained, so don't waste too much time. You must read carefully, but efficiently.

Face Value

When in doubt, use common sense. Always accept the situation in the problem at face value. Don't read too much into it. These problems will not require you to make huge leaps of logic. The test writers aren't trying to throw you off with a cheap trick. If you have to go beyond creativity and make a leap of logic in order to have an answer choice answer the question, then you should look at the other answer choices. Don't overcomplicate the problem by creating theoretical relationships or explanations that will warp time or space. These are normal problems rooted in reality. It's just that the applicable relationship or explanation may not be readily apparent and you have to figure things out. Use your common sense to interpret anything that isn't clear.

Prefixes

If you're having trouble with a word in the question or answer choices, try dissecting it. Take advantage of every clue that the word might include. Prefixes and suffixes can be a huge help. Usually they allow you to determine a basic meaning. Pre- means before, post- means after, pro - is positive, de- is negative. From these prefixes and suffixes, you can get an idea of the general meaning of the word and try to put it into context. Beware though of any traps. Just because con- is the opposite of pro-, doesn't necessarily mean congress is the opposite of progress!

Hedge Phrases

Watch out for critical hedge phrases, led off with words such as "likely," "may," "can," "sometimes," "often," "almost," "mostly," "usually," "generally," "rarely," and "sometimes." Question writers insert these hedge phrases to cover every possibility. Often an answer choice will be wrong simply because it leaves no room for exception. Unless the situation calls for them, avoid answer choices that have definitive words like "exactly," and "always."

Switchback Words

Stay alert for "switchbacks." These are the words and phrases frequently used to alert you to shifts in thought. The most common switchback word is "but." Others include "although," "however," "nevertheless," "on the other hand," "even though," "while," "in spite of," "despite," and "regardless of."

New Information

Correct answer choices will rarely have completely new information included. Answer choices typically are straightforward reflections of the material asked about and will directly relate to the question. If a new piece of information is included in an answer choice that doesn't even seem to relate to the topic being asked about, then that answer choice is likely incorrect. All of the information needed to answer the question is usually provided for you in the question. You should not have to make guesses that are unsupported or choose answer choices that require unknown information that cannot be reasoned from what is given.

Time Management

On technical questions, don't get lost on the technical terms. Don't spend too much time on any one question. If you don't know what a term means, then odds are you aren't going to get much further since you don't have a dictionary. You should be able to immediately recognize whether or not you know a term. If you don't, work with the other clues that you have—the other answer choices and terms provided—but don't waste too much time trying to figure out a difficult term that you don't know.

Contextual Clues

Look for contextual clues. An answer can be right but not the correct answer. The contextual clues will help you find the answer that is most right and is correct. Understand the context in which a phrase or statement is made. This will help you make important distinctions.

Don't Panic

Panicking will not answer any questions for you; therefore, it isn't helpful. When you first see the question, if your mind goes blank, take a deep breath. Force yourself to mechanically go through the steps of solving the problem using the strategies you've learned.

Pace Yourself

Don't get clock fever. It's easy to be overwhelmed when you're looking at a page full of questions, your mind is full of random thoughts and feeling confused, and the clock is ticking down faster than you would like. Calm down and maintain the pace that you have set for yourself. As long as you are on track by monitoring your pace, you are guaranteed to have enough time for yourself. When you get to the last few minutes of the test, it may seem like you won't have enough time left, but if you only have as many questions as you should have left at that point, then you're right on track!

Answer Selection

The best way to pick an answer choice is to eliminate all of those that are wrong, until only one is left and confirm that is the correct answer. Sometimes though, an answer choice may immediately look right. Be careful! Take a second to make sure that the other choices are not equally obvious. Don't make a hasty mistake. There are only two times that you should stop before checking other answers. First is when you are positive that the answer choice you have selected is correct. Second is when time is almost out and you have to make a quick guess!

Check Your Work

Since you will probably not know every term listed and the answer to every question, it is important that you get credit for the ones that you do know. Don't miss any questions through careless mistakes. If at all possible, try to take a second to look back over your answer selection and make sure you've selected the correct answer choice and haven't made a costly careless mistake (such as marking an answer choice that you didn't mean to mark). The time it takes for this quick double check should more than pay for itself in caught mistakes.

Beware of Directly Quoted Answers

Sometimes an answer choice will repeat word for word a portion of the question or reference section. However, beware of such exact duplication. It may be a trap! More than likely, the correct choice will paraphrase or summarize a point, rather than being exactly the same wording.

Slang

Scientific sounding answers are better than slang ones. An answer choice that begins "To compare the outcomes..." is much more likely to be correct than one that begins "Because some people insisted..."

Extreme Statements

Avoid wild answers that throw out highly controversial ideas that are proclaimed as established fact. An answer choice that states the "process should used in certain situations, if..." is much more likely to be correct than one that states the "process should be discontinued completely." The first is a calm rational statement and doesn't even make a definitive, uncompromising stance, using a hedge word "if" to provide wiggle room, whereas the second choice is a radical idea and far more extreme.

Answer Choice Families

When you have two or more answer choices that are direct opposites or parallels, one of them is usually the correct answer. For instance, if one answer choice states "x increases" and another answer choice states "x decreases" or "y increases," then those two or three answer choices are very similar in construction and fall into the same family of answer choices. A family of answer choices consists of two or three answer choices, very similar in construction, but often with directly opposite meanings. Usually the correct answer choice will be in that family of answer choices. The "odd man out" or answer choice that doesn't seem to fit the parallel construction of the other answer choices is more likely to be incorrect.

Special Report: How to Overcome Test Anxiety

The very nature of tests caters to some level of anxiety, nervousness, or tension, just as we feel for any important event that occurs in our lives. A little bit of anxiety or nervousness can be a good thing. It helps us with motivation, and makes achievement just that much sweeter. However, too much anxiety can be a problem, especially if it hinders our ability to function and perform.

"Test anxiety," is the term that refers to the emotional reactions that some test-takers experience when faced with a test or exam. Having a fear of testing and exams is based upon a rational fear, since the test-taker's performance can shape the course of an academic career. Nevertheless, experiencing excessive fear of examinations will only interfere with the test-taker's ability to perform and chance to be successful.

There are a large variety of causes that can contribute to the development and sensation of test anxiety. These include, but are not limited to, lack of preparation and worrying about issues surrounding the test.

Lack of Preparation

Lack of preparation can be identified by the following behaviors or situations:
- Not scheduling enough time to study, and therefore cramming the night before the test or exam
- Managing time poorly, to create the sensation that there is not enough time to do everything
- Failing to organize the text information in advance, so that the study material consists of the entire text and not simply the pertinent information
- Poor overall studying habits

Worrying, on the other hand, can be related to both the test taker, or many other factors around him/her that will be affected by the results of the test. These include worrying about:
- Previous performances on similar exams, or exams in general
- How friends and other students are achieving
- The negative consequences that will result from a poor grade or failure

There are three primary elements to test anxiety. Physical components, which involve the same typical bodily reactions as those to acute anxiety (to be discussed below). Emotional factors have to do with fear or panic. Mental or cognitive issues concerning attention spans and memory abilities.

Physical Signals

There are many different symptoms of test anxiety, and these are not limited to mental and emotional strain. Frequently there are a range of physical signals that will let a test taker know that he/she is suffering from test anxiety. These bodily changes can include the following:
- Perspiring
- Sweaty palms

- Wet, trembling hands
- Nausea
- Dry mouth
- A knot in the stomach
- Headache
- Faintness
- Muscle tension
- Aching shoulders, back and neck
- Rapid heart beat
- Feeling too hot/cold

To recognize the sensation of test anxiety, a test-taker should monitor him/herself for the following sensations:
- The physical distress symptoms as listed above
- Emotional sensitivity, expressing emotional feelings such as the need to cry or laugh too much, or a sensation of anger or helplessness
- A decreased ability to think, causing the test-taker to blank out or have racing thoughts that are hard to organize or control.

Though most students will feel some level of anxiety when faced with a test or exam, the majority can cope with that anxiety and maintain it at a manageable level. However, those who cannot are faced with a very real and very serious condition, which can and should be controlled for the immeasurable benefit of this sufferer.

Naturally, these sensations lead to negative results for the testing experience. The most common effects of test anxiety have to do with nervousness and mental blocking.

Nervousness

Nervousness can appear in several different levels:
- The test-taker's difficulty, or even inability to read and understand the questions on the test
- The difficulty or inability to organize thoughts to a coherent form
- The difficulty or inability to recall key words and concepts relating to the testing questions (especially essays)
- The receipt of poor grades on a test, though the test material was well known by the test taker

Conversely, a person may also experience mental blocking, which involves:
- Blanking out on test questions
- Only remembering the correct answers to the questions when the test has already finished.

Fortunately for test anxiety sufferers, beating these feelings, to a large degree, has to do with proper preparation. When a test taker has a feeling of preparedness, then anxiety will be dramatically lessened.

The first step to resolving anxiety issues is to distinguish which of the two types of anxiety are being suffered. If the anxiety is a direct result of a lack of preparation, this should be considered a normal reaction, and the anxiety level (as opposed to the test results) shouldn't be anything to worry about. However, if, when adequately prepared, the test-taker still panics, blanks out, or seems to overreact, this is not a fully rational reaction. While this can be considered normal too, there are many ways to combat and overcome these effects.

Remember that anxiety cannot be entirely eliminated, however, there are ways to minimize it, to make the anxiety easier to manage. Preparation is one of the best ways to minimize test anxiety. Therefore the following techniques are wise in order to best fight off any anxiety that may want to build.

To begin with, try to avoid cramming before a test, whenever it is possible. By trying to memorize an entire term's worth of information in one day, you'll be shocking your system, and not giving yourself a very good chance to absorb the information. This is an easy path to anxiety, so for those who suffer from test anxiety, cramming should not even be considered an option.

Instead of cramming, work throughout the semester to combine all of the material which is presented throughout the semester, and work on it gradually as the course goes by, making sure to master the main concepts first, leaving minor details for a week or so before the test.

To study for the upcoming exam, be sure to pose questions that may be on the examination, to gauge the ability to answer them by integrating the ideas from your texts, notes and lectures, as well as any supplementary readings.

If it is truly impossible to cover all of the information that was covered in that particular term, concentrate on the most important portions, that can be covered very well. Learn these concepts as best as possible, so that when the test comes, a goal can be made to use these concepts as presentations of your knowledge.

In addition to study habits, changes in attitude are critical to beating a struggle with test anxiety. In fact, an improvement of the perspective over the entire test-taking experience can actually help a test taker to enjoy studying and therefore improve the overall experience. Be certain not to overemphasize the significance of the grade - know that the result of the test is neither a reflection of self worth, nor is it a measure of intelligence; one grade will not predict a person's future success.

To improve an overall testing outlook, the following steps should be tried:
- Keeping in mind that the most reasonable expectation for taking a test is to expect to try to demonstrate as much of what you know as you possibly can.
- Reminding ourselves that a test is only one test; this is not the only one, and there will be others.
- The thought of thinking of oneself in an irrational, all-or-nothing term should be avoided at all costs.
- A reward should be designated for after the test, so there's something to look forward to. Whether it be going to a movie, going out to eat, or simply visiting friends, schedule it in advance, and do it no matter what result is expected on the exam.

Test-takers should also keep in mind that the basics are some of the most important things, even beyond anti-anxiety techniques and studying. Never neglect the basic social, emotional and biological needs, in order to try to absorb information. In order to best achieve, these three factors must be held as just as important as the studying itself.

Study Steps

Remember the following important steps for studying:

- Maintain healthy nutrition and exercise habits. Continue both your recreational activities and social pass times. These both contribute to your physical and emotional well being.
- Be certain to get a good amount of sleep, especially the night before the test, because when you're overtired you are not able to perform to the best of your best ability.
- Keep the studying pace to a moderate level by taking breaks when they are needed, and varying the work whenever possible, to keep the mind fresh instead of getting bored.
- When enough studying has been done that all the material that can be learned has been learned, and the test taker is prepared for the test, stop studying and do something relaxing such as listening to music, watching a movie, or taking a warm bubble bath.

There are also many other techniques to minimize the uneasiness or apprehension that is experienced along with test anxiety before, during, or even after the examination. In fact, there are a great deal of things that can be done to stop anxiety from interfering with lifestyle and performance. Again, remember that anxiety will not be eliminated entirely, and it shouldn't be. Otherwise that "up" feeling for exams would not exist, and most of us depend on that sensation to perform better than usual. However, this anxiety has to be at a level that is manageable.

Of course, as we have just discussed, being prepared for the exam is half the battle right away. Attending all classes, finding out what knowledge will be expected on the exam, and knowing the exam schedules are easy steps to lowering anxiety. Keeping up with work will remove the need to cram, and efficient study habits will eliminate wasted time. Studying should be done in an ideal location for concentration, so that it is simple to become interested in the material and give it complete attention. A method such as SQ3R (Survey, Question, Read, Recite, Review) is a wonderful key to follow to make sure that the study habits are as effective as possible, especially in the case of learning from a textbook. Flashcards are great techniques for memorization. Learning to take good notes will mean that notes will be full of useful information, so that less sifting will need to be done to seek out what is pertinent for studying. Reviewing notes after class and then again on occasion will keep the information fresh in the mind. From notes that have been taken summary sheets and outlines can be made for simpler reviewing.

A study group can also be a very motivational and helpful place to study, as there will be a sharing of ideas, all of the minds can work together, to make sure that everyone understands, and the studying will be made more interesting because it will be a social occasion.

Basically, though, as long as the test-taker remains organized and self confident, with efficient study habits, less time will need to be spent studying, and higher grades will be achieved.

To become self confident, there are many useful steps. The first of these is "self talk." It has been shown through extensive research, that self-talk for students who suffer from test anxiety, should be well monitored, in order to make sure that it contributes to self confidence as opposed to sinking the student. Frequently the self talk of test-anxious students is negative or self-defeating, thinking that everyone else is smarter and faster, that they always mess up, and that if they don't do well, they'll fail the entire course. It is important to decreasing anxiety that awareness is made of self talk. Try writing any negative self thoughts and then disputing them with a positive statement instead. Begin self-encouragement as though it was a friend speaking. Repeat positive statements to help reprogram the mind to believing in successes instead of failures.

Helpful Techniques

Other extremely helpful techniques include:
- Self-visualization of doing well and reaching goals
- While aiming for an "A" level of understanding, don't try to "overprotect" by setting your expectations lower. This will only convince the mind to stop studying in order to meet the lower expectations.
- Don't make comparisons with the results or habits of other students. These are individual factors, and different things work for different people, causing different results.
- Strive to become an expert in learning what works well, and what can be done in order to improve. Consider collecting this data in a journal.
- Create rewards for after studying instead of doing things before studying that will only turn into avoidance behaviors.
- Make a practice of relaxing - by using methods such as progressive relaxation, self-hypnosis, guided imagery, etc - in order to make relaxation an automatic sensation.
- Work on creating a state of relaxed concentration so that concentrating will take on the focus of the mind, so that none will be wasted on worrying.
- Take good care of the physical self by eating well and getting enough sleep.
- Plan in time for exercise and stick to this plan.

Beyond these techniques, there are other methods to be used before, during and after the test that will help the test-taker perform well in addition to overcoming anxiety.

Before the exam comes the academic preparation. This involves establishing a study schedule and beginning at least one week before the actual date of the test. By doing this, the anxiety of not having enough time to study for the test will be automatically eliminated. Moreover, this will make the studying a much more effective experience, ensuring that the learning will be an easier process. This relieves much undue pressure on the test-taker.

Summary sheets, note cards, and flash cards with the main concepts and examples of these main concepts should be prepared in advance of the actual studying time. A topic should never be eliminated from this process. By omitting a topic because it isn't expected to be on the test is only setting up the test-taker for anxiety should it actually appear on the exam. Utilize the course syllabus for laying out the topics that should be studied. Carefully go over the notes that were made in class, paying special attention to any of the issues that the professor took special care to emphasize while lecturing in class. In the textbooks, use the chapter review, or if possible, the chapter tests, to begin your review.

It may even be possible to ask the instructor what information will be covered on the exam, or what the format of the exam will be (for example, multiple choice, essay, free form, true-false). Additionally, see if it is possible to find out how many questions will be on the test. If a review sheet or sample test has been offered by the professor, make good use of it, above anything else, for the preparation for the test. Another great resource for getting to know the examination is reviewing tests from previous semesters. Use these tests to review, and aim to achieve a 100% score on each of the possible topics. With a few exceptions, the goal that you set for yourself is the highest one that you will reach.

Take all of the questions that were assigned as homework, and rework them to any other possible course material. The more problems reworked, the more skill and confidence will form as a result.

When forming the solution to a problem, write out each of the steps. Don't simply do head work. By doing as many steps on paper as possible, much clarification and therefore confidence will be formed. Do this with as many homework problems as possible, before checking the answers. By checking the answer after each problem, a reinforcement will exist, that will not be on the exam. Study situations should be as exam-like as possible, to prime the test-taker's system for the experience. By waiting to check the answers at the end, a psychological advantage will be formed, to decrease the stress factor.

Another fantastic reason for not cramming is the avoidance of confusion in concepts, especially when it comes to mathematics. 8-10 hours of study will become one hundred percent more effective if it is spread out over a week or at least several days, instead of doing it all in one sitting. Recognize that the human brain requires time in order to assimilate new material, so frequent breaks and a span of study time over several days will be much more beneficial.

Additionally, don't study right up until the point of the exam. Studying should stop a minimum of one hour before the exam begins. This allows the brain to rest and put things in their proper order. This will also provide the time to become as relaxed as possible when going into the examination room. The test-taker will also have time to eat well and eat sensibly. Know that the brain needs food as much as the rest of the body. With enough food and enough sleep, as well as a relaxed attitude, the body and the mind are primed for success.

Avoid any anxious classmates who are talking about the exam. These students only spread anxiety, and are not worth sharing the anxious sentimentalities.

Before the test also involves creating a positive attitude, so mental preparation should also be a point of concentration. There are many keys to creating a positive attitude. Should fears become rushing in, make a visualization of taking the exam, doing well, and seeing an A written on the paper. Write out a list of affirmations that will bring a feeling of confidence, such as "I am doing well in my English class," "I studied well and know my material," "I enjoy this class." Even if the affirmations aren't believed at first, it sends a positive message to the subconscious which will result in an alteration of the overall belief system, which is the system that creates reality.

If a sensation of panic begins, work with the fear and imagine the very worst! Work through the entire scenario of not passing the test, failing the entire course, and dropping out of school, followed by not getting a job, and pushing a shopping cart through the dark alley where you'll live. This will place things into perspective! Then, practice deep breathing and create a visualization of the opposite situation - achieving an "A" on the exam, passing the entire course, receiving the degree at a graduation ceremony.

On the day of the test, there are many things to be done to ensure the best results, as well as the most calm outlook. The following stages are suggested in order to maximize test-taking potential:
- Begin the examination day with a moderate breakfast, and avoid any coffee or beverages with caffeine if the test taker is prone to jitters. Even people who are used to managing caffeine can feel jittery or light-headed when it is taken on a test day.
- Attempt to do something that is relaxing before the examination begins. As last minute cramming clouds the mastering of overall concepts, it is better to use this time to create a calming outlook.
- Be certain to arrive at the test location well in advance, in order to provide time to select a location that is away from doors, windows and other distractions, as well as giving enough time to relax before the test begins.

- Keep away from anxiety generating classmates who will upset the sensation of stability and relaxation that is being attempted before the exam.
- Should the waiting period before the exam begins cause anxiety, create a self-distraction by reading a light magazine or something else that is relaxing and simple.

During the exam itself, read the entire exam from beginning to end, and find out how much time should be allotted to each individual problem. Once writing the exam, should more time be taken for a problem, it should be abandoned, in order to begin another problem. If there is time at the end, the unfinished problem can always be returned to and completed.

Read the instructions very carefully - twice - so that unpleasant surprises won't follow during or after the exam has ended.

When writing the exam, pretend that the situation is actually simply the completion of homework within a library, or at home. This will assist in forming a relaxed atmosphere, and will allow the brain extra focus for the complex thinking function.

Begin the exam with all of the questions with which the most confidence is felt. This will build the confidence level regarding the entire exam and will begin a quality momentum. This will also create encouragement for trying the problems where uncertainty resides.

Going with the "gut instinct" is always the way to go when solving a problem. Second guessing should be avoided at all costs. Have confidence in the ability to do well.

For essay questions, create an outline in advance that will keep the mind organized and make certain that all of the points are remembered. For multiple choice, read every answer, even if the correct one has been spotted - a better one may exist.

Continue at a pace that is reasonable and not rushed, in order to be able to work carefully. Provide enough time to go over the answers at the end, to check for small errors that can be corrected.

Should a feeling of panic begin, breathe deeply, and think of the feeling of the body releasing sand through its pores. Visualize a calm, peaceful place, and include all of the sights, sounds and sensations of this image. Continue the deep breathing, and take a few minutes to continue this with closed eyes. When all is well again, return to the test.

If a "blanking" occurs for a certain question, skip it and move on to the next question. There will be time to return to the other question later. Get everything done that can be done, first, to guarantee all the grades that can be compiled, and to build all of the confidence possible. Then return to the weaker questions to build the marks from there.

Remember, one's own reality can be created, so as long as the belief is there, success will follow. And remember: anxiety can happen later, right now, there's an exam to be written!

After the examination is complete, whether there is a feeling for a good grade or a bad grade, don't dwell on the exam, and be certain to follow through on the reward that was promised...and enjoy it! Don't dwell on any mistakes that have been made, as there is nothing that can be done at this point anyway.

Additionally, don't begin to study for the next test right away. Do something relaxing for a while, and let the mind relax and prepare itself to begin absorbing information again.

From the results of the exam - both the grade and the entire experience, be certain to learn from what has gone on. Perfect studying habits and work some more on confidence in order to make the next examination experience even better than the last one.

Learn to avoid places where openings occurred for laziness, procrastination and day dreaming.

Use the time between this exam and the next one to better learn to relax, even learning to relax on cue, so that any anxiety can be controlled during the next exam. Learn how to relax the body. Slouch in your chair if that helps. Tighten and then relax all of the different muscle groups, one group at a time, beginning with the feet and then working all the way up to the neck and face. This will ultimately relax the muscles more than they were to begin with. Learn how to breathe deeply and comfortably, and focus on this breathing going in and out as a relaxing thought. With every exhale, repeat the word "relax."

As common as test anxiety is, it is very possible to overcome it. Make yourself one of the test-takers who overcome this frustrating hindrance.

Additional Bonus Material

Due to our efforts to try to keep this book to a manageable length, we've created a link that will give you access to all of your additional bonus material.

Please visit http://www.mometrix.com/bonus948/csetsocialsci to access the information.